Literature in Post-Communist Russia and Eastern Europe

This book considers Russian, Czech and Slovak fiction in the late Communist and early post-Communist periods, focusing in particular on the most innovative trend to emerge in this period, on those writers who, during and after the collapse of Communism, characterized themselves as 'liberators' of literature. It shows how these writers in their fiction and critical work reacted against the politicization of literature by Marxist-Leninist and dissident ideologues, rejecting the conventional perception of literature as moral teacher, and redefining the nature and purpose of writing. The book demonstrates how this quest, enacted in the works of these writers, served for many critics and readers as a metaphor for the wider disorientation and crisis precipitated by the collapse of Communism.

Rajendra A. Chitnis studied at the University of Sheffield and at the School of Slavonic and East European Studies, University College London, from which he received his PhD in 2003. Since 1999 he has held the post of lecturer in Russian and Czech Studies at the University of Bristol. His current research includes analysis of works by Tolstaia, Sorokin and Pelevin, Hrabal, Hodrová and Kahuda, and Vilikovský, Pišťanek and Balla. Alongside research into nineteenth- and twentieth-century Czech fiction, he is also interested in the development of learning materials for the study of Czech language and culture.

BASEES/RoutledgeCurzon Series on Russian and East European Studies

Series editor Richard Sakwa

Department of Politics and International Relations, University of Kent

This series is published on behalf of BASEES (the British Association for Slavonic and East European Studies). The series comprises original, high-quality, research-level work by both new and established scholars on all aspects of Russian, Soviet, post-Soviet and East European Studies in humanities and social science subjects.

1. **Ukraine's Foreign and Security Policy, 1991–2000**
   Roman Wolczuk

2. **Political Parties in the Russian Regions**
   Derek S. Hutcheson

3. **Local Communities and Post-Communist Transformation**
   Edited by Simon Smith

4. **Repression and Resistance in Communist Europe**
   J.C. Sharman

5. **Political Elites and the New Russia**
   Anton Steen

6. **Dostoevsky and the Idea of Russianness**
   Sarah Hudspith

7. **Performing Russia – Folk Revival and Russian Identity**
   Laura J. Olson

8. **Russian Transformations**
   Edited by Leo McCann

9. **Soviet Music and Society under Lenin and Stalin**
   The baton and sickle
   Edited by Neil Edmunds

10. **State Building in Ukraine**
    The Ukranian parliament, 1990–2003
    Sarah Whitmore

11. **Defending Human Rights in Russia**
    Sergei Kovalyov, Dissident and Human Rights Commissioner, 1969–2003
    Emma Gilligan

12. **Small-Town Russia**
    Postcommunist livelihoods and identities: a portrait of theintelligentsia in Achit, Bednodemyanovsk and Zubtsov, 1999–2000
    Anne White

13. **Russian Society and the Orthodox Church**
    Religion in Russia after Communism
    Zoe Knox

14. **Russian Literary Culture in the Camera Age**
    The word as image
    Stephen Hutchings

15. **Between Stalin and Hitler**
    Class war and race war on the Dvina, 1940–98
    Geoffrey Swain

16. **Literature in Post-Communist Russia and Eastern Europe**
    The Russian, Czech and Slovak fiction of the Changes 1988–1998
    Rajendra A. Chitnis

Literature in Post-Communist Russia and Eastern Europe

The Russian, Czech and Slovak fiction of the Changes, 1988–1998

Rajendra A. Chitnis

RoutledgeCurzon
Taylor & Francis Group
LONDON AND NEW YORK

First published 2005
by RoutledgeCurzon
2 Park Square, Milton Park, Abingdon, Oxon OX14 4RN

Simultaneously published in the USA and Canada
by RoutledgeCurzon
270 Madison Avenue, New York, NY 10016

RoutledgeCurzon is an imprint of the Taylor & Francis Group

Typeset in Times by
Rosemount Typing Services, Barjarg Tower, Auldgirth, Dumfriesshire
Printed and bound in Great Britain by
Antony Rowe Ltd, Chippenham, Wiltshire

British Library Cataloguing in Publication Data
A catalogue record for this book is available from the British Library

Library of Congress Cataloging in Publication Data
A catalog record for this book has been requested

ISBN 0–415–35557–5

Contents

Acknowledgements

This book is based largely on my doctoral thesis, and I would like first to thank my supervisors Robert Pynsent and Julian Graffy of SSEES–UCL, London, for all their time, wisdom and endless encouragement during its long gestation. I would also like to thank my colleagues in the Russian Department at the University of Bristol, particularly Derek Offord and Mike Basker, for their great patience and support while this project was being completed.

During the course of my doctoral studies I was fortunate to receive two years' funding from the British Academy Arts and Humanities Research Board. Part of the section on Peter Pišťanek in Chapter 3 appeared in an earlier form in Slovak in *Romboid* XXXIV (1999), 8: 26–30.

Above all, I would like to thank my parents for all their love, faith and support, and Katka for her love, patience and understanding. This book is dedicated to them.

Author's note

Throughout this study, Russian is transcribed from the Cyrillic according to the Library of Congress transliteration system without diacritics, with the exception of certain well-known proper names where a particular spelling in English has become the norm (e.g. Dostoevsky). The study contains several references to critics who have published both in Russian and in English translation, where the transliteration of their name differs from that used here. In such cases, for clarity I have retained the Library of Congress transliterated form of the name throughout, but given the name as published in English in square brackets in the bibliography (e.g. Lipovetskii [Lipovetsky]).

Given the peculiar publishing circumstances of the period, where relevant the first reference to a work is followed by the dates of first publication abroad and at home (excluding any samizdat editions), which is often, in the Russian case, a journal publication. I have also included the stated date of writing where this differs significantly from the date of publication. The titles of classic works of Russian literature are given in their best-known English form only.

All translations are my own. References to English translations of works, where available, are included in the bibliography.

Introduction

This book constitutes the first detailed comparative study of Russian, Czech and Slovak fiction as those societies and cultures emerged from Communist autocracy in the late 1980s and early 1990s. My aim here is not to provide an exhaustive survey of the fiction of this period, but to focus on the work of those writers who, in their fiction or critical articles, characterized themselves as 'liberators' of literature. In their view, literature in the preceding period, whether sanctioned or unsanctioned, had become the servant of social, political and ideological aims, in keeping with the traditional understanding of literature in Russian, Czech and Slovak culture as the teacher of the way to live. In their work, they seek to reject this position of authority, and recast the role of the writer and literature. This study explores the principles, strategies and techniques underlying their work.

I approach this period as a 'literary situation', during which works, often written several years earlier, appeared for the first time in the country of their writers' birth and were commonly associated by commentators with the ambiguous mood of liberation and uncertainty prevalent in all three societies at the time. No single label has emerged in all three literatures to denote this type of writing, therefore I have adopted the label 'the fiction of the Changes' to reflect my focus on the period, in preference to various short-lived terms, including 'other', 'alternative', 'underground', 'independent' or 'unclassified' fiction, or the broader, problematic and ideologically charged 'postmodernism' that has come to be used in Russian and Slovak, but not in Czech, circles to denote a tendency in fiction dating back at least to the 1960s. As used here, the label 'the fiction of the Changes' does not refer to all the Russian, Czech and Slovak fiction published in this period, most of which may be said to reflect and respond to the changing situation, but specifically to that which seeks to change conventional perceptions about why literature is written and how it is read.

A loose chronological thread runs through this study, based on the dates when works were first published in their author's native country. The starting point, though it varies slightly for each literature, was essentially dictated by the socio-political and cultural liberalization of the late 1980s which allowed the fiction discussed here to be published and freed critics to explore its message. The end-point also selected itself. By the mid-1990s, commentators increasingly noted that the strategies employed by most writers discussed here seemed exhausted, and while some writers began to seek new directions, others simply took a break from publishing fiction. At the same time, new writers came to prominence who exploited these styles in order to subvert them, in effect to bring about another change. This study is therefore also underpinned by a narrative of sorts, which emerged during the course of writing and traces the anxiety about the nature and purpose of literature in the fiction of the Changes from its identification by critics in the late 1980s to its possible alleviation or at least re-definition in the 1990s.

Since not all three literatures may be equally familiar to the reader, I use Chapter 1 to place the writers discussed in the broader socio-political and literary context in which their work appeared. As the bibliography indicates, there are many more surveys and detailed studies in English of the Russian fiction of this period than of its Czech or Slovak counterparts, so in this and later chapters I include slightly more detail on the background to the latter. The remaining six chapters contain close analysis of individual works or groups of works by writers whose names featured prominently in critical discussions of the Changes period. Throughout the study I emphasize the comparative aspect. Chapters 2, 3 and 7 examine works by a Russian, a Czech and a Slovak writer. Chapters 4 and 6 focus on Russian and Slovak writers and Chapter 5 is devoted to Czech writers, reflecting their contrasting attitude to the notion of liberation. I frequently use works of fiction, criticism and theory from one literature to illuminate another. Where some previous studies have sought to impose the framework of post-Structuralist theory on this fiction, my use of theory is more pragmatic than dogmatic, acknowledging these writers' considerable interest in contemporary literary and cultural theory without, I hope, subordinating their fiction to it.

Given the limits of space, and the fact that most writers discussed here are still writing, I have chosen to concentrate on paradigmatic texts rather than provide an exhaustive analysis of each writer's work. I endeavour throughout to place these texts in the context of works by other contemporaneous writers, but some may inevitably appear under-represented. I hope, however, that this study will provide a frame of reference in which not only other Russian, Czech and Slovak literature, but also other Central and East European literatures of this period may be explored.

1 The fiction of the Changes

Context and reception

The fiction discussed in this study was published as a result of the social, political and cultural liberalization that followed the accession of Mikhail Gorbachev to the leadership of the Soviet Union and ultimately led to the collapse of Communist regimes across Eastern Europe. Gorbachev's announcement of the policies of *perestroika* (economic reconstruction) and *glasnost'* (openness, freedom of expression) signalled a decisive break with the mood and approach of the Brezhnev period, which in the jargon of the period became known as the Stagnation (*zastoi*).[1] Perhaps surprisingly, given their usual reluctance to conform to generally held positions, the Russian, Czech and Slovak writers of the Changes accept this characterization of the 1970s and 1980s, frequently contrasting their perception of reality as dynamic, ever-changing and ineffable with a fixed, arid view implicitly associated with the prevailing socio-political and cultural atmosphere of those years.

In theory, the purpose of *glasnost'* was to support Gorbachev's reforms. Richard Sakwa writes:

> On 11 February 1987, at a meeting of media figures, Gorbachev announced what was in effect a manifesto for glasnost, declaring that 'there should not be any blank pages in either our history or our literature', but warning that 'criticism should always be from a party point of view'.
>
> (Sakwa 1990: 66)

Certainly the most tangible achievement of the policy in the literary sphere was the publication for the first time, or after many years, of a huge range of twentieth-century Russian writers, including émigrés, representing several different generations and many political and artistic perspectives. However, the practical effect of *glasnost'* was a steady liberalization of the Soviet literary process, in which 'the outer limits were constantly being pushed back' (ibid.: 79). Though the making available of works by long prohibited writers restricted the space available to new writing and the former took precedence with readers, at the same time, as Galina Nefagina argues, the new writing undoubtedly benefited from the growing diversity of themes and approaches represented by the 'returned literature', which 'exerted a significant influence over the reception of literature, its aesthetics and poetics, and the demands and expectations of readers' and thus 'expanded the limits of the freedom of the word' (Nefagina 1998: 5, 9). The unity of perspective and message in Soviet literature and literary criticism that had notionally prevailed from the late 1960s until the early 1980s crumbled as the 'old guard' of writers and critics became only one, essentially conservative, element in a diverse mix of political and artistic views.[2]

For the Czechoslovak Communist regime, long used to slavishly following the Soviet line, however, Gorbachev's policies constituted a fundamental threat to its historical legitimacy. The death of Stalin in 1953 had been followed by a Thaw, during which the atmosphere in Soviet and Czechoslovak society had gradually eased, culture had liberalized and the role of intellectuals in public life had been restored. During this period, literature moved decisively away from the myth-making of Stalinist Socialist Realism in favour of more realistic, less overtly dogmatic writing. These changes were palpable in Russian and Slovak literature from 1954 onwards, but took longer to become manifest in Czech literature. With intermittent freezes, the Thaw reached its peak in the Soviet Union in 1962. Media attacks on liberal writing were renewed in 1963, as hostility to reform within the Soviet Communist Party grew, leading to the imprisonment of Joseph Brodsky (1940–96) in 1964 and of Andrei Siniavskii (1925–97) and Iulii Daniel (b.1925) in 1966.

By contrast, the warmest, most prolonged period of Thaw in Czech society and culture began in 1963, coinciding with the emergence of the most experimental generation in Slovak literature of the period. Writers were at the forefront of calls for all-embracing change which culminated in January 1968 in the accession of Alexander Dubček to the leadership of the Czechoslovak Communist Party and the beginning of the so-called 'Prague Spring' reforms. The effective ending of censorship, moves towards private enterprise and talk of multi-party elections were unacceptable to the new, hard-line Soviet leadership, and in August 1968, Warsaw Pact armies entered Czechoslovakia to halt the reform process. In April 1969, Dubček was replaced by Gustav Husák, who was charged by the Soviet Union with 'normalizing' the situation in the country, hence the term 'Normalization', conventionally used to designate the period between 1969 and 1989 in Czechoslovakia.

For the Husák regime, the resemblance between *perestroika* and *glasnost'* and Dubček's reforms was uncomfortably close. Karen Henderson writes:

> Since most [of the Czechoslovak government] had come to power after putting down the 'counter-revolution' of 1968 [...], conceding the legitimacy of the 1968 reform attempts would mean that they had no right to rule [...] and it was hard for them to pursue the Gorbachev direction in any intellectually coherent fashion while hiding the similarities to earlier Czechoslovak efforts. Consequently official Czechoslovak support for *perestroika* was muted.
>
> (Henderson 2002: 26)

Moves towards liberalization were more evident in Slovakia, where the situation in the 1970s and 1980s had in practice been less fraught, as Henderson indicates:

> There was a less clear divide [in Slovakia] between the state on the one hand and the dissidents on the other. The greater informality and lower level of paranoia prevailing in official organizations in Slovakia allowed some expression of alternative views: state structures were more easily penetrable than in Prague.
>
> (Ibid.: 27)

The Czechoslovak Party's half-hearted efforts from late 1988 onwards to adopt Gorbachev's rhetoric were soon overtaken by events. Following the fall of Communist governments in Hungary, Poland and East Germany, Czechs and Slovaks took to the streets in November 1989, and Gorbachev ordered the resident Soviet troops not to intervene. By January 1990, a new, non-Communist government had been established under the presidency of the former playwright and dissident, Václav Havel. The political censorship of literature ended, and the return of long prohibited literature finally began in earnest. One further major change, however, awaited the inhabitants of both the Soviet Union and Czechoslovakia, of only minor relevance to the literature discussed here. In January 1992, the Russian Federation emerged with the dissolution of the Soviet Union, while the independent states of the Czech Republic and Slovakia came into being in January 1993 following the failure of efforts to find a way of governing Czechoslovakia that met the aspirations of both Czechs and Slovaks.

The first serious attempts to explore the nature of the 'new' writing of the *glasnost'* period appeared in Russian literary journals in 1989. Early that year, *Literaturnaia gazeta* published two articles reflecting on recently published Russian fiction, prefaced by a reader's letter, worth quoting since it typifies the perception of the role and nature of literature challenged by the writers of the Changes. Citing works she has just read by Valeriia Narbikova (b.1958), Viacheslav P'etsukh (b.1946) and Tat'iana Tolstaia (b.1951), the reader remarks:

> It seems to me that some of the writers (and especially female writers – which surprises me most!) have exploited *glasnost'* in order to display for general inspection only what is filthy and disgusting. There you go, they say, take that! Can anything be gained from such 'truth'? Can writers have forgotten that literature should elevate and enlighten the human being, not bend him to the ground?
>
> (Chuprinin 1989a: 4)

The very title of the second article, 'Plokhaia proza' (Bad fiction), left the reader in no doubt about its author's views (see Urnov 1989: 4). However, the first article, by Sergei Chuprinin, entitled 'Drugaia proza' (Other fiction), gave the emerging 'new' writing its first label.

Chuprinin dates the origins of 'other fiction' back to the late 1970s, when literature that failed to commit itself to the service either of the regime or of its opponents 'really felt itself to be other, that is to say emphatically and provocatively alternative in its relationship both to the reigning morality and, in fact, to all that was considered literature in Russia' (Chuprinin 1989a: 4). The first collective expression of this position came, according to Chuprinin, with the abortive attempt in 1978 by Vasilii Aksenov (b.1932), Andrei Bitov (b.1937), Viktor Erofeev (b.1947), Fazil' Iskander (b.1929) and Evgenii Popov (b.1946) to secure the uncensored publication of an anthology of 'non-committed' literature called *Metropol'* (Ann Arbor, 1979).[3] *Metropol'* united writers from different generations who had difficulty publishing in Brezhnev's Soviet Union, including prominent figures from the height of the Thaw, like Aksenov, Bitov and Iskander, whose major post-Thaw works did not appear until the *glasnost'* period, and those, like Erofeev and Popov, whose fiction, though written in the 1970s and early 1980s, would be considered central to the 'new fiction' of the late 1980s.

Despite this continuity, critical discussions of 'other fiction', while noting precursors, focused almost exclusively on writers whose work was not associated with an earlier period, even though it had often been written in the 1970s or early 1980s. The major anomaly was *Moskva–Petushki* (Paris 1973, Moscow 1989, dated as written 1969) by Venedikt Erofeev (1938–90, no relation of Viktor), which had already been published and reviewed abroad and in *samizdat*, but became for critics a defining example of the 'new' aesthetic. The core names listed by Chuprinin or other critics included both Erofeevs, Narbikova, P'etsukh, Popov, Tolstaia, Zufar Gareev (b.1955), Aleksandr Ivanchenko (b.1945), Liudmila Petrushevskaia (b.1938) and Vladimir Sorokin (b.1955). In the peculiar situation of Soviet literature at the height of *glasnost'*, some, like Ivanchenko and Tolstaia, had first been treated by critics as a continuation of the development of sanctioned literature; others, like the Erofeevs, Petrushevskaia, P'etsukh and Popov, were accepted as 'delayed' arrivals who had not been able to publish, not submitted their work for publication or published only rarely; and yet others, notably Narbikova, were seen as new writing reflecting the liberalization of literary themes and method.

In his attempt to delineate what unites these writers and distinguishes them from other contemporaneous writing, Chuprinin focuses on their characters, 'almost exclusively wretched, luckless, damaged people' (Chuprinin 1989a: 4). Whereas, Chuprinin argues, similar types, when they appeared in sanctioned fiction of the 1970s and early 1980s, represented a deviation from the norm, in 'other fiction' they suggest that a 'distorted, rotten, phantasmagoric reality' had become the norm. Chuprinin considers the 'other fiction' writers as the 'artists-diagnosticians and naturalists [*estestvoispytateli*]' (ibid.) of this reality. Writing in 1991, Mikhail Epshtein similarly concentrates on characterization, contrasting the 'weirdoes' ('chudiki') depicted in the fiction of the Thaw and early post-Thaw writer, film-actor and director, Vasilii Shukshin (1929–74), with the more extreme 'wankers' ('mudaki') including Popov, Viktor Erofeev and P'etsukh. For

Epshtein, while the 'chudik' represented an 'individual deviation from the over-constricting norms of social life', the 'mudak', the 'worn face of social madness', 'also deviates from the norms of common sense, but this is the characteristic not of an individual, but of a collective being that has rolled off the rails of reason and history' (Epshtein 1991: 220).

Both Chuprinin and Epshtein focus on the 'taboo-breaking' in 'other fiction', exemplified by Epshtein's use of the taboo word 'mudak' and regarded by Robert Porter as its 'most salient characteristic' (Porter 1994b: 19). However, the flouting of prohibitions concerning the type of language or subject matter appropriate to literature, and the way a human being should be portrayed, occurred in a broad range of 'new' Russian writing in the period, in particular the grim social realism of writers like Sergei Kaledin (b.1949), which more closely fits Chuprinin's perception of 'other fiction' as a form of social criticism. Moreover, this type of taboo-breaking is not really relevant to writers like Tolstaia and Ivanchenko. Natal'ia Ivanova found the type of character and reality described by Chuprinin and Epshtein so widespread in contemporaneous Russian fiction that she wrote of the 'literary hegemony of the catastrophe genre'. In her view:

> Motifs associating the end of the century and the millenium with the end of the world – fatal illness, collapse, death, madness, doom – are concentrated in the image of the hospital and the madhouse, the place where a contemporary novel's hero is likely to be found, since he is characterized by a sick imagination and morbid fantasy (including historical fantasy), by the collapse of consciousness.
>
> (Ivanova 1998: 80)[4]

A more effective means of differentiation was proposed by Vladimir Potapov, who defines 'other fiction' as 'literature which feels and acknowledges itself as only and nothing more than a phenomenon of language' (Potapov 1989: 252) or, in other words, breaks the convention that literature is the source of truth about how to live. In Potapov's view:

> 'Other fiction' is least inclined to consider itself a collective organizer or propagandist, a mouthpiece or transmitter of ideas, hence its refusal to commandeer in any way, hence the unusual character of its dialogue with the reader […]. 'Other fiction' writers almost never set themselves the task of creating a substantial, multi-coloured, plastically perfect world, existing as it were independently of the author. A 'mediator-voice' is always present between reader and author, evoked to remind the reader that all that is being communicated is merely 'words, words, words', merely literature.
>
> (Ibid.: 254)

This point of view was expressed in a more belligerent way by Viktor Erofeev, in his controversial essay, 'Pominki po sovetskoi literature' (A funeral feast for Soviet literature), first published in *Literaturnaia gazeta* in July 1990, which announced the death of Soviet literature. In his essay, Erofeev asserts:

> In Russia the writer was often called upon to carry out several duties at the same time: to be a priest, a prosecutor, a sociologist, an expert in questions of love and marriage, an economist and a mystic. He was so much everything that he frequently turned out to be nobody as a writer, unable to sense the peculiarities of literary language and figurative paradoxical thinking.
>
> (Erofeev 1996: 432)

Erofeev considers the focus of writing in this dominant understanding to be directed outwards, towards shaping a notion of the human being. By contrast, the focus of the 'new' literature was, in his view, directed inwards, towards words. Erofeev writes: 'In a novel it is important to create not so much a definite human image or character, as something about which I would simply say *literature*' (ibid.: 433).

Erofeev's essay evokes not only Roland Barthes's 'The death of the author', but also Francis Fukuyama's *The End of History?*, published in Russian in *Voprosy filosofii* in early 1990, which, often misunderstood as a programmatic rather than a speculative statement, greatly influenced intellectuals in former Communist countries in the early Changes period. Above all, however, the notion of artistically compromised literature recalls Abram Terts's prescient essay 'Chto takoe sotsialisticheskii realizm?' (What is Socialist Realism?, Paris 1959), itself titled in imitation of Jean-Paul Sartre's *Qu'est-ce que la littérature?* Terts, the pseudonym of Andrei Siniavskii, sarcastically condemns Socialist Realism as a 'half-classicist half-art' (Terts 1982: 214), and advocates a notion of art close to that propounded by the writers of the Changes. Sharing the optimism of Barthes, Fukuyama and Terts, Erofeev's essay presents the 'liberated' literature as a new beginning. By contrast, for Epshtein it is symptomatic of what he considers a recurring 'aesthetic' stage in Russian literature, in which literature surrenders or loses all other functions and drifts into self-contemplation. He writes: 'What is left for a literature that is no longer politics, religion or philosophy? It is left with language, a kind of minimum, a final bridgehead on which to set the conditions for its capitulation' (Epshtein 1991: 226).

The notion that literature was suffering from a loss of purpose also formed the basis of Pavel Janoušek's assessment of Czech literature in the early post-Communist period. In 1990, he asserted that Czech literature was, in basketball parlance, taking a 'time-out' to come to terms with its past, and not only with the works which had not been sanctioned for publication before the Changes, but also with those which had (see Janoušek 2001: 69–79). In his view, under Communism, readers and critics had judged a work above all on the extent to which it told the truth about the reality of life in contemporary Czechoslovak society. In the post-1989 period, however, that truth-telling function had passed to the media, leaving literature, according to Janoušek, uncertain of what to say instead (see Janoušek 1994: 3). Janoušek subsequently argued that with the loss of the enemy (Communism), Czech literature had lost the 'need to communicate', with the result that 'individual works are interpreted only as the personal *plaisir* of the author' (Janoušek 1996: 10).

The accession of Gorbachev saw a slight change of atmosphere in Czech literature, with the publication in 1986 of works like *Simulanti* (Malingerers) by Milan Pávek (b.1941), delayed since 1983, *Jak potopit Austrálii* (How to sink Australia) by Petr Šabach (b.1951) and *Knížka s červeným obalem* (A little book with a red cover) by Alexandra Berková (b.1949) that combined relatively strong political satire with an inventive, comic approach to narrative. However, in an article about new Czech writing published in August 1989, Ivo Slávik suggested that the short-story collections by Šabach and Berková were more or less the only new works worthy of note, commenting:

> The literary vivaciousness and the vitality of the heroes of these debuts, like the flexibility and range of expression of the authors, form the basis for the emergence of an antithesis to the schematicism in which part of the literary production of younger writers who entered literature in the 1970s drowned.
> (Slávik 1989: 22)

Slávik's remarks demonstrate the altogether more liberal situation in Slovakia, to which I shall shortly return. The ironic, playful, female perspective of Berková's collection in particular appeared refreshingly unusual in the context of Czech sanctioned fiction in which humour was often restricted to male adolescent sarcasm.[5] In the second edition, published in 1988, Berková supplied a typically quirky account of her method that looked both back to the 1960s and forward to the fiction of the Changes:

> Working with television has taught me (*oh it has, yes, it has*) above all to build a whole through the association of situations according to their internal homogeneity, without explanation, without justification and without the hopelessly boring strings of monotonous informative narration that I don't like reading and that manage to ruin even the liveliest subject. Fear and humour belong together.
> (Berková 1988: back cover)

The impact of *glasnost'* was first felt in Czech literature only in late 1988, when the Union of Czech Writers began in earnest to seek a way of 'reuniting' sanctioned, *samizdat* and *tamizdat* literature. Representatives of the regime hoped to achieve this 'reunification' in the manner of their Soviet counterparts a few years earlier, as Janoušek indicates in his discussion of this process:

> Though they admitted the necessity of coming to terms in some way with the disowned, they imagined it as a gradual and painless integration of 'minor' branches into the 'main' branch, as an 'opening of doors' to books which were not entirely in conflict ... let's say, with Communist ideals (more precisely, with the definition ordained by their higher organs at the time).
>
> (Janoušek 2001: 60)

The Party-led liberalization of literature was highly unpredictable. *Literární měsíčník*, the mouthpiece of official literature in the 1970s and 1980s, made a great virtue of its serialization in the summer of 1989 of *Rozhovory s útěkem* (Conversations with escape, 1990), a novel describing a lesbian affair, by the superficially non-conformist rock singer Bára Basiková (b.1963). The same year, however, Daniela Hodrová (b.1946), a leading literary theorist and novelist in the post-Changes period, could publish her theory of the novel, *Hledání románu* (In search of the novel), only in censored form. She did secure agreement for the publication of her novels *Podobojí* (In both kinds) and *Kukly* (Pupae), completed in the early 1980s, but these were then paradoxically delayed by the fall of the regime until 1991. The most significant event of this period was the sanctioned publication in early 1989 of two major novels by Bohumil Hrabal (1914–97) – *Obsluhoval jsem anglického krále* (I waited on the King of England, Cologne 1980) and *Příliš hlučná samota* (Too loud a solitude, Cologne 1980) – both completed in the early 1970s and previously published abroad and in *samizdat*. Associated with the liberalization of literary method in the 1960s, when he first came to prominence, Hrabal was not permitted to publish following the collapse of the reforms process until 1975, when he gave a 'self-critical' interview to the Party cultural weekly, *Tvorba*, declaring his support for Socialism.[6] Even after that, however, those works sanctioned for publication were stylistically and thematically his least challenging. As Vladimír Novotný pointed out in his survey of Czech literature since 1989, Hrabal, as the most popular writer in sanctioned, *samizdat* and *tamizdat* literature, effectively embodied the unity of Czech literature on his own (Novotný 1995a: 24), and he casts a long shadow over post-1989 Czech fiction.

The first attempt to end the 'time-out' in Czech literature came with the essay 'Obnovení chaosu v české literatuře' (The renewal of chaos in Czech literature) by Jiří Kratochvil (b.1940), published in *Literární noviny* in November 1992. As Milan Jungmann noted in his response, Kratochvil's provocative assertions closely resembled Erofeev's in his 'Pominki po sovetskoi literature', which had appeared in Czech in *Světová literatura* earlier in the same year (see Jungmann 1993a: 7). Like Erofeev, Kratochvil emphasizes that, in his view, the Marxist-Leninist understanding of literature is merely an example of the conventional notion of literature in Czech culture as a collectivizing tool, demonstrated also by the use of literature by the dissidents in the 1970s and 1980s:

> After a long time Czech literature is not only free again and rid of all social commitments and national expectations, but also has its 'generation', which is turning its back on both the literature of the 1960s and the official and unofficial literature of the twenty years of occupation. It is a literature which with relish scorns all ideologies, missions and services to the people or to anyone.
>
> (Kratochvil 1995: 83–4)

As far as fiction is concerned, the writers of the literature to which Kratochvil refers came essentially from two distinct groups, who together make up the Czech counterpart to what Soviet critics in the late 1980s called 'other fiction'. The first was drawn from Kratochvil's own generation, and consisted of writers born during or shortly after the Second World War, for whom the Thaw had ended before they could make a substantial impact. They included Hodrová and Michal Ajvaz (b.1949), to whom Novotný added, among others, Berková, Vladimír Macura (1945–99), Ivan Matoušek (b.1948) and Václav Vokolek (b.1947) (see Novotný 1995b: 24). Of these, only Berková and Macura had had fiction sanctioned for publication before November 1989, though like Berková's *Knížka s červeným obalem*, Macura's short story collection *Něžnými drápky* (With tender claws), published in 1983, scarcely conformed to ideological expectations. Some, like Hodrová and Macura, had pursued careers in literary studies during the 1970s and 1980s; most, however, had been not only excluded from the sanctioned literary process, but also, while publishing in *samizdat* and *tamizdat*, peripheral to major dissident activities. The second group was made up of underground writers who emerged in the 1980s, particularly those, like Vít Kremlička (b.1962), Petr Placák (b.1964) and Jáchym Topol (b.1962), associated with the *samizdat* journal *Revolver Revue*,[7] to whom Zuzana Brabcová (b.1960), though not strictly 'underground', was frequently added because of close stylistic similarities.[8]

In his brief survey of Czech fiction of the early 1990s, first published in *Literární noviny* in 1995, Aleš Haman identified two main tendencies:

> one aimed for authenticity, the instant expression of bare, existential transience, the demystification of all illusions and demythicization of all ideals which could provide something to hold on to in the flow of time; the other tendency was formed of fiction which bet on the destruction of *histoire* by means of a refined game of imaginary associations and the merging of fantastic visions and realistic ideas.
>
> (Haman 2001a: 10)

Haman's division of writers into one or other tendency is over-simplified, since in practice they were not necessarily mutually exclusive. However, Czech literature in the 1990s, to a greater extent than either Russian or Slovak, was dominated by explicitly or implicitly autobiographical works seeking to give an 'eye-witness' account of the experience of the 1970s and 1980s, and at the same time to assert the writer's own anti-Communist credentials. These works were often either written by formerly controversial sanctioned writers like Zdeněk Zapletal (b.1951), or had been published previously in *samizdat* or *tamizdat*, like, for example, the novels of émigré writers such as Iva Pekárková (b.1963) or Jan Pelc (b.1957). This tendency may therefore be seen to represent a continuation of what Janoušek describes as the 'truth-telling' approach called for by both official and dissident establishments – for diametrically opposed ideological reasons – in the preceding period. What Kratochvil presents as the 'new' Czech writing, though it rarely dissented from the characterization of the 1970s and 1980s as a 'traumatic' period, nevertheless represented an attempt to break with this approach, to cease the perpetuation of shared versions of reality and foreground instead their constant disintegration and recreation. For this reason, Kratochvil describes this writing as the 'literature of chaos, that is, of the beginning', the writers of which

> are not only consciously and systematically returning to artistic and 'artificial' literature (and logically at the same time to its opposite, Gellnerian literature and aesthetic brutalism), but, above all, aim to create some kind of individual myths, replacing the collective myths which have thus far dominated in Czech literature from the time of the Revival through the left-wing avant-garde to ideologized literature and literature of the 'political opposition' of the 1960s.
>
> (Kratochvil 1995: 84)[9]

The attempt by Erofeev, Kratochvil and other Russian and Czech writers of the Changes to present their writing as a complete break with the principles and techniques underpinning literature in the preceding period arose essentially from a sense that they and their way of thinking had been egregiously excluded both from mainstream sanctioned and from unsanctioned literature during the 1970s and 1980s. In his critique of Kratochvil's theoretical writing, Haman comments:

> In Kratochvil's opinions, the experience of the time of Normalization, which shut creative personalities (of his type) in 'internal emigration' on islands of loneliness far from the madding crowd, is mixed with euphoria at the freedom after November 1989. The confinement of non-conformist isolation was transposed into a notion of the absolute autonomy of artistic creation rid of all secondary functions.
>
> (Haman 2001b: 4)

In an article published in 1990, Jungmann, the editor-in-chief of *Literární noviny* from 1964 to 1967, at the height of the Czech Thaw, described the policy of Normalization, applied to literature, as the regime's 'revenge' on writers for the prominent role they had played in calls for reform (see Jungmann 1990: 145).

During a conference panel discussion in Tampere in July 2000 on the work of the sanctioned but hardly conformist writer Vladimir Makanin (b.1937), Natal'ia Ivanova used the same word in characterizing the late *glasnost'* period in Russian literature as the 'revenge of the underground', during which writers like Makanin were temporarily swept aside by the 'new' writers and often could not or chose not to publish. As much as it heralded the future, then, the Russian and Czech fiction of the Changes also represented the culmination of a period of disinformation and misrepresentation, when not only writers, but also critics served 'extra-literary' purposes, the 'final' caricaturing of the recent and distant literary past necessary to liberate writer and critic from this service.

Nowhere is this caricature more apparent than in Erofeev and Kratochvil's accounts of literature since the Thaw, which provoked the greatest controversy at the time. Kratochvil's use of the term 'official literature' implicitly to refer to everything sanctioned for publication in the 1970s and 1980s reflects the prevalent Czech dissident view that all sanctioned literature was artistically compromised and, moreover, complicit in the maintenance of the autocratic regime. This view has fundamentally shaped the conventional wisdom about the literature of the Normalization in Czech criticism since 1989, and undoubtedly derives from the particular sense of betrayal and injustice experienced by those excluded from the literary process in the aftermath of August 1968. For commentators like Jungmann, those few writers closely associated with the literary experimentation of the Thaw, like Ladislav Fuks (1923–94) and Vladimír Páral (b.1932), who continued to have their work sanctioned for publication, had sold their talents and reputations to the regime. Of Fuks and Páral, Jungmann wrote:

> it was evident that the writer no longer vouched for his work, that he had failed in that most fundamental thing; literature for him was no longer a struggle for a deeper knowledge of the human being and society, it was a means to the end of profitable self-realization.
>
> (Ibid.: 148)

Jungmann was equally scathing about attempts to establish a new generation of writers to replace the one that had been discredited, and his rejection of these writers as artistically weak is reiterated in ostensibly more analytical surveys (see Bock 1992: 67–84).[10]

Responding to the blanket rejection of sanctioned literature in Kratochvil's essay, however, Věroslav Mertl (b.1929) defended writers like himself, whom sanctioned critics described as the 'grey zone' because their work, though sanctioned for publication, lacked the overt optimism and commitment which Party ideologues demanded. These included, for Mertl, the older generation of poets like Ludvík Kundera (b.1920), Oldřich Mikulášek (1910–85) and Jan Skácel (1922–89), as well as writers of historical fiction like Vladimír Körner (b.1939) and Jiří Šotola (1924–89) (see Mertl 1993: 7). To this so-called 'grey zone' might be added writers of 'rural fiction' like Zeno Dostál (b.1934) and Jiří Navrátil (b.1939), writers of 'urban fiction' like Václav Dušek (b.1944) and comic writers like Miroslav Skála (1924–89).[11] Perhaps, however, it is sufficient to quote Janoušek, who, in an article surveying the literary situation nearly a year after the fall of the Communist regime, commented:

> The consequences which the subjugation of official literature to politics had on its quality are undeniable. I strongly object, however, to the blind partiality of apostles of the new faith casting judgements without reading books, or having read books, but through 'aprioristic' glasses. I am convinced that worthwhile works emerged in all branches of Czech literature, as well as trash and junk.
>
> (Janoušek 2001: 76)

In contrast to Kratochvil, Erofeev provides a more detailed survey of the main trends which emerged in Russian literature during the Thaw, attacking both the chauvinism and extreme conservatism of 'official' and 'Village' literature, which in his view enjoyed its heyday serving the ideological positions of the Brezhnev period, and the 'hyper-moralizing' of 'liberal' literature, which took centre-stage with the officially approved 'truth-telling' of the *glasnost'* period. This greater detail, and in particular his differentiation between 'official' and 'liberal' trends reflects the fact that literary scholars had found enough continuity from the artistic approaches of the Thaw in sanctioned Soviet literature of the 1970s and 1980s for it not to be completely discredited. The qualities of writers like Chingiz Aitmatov (b.1928), Valentin Rasputin (b.1937), Vasilii Shukshin (1929–74), Iurii Trifonov (1925–81) and others have already been well-documented in Russian and Western criticism, and therefore my description of Soviet literature in this period will contain less detail than my preceding account of the Czech situation.

By 'official literature', Erofeev means only that sometimes called 'secretarial' literature, since its most prominent exponents were members of the Secretariat of the Writers' Union. By 'liberal' literature, at least until the *glasnost'* period, Erofeev appears to mean sanctioned urban realist writing – so-called *bytovaia proza* – epitomized in the 1960s and 1970s by Trifonov, and subsequently by the so-called *sorokaletnie* (the 'forty-year-olds'), a loose category invented by critics to take in disparate writers like Makanin, Anatolii Kim (b.1939), Ruslan Kireev (b.1941) and Anatolii Kurchatkin (b.1944). Deming Brown comments of their fiction:

> About all of these writers there is an absence of dogmatism, an ideological tentativeness and lack of doctrinal certainty. They do not fear ambiguity and ambivalence, and in some cases they in fact cultivate such attitudes. To a great extent they seem to feel that as artists their task is investigative and cognitive, not didactic.
>
> (Brown 1993: 101)

This type of writing, which may be said to correspond to the so-called 'grey zone' of Czech sanctioned fiction, only irritates Erofeev, who mocks its 'obtrusive reliance on allusions', commenting:

> readers grew addicted to a 'treasure hunt' for hints, to seeking out places where the writer had his tongue in his cheek. The result was that writers got carried away with all this tongue-in-cheek parody and forgot how to think.
> (Erofeev 1996: 433)

It might equally be argued, however, that this withdrawal of implied authorial judgement and guidance in sanctioned fiction of the 1970s and 1980s marked the 'birth of the reader' which, according to Barthes, accompanies the 'death of the author', understood as a figure imparting a 'single "theological" meaning (the message of the Author-God)' (Barthes 1977: 146). Indeed, as this study shows, the writers of the Changes frequently appear far more confident about their understanding of the nature not only of art, but also of human existence, than much 'liberal' literature of the preceding period. As in Czech reactions to Kratochvil's essay, Russian commentators responding to Erofeev's essay were most exercised by his treatment of these writers, whom readers and critics perceived to have striven in difficult circumstances to resist what Igor' Dedkov terms the 'degradation of reality' in ideologized literature (Dedkov 1991: 236). Dedkov, who cites Trifonov and the Village fiction writer Viktor Astaf'ev (1924–2002) as examples, closely resembles Janoušek in his approach, and displays a weariness with the trendy apocalyptic view of the literary situation expressed by commentators like Erofeev and Epshtein.[12]

In contrast to the prevailing Russian and Czech view of their literary histories since the death of Stalin as a series of ruptures, of which the 'fiction of the Changes' is, for now, the last, Slovak writers and commentators emphasize the continuity in their literary development in the same period, which a brief 'freeze' in the early 1970s could not disrupt (see, for example, Jenčíková and Zajac 1989: 45–71). As a result, the Slovak fiction of the Changes produced no statement comparable to those of Erofeev and Kratochvil, seeking to dissociate post-1989 Slovak literature from that of the preceding period. From the outset, the concerns of the Russian and Czech fiction of the Changes are presented in a Slovak context as the expression of the sense of the 'exhaustion of literature' consuming Western culture as a whole. For example, the short story collection *Chliev a hry* (Byre and circuses, 1990) by Pavel Hrúz (b.1941), his first publication since 1968, included a note from the author reflecting on how the writer should respond to the long-drawn-out decline in the importance of literature as the bearer of absolute truth. Hrúz writes:

> With each generation the human being is wiser and has learnt his lesson better, his descendants no longer burden themselves with thoughts about the inflatedness of words, knowing all too well about the growing disorder of

> informatics, of which for them *belles-lettres* is an inferior, indeed negligible part. What should the incorrigible man of letters do with himself now? [...] From the bottom of my heart I think that the poor old writer (though clearly now no more than a graphomaniac) should not give up his gift of negative entropy. He should give up only his omniscience and didacticism, he should mask all fictions and give the reader the greatest possible chance of co-creation. (And deeply conceal the insistent feeling that he is striking up a dialogue with a blank face.)
>
> (Hrúz 1990: back cover)

In the early 1970s, as in Czech literature, many of the most prominent Slovak writers from the generation which had emerged in the mid-1960s, including Hrúz, Ján Johanides (b.1934), Vincent Šikula (1936–2001) and Pavel Vilikovský (b.1941) were similarly not permitted to publish. During this period, however, works by two other members of this generation, Peter Jaroš (b.1940) and Rudolf Sloboda (1938–95), continued to appear, alongside the first publications of Dušan Dušek (b.1946) and Dušan Mitana (b.1946), who continued in the spirit of the literary experiment of the Thaw. Eva Jenčíková and Peter Zajac perceive the turning-point in Slovak literature to be the return of Šikula with *Majstri* (The master carpenters) in 1976, followed by the widely admired *Pomocník* (The butcher's assistant, 1977) by Ladislav Ballek (b.1941), a rising functionary in the literary establishment, and Jaroš's *Tisícročná včela* (The thousand-year-old bee, 1979) (see Jenčíková and Zajac 1989: 62). Johanides published for the first time in twelve years in 1978, and in 1983 came his most complex and ambitious work, the historical novel *Marek koniar a pápež uhorský* (Marek the Master of Horse and the Hungarian Pope), the same year as Vilikovský's only publication between 1965 and 1989, the detective novel *Prvá veta spánku* (The first movement of sleep, 1983).[13] Though all these writers at times encountered difficulties – for example, distribution of Sloboda's novel *Rozum* (Reason, 1982) was temporarily halted in 1982, and Mitana had to alter the ending of his novel *Koniec hry* (The end of the game, 1984) – they undoubtedly enjoyed greater artistic freedom than their Czech counterparts. Consequently, though writers like Ivan Kadlečík (b.1938), Martin Šimečka (b.1957) and Dominík Tatarka (1913–89) were closely associated with the leading Czech dissidents, Slovak *samizdat* and *tamizdat*, unlike its Russian and Czech counterparts, could never claim either in quantity or significance to represent the 'real' Slovak literature in this period.

Nevertheless, writing in early 1989, Jenčíková and Zajac pointed to an 'urgent need to release the human creativity blocked up by the stigma of the previous decades', noting that the 'detabooization' of certain subjects, a central element of *glasnost'*, was one way of achieving this (Jenčíková and Zajac 1989: 71). By linking their article back to a discussion in 1965 in the same journal, *Slovenské pohľady*, about a perceived 'crisis' in Slovak literature, they perhaps deliberately suggest that, as at that time, new works had already appeared indicating the direction that Slovak literature would take. The emergence of a new generation of writers began with the publication of collections of verse by Jozef Urban (1964–99) in 1985 and Ivan Kolenič (b.1965) in 1986, together with the appearance in periodicals of verse by poets including Taťjana Lehenová (b.1961), Ján Litvák (b.1965), Andrijan Turan (b.1962) and Kamil Zbruž (b.1964).[14] This liberalization may be said to have culminated in the publication in 1988 in *Dotyky* of Lehenová's poem 'Malá nočná mora' (A little nightmare), parodically describing female penis fascination, which begins:

> With unquietening amazement
> I intimately observe how you grow
> I want it.
> I want you to be big and powerful
> I want you to be king
> (Lehenová 1989: 38)

The poem provoked enormous debate, with some critics condemning it as 'no longer literature', rather as Urnov condemned Narbikova in his 'Plokhaia proza', but its appearance, and that of Lehenová's first collection the following year, suggested that meaningful literary censorship in Slovakia was at an end.[15]

Sanctioned poets in all three literatures in the 1980s were the first to explore – or be permitted to explore – the themes and techniques which would later typify the 'fiction of the Changes', but their impact was greatest in the Slovak context, not least because several of the new generation, in particular Urban, were also prominent critics.[16] In their reviews, published, for example, in the literary supplement to the daily newspaper *Smena*, the journal *Romboid* and its supplement for young writers, *Dotyky*, which was established in 1987 and became a separate periodical in 1989, Urban and others attacked manifestations of what they perceived as unthinking literary conformism, provoking often unmeasured reactions from establishment critics.[17] The launch of *Literárny týždenník* in September 1988, explicitly to support the Slovak literary establishment's 'own programme of *perestroika*' (Solovič 1988: 1),[18] merely cemented the process of liberalization which had been taking place. As far as fiction was concerned, the decisive moment was the publication in the spring of 1989 of Vilikovský's satire *Večne je zelený...* (Forever green is..., 1989) and two other volumes of his fiction, all dating from the early 1970s.

In the 1990s, formerly sanctioned writers like Dušan Dušek, Johanides, Mitana and Vilikovský remained central to new Slovak fiction, alongside new writers like Kolenič, Viliam Klimáček (b.1958), whose first collection of verse was published in 1988, Peter Pišťanek (b.1960), who had published stories in *Slovenské pohľady* since 1988, Jana Bodnárová (b.1950), the feminist Jana Juráňová (b.1957) and Tomáš Horváth (b.1971), the first to emerge of the writers whom Robert Pynsent later labelled the Genitalists. These writers, who also included Vlado Balla (b.1967), Tom von Kamin (b.1971) and Marek Vadas (b.1971), had studied Slovak literature and aesthetics at Bratislava University and, like the slightly older Urban/Barbarian 'generation', were often critics too. Pynsent notes that their writing is marked by an 'ironization of male genitalia and an explicit concern in their fiction with modern Theory, especially French varieties' (Pynsent 1999: 22). This ironizing of the phallus, as a symbol of the Slovak stereotype of male potency, already present in Lehenová's verse, may be seen as a unifying motif in the Slovak fiction of the Changes, with male sexual impotence reflecting the impotence of the writer in works by Johanides and Kolenič, as well as the Genitalists, or the potent imagination in Klimáček's *Panic v podzemí* (A virgin in the underground, 1997). Johanides's *Trestajúci zločin* (Crime that punishes, 1995) takes the form of a monologue by a former police archivist to a young man who has come to discover the fate of his parents during the 1950s. It transpires that the archivist himself had been tortured in that period and castrated. The empty scrotum in the novel symbolizes not only his submission to the regime, but also the writer's inability ever to tell a truth uncompromised by allegiance to one perspective or another, a theme in Johanides's writing since the 1960s. Though Juráňová does not explicitly refer to the phallus in her fiction, she repeatedly sets an explicitly Slovak coarse masculinity, often expressed as a latent threat of violence, against a wise, playful, somewhat melancholy femininity reminiscent of Berková's *Knížka s červeným obalem*. In Juráňová's work, the 'victories' of that masculinity, achieved through verbal or physical violence, are illusory compared with the resilient independence of that female perspective.

The Slovak emphasis on the continuity between the writers of different generations reflects the emergence of a more urgent confrontation in Slovak literature between those writers who had a liberal, pluralist understanding of culture, and those who propagated a conservative nationalist view.[19] This confrontation was scarcely evident in mainstream Czech culture, which was dominated by a 'politically correct', anti-Communist, pro-Western perspective, but certainly manifested itself in Russian culture of the period, though in literature less fiercely than in Slovakia because the 'liberals' were in power rather than in opposition.[20] Under the premiership of Vladimír Mečiar, who took Slovakia to independence and remained in power for much of the 1990s, the nationalists forcefully promoted a very specific, chauvinist understanding of Slovak culture and history, creating or re-creating publications, publishing houses and cultural institutions in their image. The major periodicals, with the crucial exceptions of *Romboid* and *Dotyky*, later augmented by *Vlna* and *RAK*, and the daily newspaper *SME*, simply excluded all writers who failed to fit this understanding, while their books sometimes carried warnings to the reader from the Ministry of Culture, indicating that they had been deemed 'not suitable for Slovak readers'. In Russia in the 1990s, critics tended to divide along liberal and conservative lines, with the former publishing in journals like *Druzhba narodov*, *Iunost'*, *Novyi mir*, *Znamia* and the newly established *Novoe literaturnoe obozrenie*, and the latter in, for example, *Nash sovremennik* and *Molodaia gvardiia*.

Though, like their Czech counterparts, the Russian and Slovak writers of the Changes frequently satirized the West and the process of economic and political 'westernization' in their countries, their commitment above all to creative freedom meant that they could not but be associated with the liberal camp. Writing preoccupied with the examination of its own limitations, understood as a metaphor for the limitations of the human being, was, moreover, plainly at odds with the nationalist view of culture as a shaping, collectivizing force. In an essay comparing the perception of literature in Russian and in Western European culture, translated in an early issue of *Literárny týždenník*, Iurii Lotman argues: 'In Western European culture, no bridge connects how a human being writes and how he lives. In Russian culture, however, this link is very close' (Lotman 1988: 9). The comments of Hrúz, Kratochvil and others quoted above indicate that this link was also perceived to be very close in Slovak and Czech culture. The attempt by the writers of the Changes to sever this link and focus on what Lotman calls the 'problem of the relativity of the word' (ibid.) thus represented for both its advocates and its opponents an attempt to 'westernize' literature.

Writers and critics reflected their 'westernizing' allegiances most demonstratively through their interest in Western post-Structuralist and postmodernist theory, which is much more overt in Russian and Slovak literature and criticism than in its Czech counterpart. In his exhaustive survey of new Czech fiction in the 1990s, Lubomír Machala comments:

> The high frequency with which the term [postmodernism] occurs in texts of the most varied provenance indicates that postmodernism became very fashionable in Czech circles in the first half of the 1990s, but a retrospective glance also reveals that still today Czech literature lacks a systematic reflection of the problems of postmodernism comparable to that found even in neighbouring Slovakia.
>
> (Machala 2001: 20)

Machala's book contains the first serious attempt to place Czech literature in this context; it was followed in 2002 by Vladimír Novotný's *Mezi moderností a postmoderností*, which includes a brief comparative study of Jáchym Topol's *Sestra* (Sister, 1994) and Viktor Erofeev's novel *Russkaia krasavitsa* (A Russian beauty, 1990, dated as written 1980–2), published in Czech in 1992 (see Novotný 2002: 45–59).[21] By contrast, Timothy Beasley-Murray argues of writers exploiting post-Structuralist theory in Mečiar's Slovakia:

> The import of theory is the passport to the cosmopolitan zone of pan-European culture. Put in specific terms: using literary theory means not being a nationally-oriented writer such as Andrej Ferko [b.1955], Štefan Moravčík [b.1943] or Rudolf Čižmárik [b.1949], but rather putting oneself in the same arena as, say, Salman Rushdie.
>
> (Beasley-Murray 2000: 81)

Discussion of postmodernist theory in sanctioned periodicals in this period began earliest in Slovakia, with Peter Zajac asserting in *Romboid* in the spring of 1989 the relevance of postmodernism to Slovak culture as an aesthetic associated with times of transition, thereby seeking to return Slovak literature to the currents of Western culture where, in his view, it belonged (see Zajac 1989b: 102).[22] Later the same year, Tibor Žilka, the most prolific theorist of postmodernism not only in Slovak, but also in Czech periodicals in the 1990s, published an article in which he traces postmodernism in Slovak literature back to writers of the 1960s like Hrúz, Jaroš, Johanides, Vilikovský and Sloboda (see Žilka 1989: 18–24).[23] Similar efforts in the early 1990s to 'reconstruct' a canon of Russian postmodernism by Russian critics including Epshtein, Mark Lipovetskii and Viacheslav Kuritsyn culminated in Lipovetskii's *Russkii postmodernizm*, published in 1997, and Irina Skoropanova's *Russkaia postmodernistskaia literatura*, published in 1999. Both dated postmodernist fiction back to works written but unsanctioned for publication in the 1960s by Bitov, Venedikt Erofeev and Terts, through émigré writers like Brodsky and Sasha Sokolov (b.1943) to the 'other fiction' writers of the late 1980s.[24]

As Lipovetskii argues in his contribution to a discussion of postmodernism in Russia published in *Voprosy literatury* in late 1991, commentators found in Western postmodernist theory a new critical framework in which to explore recent writing (see Lipovetskii 1991: 4). Beasley-Murray suggests that conformist Slovak intellectuals espoused either nationalism or Western theory in an attempt to fill the ideological vacuum left by discredited Marxist-Leninist theory, and cites a satirical episode from the novel *Univerzita* (University, 1996) by Vadas and Eman Erdélyi (b.1972), in which a female lecturer decides in the lift one evening after work that she will give up being a Marxist and become a phenomenologist, radically transforming her whole demeanour (see Beasley-Murray 2000: 80). At the same time, however, by tracing postmodernism in Russian or Slovak literature back to the 1960s, when it supposedly appeared in Western literature, critics implicitly sought to demonstrate that Russian or Slovak literature had not, as suspected, fallen behind the dominant currents in Western literary culture. Other commentators from Russia or former Soviet Bloc countries, indeed, went as far as to suggest that the 'postmodern condition', which comes about, according to Jean-François Lyotard, as a result of the 'decline of the unifying and legitimating power of the grand narratives' (Lyotard 1984: 38), found a unique expression in those cultures which had experienced the disintegration of Marxism-Leninism.

The accounts of Russian postmodernism by Lipovetskii, Skoropanova and others, while overcoming the 'extra-literary' division between unsanctioned literature written inside or outside Russia, do not include a single work sanctioned for publication in the Soviet Union before 1986. In his *Early Soviet Postmodernism*, Raoul Eshelman rejects this perspective as a perpetuation of what he calls the 'deformation model', which 'assumes that Soviet [i.e. sanctioned] literature was twisted and turned by political pressures to such an extent that it set out on a history of its own, independent of Western epochal development' (Eshelman 1997: 30). Eshelman continues:

> There are, of course numerous differences between Western and Soviet literature. These differences arise not because Soviet literature functioned in an essentially different way from Western literature, but because Soviet writers were not allowed to experiment with style or express their political opinions openly. These restrictions did not, however, prevent Soviet writers from taking recourse to the same postmodern figures of thought as their Western counterparts.
>
> (Ibid.)

Eshelman suggests that mainstream sanctioned fiction, by failing in its attempts to repair or reconstitute the Marxist-Leninist 'grand narrative', constitutes the first stage in the development of a peculiarly Russian 'postmodernism'. These writers' concern for the integrity of units like the individual or the collective in later stages gives way to authorial self-irony about the attempt to repair these notions and culminates in the foregrounding of their fictionality. By describing how the principles and techniques claimed as their own by the writers who came to prominence in the late 1980s can be traced in their development in sanctioned fiction since the Thaw, Eshelman not only undermines conventional accounts of 'Russian postmodernism', but in effect reveals the sheer arbitrariness of the term 'postmodernism'.

The term 'postmodernism', whether it is used to refer to the contemporary period itself or to the dominant artistic approach of that period, implies a linear chronology in which 'postmodernism' represents a new stage, despite the frequent, serious objection to the term that its defining features may be identified in literature of many other periods. For example, Lipovetskii asserts that postmodernism marks a new stage in culture, in which art enters into a 'dialogue with chaos'. He writes:

> Postmodernism demonstrates a major artistic and philosophical attempt to overcome the binary opposition of chaos and cosmos, which is fundamental for classical and modernist types of culture, and to redirect the creative impulse toward a compromise between these universals [...]. Rather than resolving contradictions, [postmodernist compromises] lead to a new intellectual space for the constant interaction of binary oppositions. Of course, such a space cannot help but be the source of new conflicts and new contradictions; yet such constant interaction is also the inexhaustible source of new artistic and philosophical meaning.
>
> (Lipovetskii 1999a: 30–1)

In *...na okraji chaosu...*, her poetics of the twentieth-century literary work, however, Hodrová, in effect seeking to overcome problematic terminological distinctions like 'modernism' and 'postmodernism', coincidentally argues that the quintessential twentieth-century work, which need not necessarily be the most numerous type, is based throughout the century on this 'dialogue'. She writes: '[the work is a] creation and manifestation of chaos. It is a construct that sometimes appears to succumb to chaos; however, at the same time, by finding elements of its hidden other order, the work shapes and overcomes chaos' (Hodrová 2001: 134).

By opening itself up to chaos and change, rather than reaffirming and perpetuating the existing notion of the cosmos, the twentieth-century work, in Hodrová's view, epitomizes what she terms an 'aesthetics of otherness'. This notion is derived from Lotman's contrast between an 'aesthetics of identity', which he associates with Classicism, and an 'aesthetics of confrontation', emerging with Romanticism. According to Hodrová, whereas in the 'aesthetics of identity', 'the most highly valued features in a work were those held in common with paradigmatic works, "identity" was a pre-requisite of value and whether a work could be considered ideal' (ibid.: 115), in the 'aesthetics of otherness':

> The source of aesthetic value is declared to be variability, deviation, the foregrounding [*aktualizace*] and deformation [of methods], and defamiliarization, which are in fact different terms for more or less the same phenomenon and principle. The value of a work, if it is mentioned at all, is connected above all with the features which run counter to the norm and emphasize its uniqueness, newness and originality.
>
> (Ibid.: 116)

Hodrová associates the 'aesthetics of identity' with utopian writing, 'doctrines of totalitarian regimes and times of stability', and perceives the 'aesthetics of otherness' to be 'thriving and reflected in works arising from and considered outside "official" art, being born on the joins between eras, in unsettled times' (ibid.). The 'aesthetics of otherness' may be associated with the figure who, in Lotman's description, 'stands on the margins, talks nonsense, says unexpected things or speaks in paradoxes, who likes the things that no one likes'(Lotman 1988: 9). Lotman associates this figure with the author of paradoxes, the jester, and, echoing Evgenii Zamiatin (1884–1937), the heretic and the martyr.

The attraction of the model advanced by Hodrová on the basis of Lotman's theory is that it posits in place of the notion of a linear movement forward, implied by 'postmodernism', a notion of literature 'swinging' between two extremes. This movement is, however, accompanied by a notion of movement forward in which what went before is not really supplanted, but remains preserved. In her theory as in her fiction, Hodrová resists the notion that, as time passes, concepts are replaced by other concepts, instead presenting words as masks through which the patient and careful observer may perceive its previous guises. In her poetics of the twentieth century, she writes: 'development is never the mere substitution of types; in the new stage, the preceding state remains preserved as a possibility, so that the variety of possibilities (types) in fact grows constantly and in a relatively unlimited way, because little in literature perishes entirely and forever' (ibid.: 243).

The fiction of the Changes exemplifies this simultaneously cyclical and accumulatory understanding of literary development, displaying a heightened awareness on the one hand of the 'preceding state', understood as an apparently alien aesthetics which the writer seeks to subvert in the text, and on the other of previous manifestations of the 'aesthetics of otherness', recalled, for example, through intertextual references. As precursors to the Russian fiction of the Changes, Chuprinin lists the philosopher Vasilii Rozanov (1856–1919), and twentieth-century non-conformist writers like Nabokov, Zamiatin, Andrei Belyi (1880–1934) and Konstantin Vaginov (1899–1934) (see Chuprinin 1989a: 5), to whom other critics added other Symbolists, members of the Oberiu avant-garde movement, particularly Daniil Kharms (1905–42), and so-called 'fellow-travellers' of the Revolution, particularly Iurii Olesha (1899–1960). The Czech writers of the Changes owe much to the Decadents, while the Czech and Slovak writers of the Changes exhibit the influence of the early twentieth-century philosopher and fiction writer Ladislav Klíma (1878–1928), the Poetist Avant-garde, and experimental fiction writers of the late 1930s and 1940s like Milada Součková (1899–1983). Though writers in all three literatures seek to associate themselves with an international 'canon' including, for example, the Comte de Lautréamont, Franz Kafka, Jorge Luis Borges, Samuel Beckett, and French 'nouveau roman' and 'nouveau nouveau roman' writers, this appeal to a supranational culture is most evident in the Slovak fiction of the Changes. This may be attributed not only to the contemporary political situation already described, but also to a certain sense of a lack of what Beasley-Murray calls an 'Urbanist' tradition to counter the 'Ruralist' 'aesthetic of identity' (Beasley-Murray 2000: 81).

For Hodrová, the exceptional periods in twentieth-century literature have been those when the work has closed itself off to chaos and become preoccupied with the 'reinforcement of composition and everything connected with it (reinforcement of genre, a return to *histoire* and to a single Meaning)' (Hodrová 2001: 103). As far as Czech literature is concerned, this occurred before and during the Second World War, when, in Hodrová's view, it reflected an attempt to withstand the 'total destruction of values', then in the 1950s and again in the Normalization period, when it was fundamentally motivated by political expectations. For Hodrová, the so-called 'literature of dissent' in the 1970s and 1980s was also founded on an 'aesthetic of identity', in her view connected 'not only with its latent inclination towards ideologization, but also with its emphasis on the importance of the reader, for whom the "aesthetic of otherness" sets greater obstacles to understanding the text than the "aesthetic of identity"' (ibid.: 116). Despite her insistence that her poetics make no value judgements about different approaches to the creation of literature, by asserting the 'aesthetics of otherness' as the 'natural' aesthetics of the century, she, like Erofeev and Kratochvil, ultimately reveals the bias of those sidelined in the 1970s and 1980s. Perhaps, however, rather than the triumph of one aesthetics over the other, literature is constantly seeking not a compromise, but an equilibrium between them. The swing perceived by the writers of the Changes in Russian, Czech and Slovak literature towards an extremely fixed model of the world and an extremely self-confident view of the capabilities of the human being results in a comparable swing to the opposite extreme. That swing forms the subject of the following chapters.

2 Deaths of authors

Venedikt Erofeev, Bohumil Hrabal, Pavel Vilikovský

In the early months of 1989, three novels written in the early post-Thaw period – Venedikt Erofeev's *Moskva–Petushki*, Hrabal's *Příliš hlučná samota* and Vilikovský's *Večne je zelený...* – were sanctioned for publication in full for the first time in the country of their writers' birth.[1] In the case of *Moskva–Petushki* and *Příliš hlučná samota*, the significance of their publication rested on the fact that they were well-known to critics, having already been published and reviewed abroad and in *samizdat*, but Vilikovský's failure to publish more than one work of fiction during the Normalization had served as a particular reminder of the restrictions facing Slovak writers. In an early review of *Večne je zelený*, Milan Šútovec suggests that Vilikovský suffered from writer's block (see Šútovec 1989: 258), but the more common view, contained in Peter Darovec's study of the novel, is that Vilikovský was not prepared to tailor his work to prevailing political expectations in order to be published (see Darovec 1996: 31).

The enthusiastic reception which critics accorded *Večne je zelený...* reflected a sense that, with the work's publication, the authority of these restrictions had essentially gone. Milan Resutík, noting the work's exceptional popularity among critics, wrote: 'against the background of our good old, calm and to some extent stagnant fiction, I would say that we could speak of a break-through book' (Resutík 1990: 124). Darovec describes its impact in terms similar to those used by Viktor Erofeev or Kratochvil in their articles declaring the liberation of Russian and Czech literature respectively:

> [*Večne je zelený...*] plays with the very essence of the understanding of literature rooted in the broad mass of the Slovak reading public, brought up on texts which were always dominated by a clear ethical or moral objective. That purpose may have changed according to socio-political requirements (texts of national awakening, texts building the nation or Socialism), but the principle of 'using' literature for an extra-literary purpose remained.
>
> (Darovec 1996: 34)

From the earliest reviews, *Večne je zelený...* was presented by Slovak critics as a defining example of postmodernism in Slovak literature (see, for example,

Halvoník 1989: 4, Zajac 1989a: 4 and Žilka 1990: 83–91).[2] Similarly, *Moskva–Petushki*, initially presented by critics as a defining example of the emerging category of 'other fiction', is now conventionally considered one of the first works of Russian postmodernist fiction (see, for example, Bogdanova 2002). By contrast, Czech critics placed *Příliš hlučná samota* in the context of Hrabal's own literary development, which was perceived not only to culminate, but also to be questioned in *Příliš hlučná samota*. Jiří Holý, however, notes the proximity of the novel's themes and motifs to the works of writers from the 1980s underground (see Lehár *et al.* 1998: 860).

Moskva–Petushki and *Příliš hlučná samota* have both been associated by critics with the mood of despair among intellectuals following the Warsaw Pact intervention in Czechoslovakia in August 1968, which Mark Lipovetskii and Konstantin Kustanovich, following a general tendency, suggest marked the symbolic end of hope not only in Czechoslovakia, but also in the Soviet Union (see Kustanovich 1997: 132 and Lipovetskii 1999a: 5). For example, Andrei Zorin writes: 'if we are interested in the social state of mind following the collapse of the illusions of the Sixties, *Moskva–Petushki* is an invaluable source' (Zorin 1989: 256), while Radko Pytlík comments: '*Příliš hlučná samota* is one of the most convincing expressions of the situation at the time of the entry of the Soviet occupation forces and subsequent events' (Pytlík 1998: 93).

In *Moskva–Petushki*, Erofeev suggests that August 1968 marks the end of history, understood as linear progress towards an ideal world. In the novel, which, like *Příliš hlučná samota* and *Večne je zelený…*, takes the form of a monologue, the narrator, Venichka, is making a regular journey on a suburban train from Moscow to Petushki, where both the woman he loves and his young son live. Each week he avoids paying for his ticket by recounting part of the history of the world to the conductor, but this week he has reached the last part of his account: 'every story has an end, and world history too… Last Friday I got as far as Indira Gandhi, Moshe Dayan and Dubček. There was nowhere to go beyond this' (Erofeev 1995: 103). Since the text of *Moskva–Petushki* is dated 1969, Venichka's remark is factually true, but in the context of the work it acquires apocalyptic significance. At the end of *Moskva–Petushki*, Venichka is murdered by four thugs who, according to Svetlana Gaiser-Shnitman, simultaneously represent the Four Horsemen of the Apocalypse and Marx, Engels, Lenin and Stalin (see Gaiser-Shnitman 1989: 229), thus equating the failure of the Communist ideal with the final defeat of human attempts to perfect themselves. The conductor's reference to Venichka as Sheherezade strengthens the implication that the intellectual has sought to ward off the inevitability of death with a fairy-tale about the teleology of human history which can no longer be sustained.

The linear perception of history is also disrupted in *Příliš hlučná samota*, reflecting the fact that the narrator, Haňťa, has retreated from the 'outside world, the world of history' (Rothová 1993: 151) into a cellar where he has spent the past thirty-five years pulping books. From references to university teachers and others who have been expelled from their jobs, the reader infers that the action of the work takes place in the period following the events of 1968, but the dating is never made explicit. The resulting uncertainty draws attention to the fact that, after 1939, 1945 and 1948, this is the fourth time since Haňťa has been in his cellar that people in Czechoslovakia have been forcibly removed from their jobs. In this way, not only are the particular socio-political circumstances shown to be irrelevant, but also the notion of linear time as an indicator of progress is exposed as illusory, since in the pursuit of a perfect world, human beings simply repeat themselves. At the end of the novel, Haňt'a indulges in an apocalyptic fantasy in which he pulps the whole of Prague, like Moscow in *Moskva–Petushki*, a metaphor for history, before dreaming of pushing himself through his press.

In the novels under discussion, Erofeev, Hrabal and also Vilikovský seek simultaneously to express sympathy with and to question the desire of the intellectual to retreat from the external world of everyday mortal existence into a private paradise of ideas. As Gaiser-Shnitman points out in her analysis of *Moskva–Petushki*, Moscow, represented by the Kremlin, is 'the symbol of secular reality and history', while Petushki is an 'Eden on earth' (Gaiser-Shnitman 1989: 45), of which Venichka says: 'Petushki is a place where day or night the birds never fall silent, where winter or summer the jasmine never ceases blossoming. Original Sin may have existed, but it does not weigh heavily on anyone there' (Erofeev 1995: 56). In *Příliš hlučná samota*, Haňťa's cellar, his 'too loud a solitude', is similarly described in terms of Eden:

> my boss sometimes cuts through the old paper with a hook and calls down to me through the opening, his face purple with rage: Haňťa, where are you? For goodness' sake, stop gawping at books and get on with it! The yard is full and you're down there mucking about in dreamland! Meanwhile I'm crouching at the foot of a mountain of paper like Adam amongst the trees of the garden, with a book in my fingers I open anxious eyes into a different world from the one in which I have just been, because, you see, when I get absorbed in a book, I'm somewhere completely different, I'm in the text, I'm surprised at this myself and I must guiltily admit that I really was in a dream, in a more beautiful world, that I was at the very heart of truth.
>
> (Hrabal 1994b: 13)

Haňťa feels guilty not because he has been caught shirking, but because he is reminded of his enduring existence in the terrestrial world. Reading, for him, has the status of transgression, since what he seeks in books is forbidden knowledge, a 'message from the heavens' about the meaning of existence. In *Moskva–Petushki*, Venichka stubbornly ignores the entreaties of angels who warn him that Petushki is not open to him or to them, indicating that his journey is also an act of transgression.

Mark Al'tshuller describes *Moskva–Petushki* as the 'symbolic journey of the soul from darkness to light, along which Gogol wanted to lead Chichikov, and which Dante completed' (Al'tshuller 1982: 82). As Gaiser-Shnitman shows, from the beginning of Venichka's journey Erofeev's text contains references to Christ's Passion, suggesting that his journey through torment may end in resurrection in Petushki. In contrast, Haňt'a's retreat into his cellar signifies his movement away from physical existence towards re-absorption in the universe. The contrast between Venichka and Haňt'a is encapsulated in the scene in *Příliš hlučná samota* in which Haňt'a dreams that he is visited by Christ and Lao T'se. While the old man, Haňt'a, identifies with the passive resignation of Lao T'se, Christ, like Venichka, is the embodiment of hope for the future:

> I saw the bloody corporeality of all Jesus's ciphers and symbols, while Lao T'se was standing in a shroud and pointing to a beam of uncarved wood [...]. I saw how romantic Jesus is, while Lao T'se is classicist. Jesus as the high tide, Lao T'se as the low tide, Jesus as spring, Lao T'se as winter, Jesus as effective love for one's neighbour, Lao T'se as the peak of emptiness, Jesus as *progressus ad futurum*, Lao T'se as *regressus ad originem*.
>
> (Hrabal 1994b: 36)

As Haňt'a later indicates when he muddles up the two Latin phrases, the outcome of human hope and human resignation is the same; all that differs is the philosophical approach (and perhaps the age of the human being).

In the context of several commentators' comparison of Venichka with the 'holy fool' (*iurodivyi*) of Russian medieval society, Venichka and Haňt'a may be seen to represent, respectively, the active and passive aspects of the holy fool's behaviour. Both Venichka's drunken antics in the railway carriage, and Erofeev's text itself in the context of late 1960s Soviet literature and society recall the holy fool's attempts to shock people from their absorption in the 'vanity' (*sueta*)[3] of the terrestrial world and think of the salvation of their souls. Early in the work, Venichka rejects society's fixation with heroic concepts and terminology in language which parodies exhortative Soviet rhetoric, but calls instead for human beings to consider their weakness:

> Oh, if only the whole world, if only everyone in the world were quiet and anxious, as I am now, and just as unsure of everything – of themselves, of the seriousness of their place beneath the heavens – how good it would be! There would be no enthusiasts, no heroic deeds, no conviction, just a universal faint-heartedness. I would agree to live on earth for the whole of eternity if beforehand someone showed me a little corner where there was not always room for a heroic deed. 'Universal faint-heartedness' is, after all, salvation from all troubles, a panacea, the pre-requisite of the greatest perfection.
>
> (Erofeev 1995: 41)[4]

Venichka's advocacy of 'universal faint-heartedness' is matched by Haňťa's affection for the *Tao Te Ching*. In the *Tao*, things are understood to be in a constant state of imperceptible growth and change, and human beings are discouraged from acting since this may interfere in the spontaneous development of things and hasten their return to nothingness. The human being should rather sit in contemplation, constantly making peace with the universe for the harm his existence inevitably causes. Haňťa is troubled by the fact that he inadvertently crushes mice in his press when he pulps packages of paper. Another of Haňťa's favourite works is *In Praise of Folly*, in which Erasmus advocates the Christian way of life, though it may seem madness to those absorbed in the values of earthly life. In contrast to Venichka, Haňťa represents the passive aspect of the holy fool, remaining awake in contemplation of the wretchedness of humankind (see Likhachev (ed.) 1984: 81).

In calling for humility, both Venichka and Haňťa express their anxiety that concern for the soul is being effaced in contemporary life, as manifested for both of them by the drinking habits of young people. Venichka declares that because they do not know how to drink alcohol, they do not care about anything. Throughout the work, alcohol and the ability to grieve at the state of the world are intimately linked with the soul. At the beginning, Venichka comments that everyone knows the burden which he carried up the steps of the entrance hallway where he spent the night. In the context he is referring to his hangover, but later the grief he feels at the state of the world is also described as a burden. Moreover, Viacheslav Kuritsyn notes that the forty steps of the staircase correspond to the forty days before the soul leaves the body in the Orthodox tradition (see Kuritsyn 1993: 298), giving credence to Al'tshuller's suggestion that the whole text takes place inside Venichka's head as he staggers up the staircase from the moment of his stabbing to his death, and thus represents the passage of his soul from his body (see Al'tshuller 1982: 85).[5] The inability to drink, indicating an inability to feel sorrow, thus represents an absence of soul, reflected in the empty, expressionless eyes of Venichka's fellow passengers on the train. Towards the end of the work he rails against those responsible for this loss of soul, implicitly those who imposed Marxist-Leninist ideology on Russia:

> Oh the shameful people! They've turned my earth into the shittiest hell – they even force us to hide our tears from people and show off our laughter! Oh the vile bastards! They've left people with nothing but 'sorrow' and 'fear', and then after this, laughter for them is public, and tears are banned!
> (Erofeev 1995: 124)

Haňťa, whose Gipsy sweetheart dies in Auschwitz, takes great pleasure after the war in pulping the cheering faces on Nazi propaganda. The implied reader may infer a link between these cheering faces and those on Communist propaganda.

In *Příliš hlučná samota*, the young workers who operate the enormous new hydraulic press which will put Haňťa out of work drink milk, not beer, reflecting the fact that the process of modernization in the novel is the pursuit of whiteness, the eradication of stains. The epigraph to Hrabal's novel is taken from Goethe's *Faust*: 'Only the sun has a right to its spots'. Stains in the work indicate the inherent imperfection of human beings, symbolizing the sin which caused them to be cast from Paradise. On two occasions Haňťa's sweetheart discovers that she has excrement on her clothes, first at a village dance and second at a fashionable ski resort, reminding them both in a moment of happiness and personal pride of the wretchedness of the human condition. Haňťa refers ironically to Nietzsche – 'what happened to her was human, all too human' – and suggests that while Goethe, Schelling and Hölderlin would have forgiven their lovers this revelation of their humanity, Leibnitz, who suggested that human beings lived in the 'best of all possible worlds' would not (see Hrabal 1994b: 27). The removal of stains, the pursuit of perfection through rational progress, is the eradication of humanity. The huge new hydraulic press can transform vast numbers of books into blank paper. The blank paper equates with the blank faces of the new generation of workers, unlike Haňťa, uninterested in those who worked to produce the books they are destroying. The erasure of the print in the books is the erasure of their human element. The effacement of the spiritual dimension to existence is reflected in the treatment of Haňťa, who, with the advent of the new machine, is sacked from his job in the cellar and given the task of packing the blank paper. The process of modernization invades and destroys his 'too loud a solitude', leaving him to contemplate suicide.

Vilikovský's fiction is also marked by what Pynsent calls 'despair at the contemporary lack of spirituality' (Pynsent 1990: 126). Vilikovský's treatment of the theme in *Večne je zelený...*, however, differs from that of Erofeev and Hrabal in *Moskva–Petushki* and *Příliš hlučná samota* in that this lack of spirituality is not opposed, but rather embodied by the narrator, an old man recounting his adventures as a spy in Central Europe before and after the First World War. Zajac, whose early review of the novel expresses the most overt disgust of any towards the narrator, suggests that Vilikovský's narrator bears witness to the fact that the 'human being is definitively becoming an animal' (Zajac 1989a: 5).

The title of the novel is taken from the scene in Goethe's *Faust* in which Mephistopheles is asked for academic advice by an especially earnest student, consumed by a thirst for knowledge. The bored Mephistopheles tells the student: 'My friend, all theory is grey, and green the golden tree of life' (Goethe 1998: 61). By quoting only part of the line, Vilikovský in effect defines the implied reader as an intellectual for whom familiarity with the quotation has perhaps bred contempt for its meaning. *Večne je zelený...* may be read as a parody of the encounter in *Faust*, not only at the level of the narrator and his listener, who, never given his own voice, is characterized by the narrator as an earnest, naive young man who has come in search of knowledge, but also at the level of author and reader.[6] In his discussion of the novel as a literary game between author and reader, Darovec writes:

> Vilikovský's *Večne je zelený...* is not a game in which the reader is given many opportunities to co-operate with the author. Rather, he is constantly surprised by him and mercilessly mocked for his clumsiness and slowness, thanks to which the text, directed by the author, is always one step ahead of him.
>
> (Darovec 1996: 41)

In *Faust*, the student says to Mephistopheles: 'I'm so confused by all you've said / It's like a millwheel going round in my head' (Goethe 1998: 59). In this respect, the text represents the human experience of reality, which, according to the narrator, is 'often harsh, implacable and takes little care of us' (Vilikovský 1989a: 39). At the beginning of the work, the narrator, apparently referring to his attempted seduction by – or of – an Austrian Colonel, but at the same time reflecting the human response to this ineffable reality, comments: 'In this game whose rules I did not know, and which, moreover, were deliberately to remain a mystery to me until the end, I decided to invent my own rules' (ibid.: 10). To survive, Vilikovský suggests in the novel, the human being may either learn to adapt endlessly to the rules of others, or, as Beasley-Murray argues, constantly strive in vain to 'create individual, provisional rules' of his or her own (Beasley-Murray 1998: 276). The narrator embodies the former approach, while Vilikovský advocates the latter as the only authentic way of being.

In an implied authorial parody of the spy persona, the narrator presents himself as the essence of life, a devastatingly handsome and potent lover of danger, women and, if necessary, men; at one point, he comments, implicitly referring to himself in contrast to his listener: 'The man who knows how to taste life in all its forms, though he may not live longer, undoubtedly lives more intensively' (Vilikovský 1989a: 41). Throughout his monologue, he asserts the superiority of his life experience over what his listener may have read in books. For example, after apparently citing the anthropologist Bronislaw Malinowski's account of the dominant role of women in sexual intercourse in Oceania, he comments: 'I, having worked in the aforementioned field more practically than theoretically, on the basis of my own experiences can but confirm his observations' (ibid.: 33). His ability to escape from the most precarious situations appears, however, to rest not so much on heroic actions as on his own mastery of language, specifically his ability to tell stories:

> The basic rule for the person who enters that form of human intercommunication called an interrogation in the role of the interrogated is: the interrogator must get what he's after. He must be amused and entertained, he must enrich himself with new information, and he must enjoy himself sensually. Indeed, there are even individuals – I'd call them geniuses of interrogation – who manage in the course of an interrogation to educate the interrogator.
>
> (Vilikovský 1989a: 44)[7]

In *Večne je zelený...*, Vilikovský effectively identifies the two literary types destined to dominate Slovak fiction in the 1990s. The narrator represents the amoral, self-seeking potentate epitomized by Rácz in Pišťanek's *Rivers of Babylon* trilogy (see Chapter 3) and also the narrator of *Kniha o cintoríne* (A book about the cemetery, 1998) by Samko Tále (the pseudonym of Daniela Kapitáňová), which might be considered a *Večne je zelený...* for the post-Mečiar period. By contrast, his listener represents the sexually and scriptorially impotent intellectual portrayed by Kolenič and the Barbarians (see Chapter 6) or the Genitalists (see Chapter 7). Indeed, the contrast is expressed phallically in *Večne je zelený...*, in which the narrator, before referring to his own resplendent erection, comments: 'the late-starter intellectual – but this won't be your case – after his first, unsuccessful attempt at coitus is often psychologically traumatized. The over-sensitivity of today's men is acquiring terrifying proportions' (Vilikovský 1989a: 51).

Večne je zelený... may be compared with Hrabal's *Taneční hodiny pro starší a pokročilé* (Dancing lessons for the older and more advanced, 1964), where the stream of language pouring from the narrator's mind represents life and resistance to the positivist use of language which seeks to restrict that life. In *Taneční hodiny*, where the narrator is also an old man reminiscing about the period before and after 1918, Hrabal constructs the narrator's monologue from what Susanne Roth calls a 'literary montage' of quotations and allusions, outside which the narrator has no existence. Sylvia Richterová writes: 'The characters in Hrabal's stories live to speak, because they speak, to the extent that they speak and thanks to the fact that they are spoken about' (Richterová 1991: 76). This strategy is replicated by Vilikovský in *Večne je zelený...*, in which the narrator's monologue is a patchwork of quotations not only from works of 'high literature', but also from political and advertising slogans, psychoanalytical and political texts, 'manuals, travelogues, recipe books, popular science and even rhetorical declamations, in which our hero so clearly delights' (Zajac 1989a: 5).

In *Taneční hodiny*, however, the use of the montage technique does not express the loss or impossibility of originality or authenticity, but rather constitutes an attempt to locate that originality and authenticity not in the meaning of what is said, but in how it is put together anew. Roth views literary montage as more a borrowing than a quotation, a distinction defined by Herman Meyer:

> A borrowing differs from a quotation in that it does not have the character of a reference; it is not intended to be placed in relation to its original source, and that is good, because although a return to the source has a philosophical explanation, it does not enrich semantically and does not provide any aesthetic surplus value.
>
> (Meyer quoted in Rothová 1993: 81)

The narrator, rambling to a certain Kamila as she picks cherries, conveys his individuality through the fleeting uniqueness of composition, just as the sound and rhythms of his narration convey being itself. Hodrová argues that Hrabal's 'streams' of narration constitute a 'means of expressing the maximum interconnectedness of speech and the world, pulsating in the same rhythm' (Hodrová 2001: 37). According to Hrabal, the wholly innocent objective of the narrator of *Taneční hodiny* is to gain Kamila's 'acknowledgement and respect and admiration' (quoted in Rothová 1993: 152), and he is rewarded at the end when she takes her clothes off and washes in front of him. The ending may be seen as a parodic return to Eden, granted to the old man in reward for a lifetime in the shade of the tree of life, reflected by his narration.

By contrast, Vilikovský's narrator is a comic Frankenstein's monster, a 'dummy put together from language which signifies nothing but is none the less a real force' (Mikula 1989: 45). Early in his monologue, explaining his motivation for being a spy, he declares: 'The only reward really is the awareness that you helped to turn the wheel of history; whether here or there, it doesn't matter, the main thing was to make sure it moved' (Vilikovský 1989a: 10). Like Erofeev and Hrabal, Vilikovský thus rejects the notion of history as an inexorable process towards an ideal, positing instead an 'understanding of historical development as an irrationally connected sequence of events which unwind from a multitude of coincidences working against each other' (Darovec 1996: 39). In practice, the narrator has not moved the wheel, but has moved with it, endlessly adapting to the prevailing doctrine, adding it, in effect, to his repertoire, in order to survive. Through the consequent mixture of nationalist, anti-nationalist, Fascist and Marxist-Leninist rhetoric in his monologue, he becomes, in Zajac's view, the embodiment of 'central European consciousness'. Zajac writes: 'the adoration of "the best of all possible worlds" at every instant of its existence no longer has the appearance of masochism [as in *Candide*], but has become total, generally acceptable and accepted opportunism' (Zajac 1989: 5). In this respect, Vilikovský's narrator resembles the amoral, self-seeking Dítě, the central character of Hrabal's *Obsluhoval jsem anglického krále*, written at a similar time to *Večne je zelený...*, who represented for Hrabal 'the eternal adaptability of the Czechs'.

Whereas so much sanctioned and unsanctioned fiction not only of the Thaw, but also of the 1970s and 1980s, reflected on the failure of people to live up to ideas and the failure of ideas to live up to people, in all three of the novels under discussion the notion that ideas and people should ever be expected to live up to one another is presented as a grotesque confusion, embodied by Vilikovský's narrator. A product of the attempt to impose theory on life, he represents not the spirit of life, but the soullessness of ideologized life, as empty as what Valér Mikula calls the 'desemanticized' quotations of which it is compiled (Mikula 1989: 45). His monologue constitutes, in effect, the revenge of that ideologized life on the minds which created it. At the end of the novel, the narrator, ostensibly demonstrating a series of knots, ties his listener up, the literal representation of what has happened metaphorically through the work, before sarcastically remarking: 'Now you can see where your reckless desire for knowledge has brought you' (Vilikovský 1989a: 85).

The same remark might have been uttered to Venichka by the thugs who murder him. Through Venichka, Erofeev parodies himself as the epitome of the sentimental Russian intellectual, moved by sorrow at the condition of the world to drink and to dream. Liviia Zvonnikova suggests that in the novel Erofeev satirizes the Russian intelligentsia's 'revolt against God', whom they blamed for the plight of the human being (see Zvonnikova 1996: 220). This revolt is recalled in Venichka's refusal to buy a ticket on the train, which parodically evokes Ivan Karamazov's respectful refusal of a ticket to God's future in Dostoevsky's *The Brothers Karamazov* (1881). The repeated identification of Venichka with Christ, culminating in his late, despairing cries of 'Eli, Eli, lama sabachthani', reflects how this revolt ultimately resulted in the intellectual taking the salvation of humanity upon himself. Like the listener-intellectual in *Večne je zelený...*, however, his quest fails. Instead of reaching Petushki, Venichka falls into a drunken stupor, and when he awakes, apparently on the way back to Moscow, his journey is plunged into chaos. The chapter titles, which throughout the novel break into Venichka's monologue to indicate stations on the train's route, start to merge Moscow and Petushki. Venichka's return to Moscow not only indicates the impossibility of perfecting human existence, but also suggests that the result of the attempt to create heaven on earth is 1960s Communist Moscow.

Venichka's journey represents the culmination of the Russian intellectual's yearning for the celestial, which Erofeev implicates in the establishment of Communism through his use of literary montage. As Gaiser-Shnitman and other critics have documented, Venichka's monologue is, like that of Vilikovský's narrator, composed of quotations and allusions, in this case to the Bible, Greek myths, slogans, popular songs, films, fairy-tales, children's literature and scientific and political texts, but above all the canon of world and, particularly, Russian literature.[8] In *Moskva–Petushki*, Erofeev expresses his intention to resist the temptation to follow those writers who have gone before him by despatching in his stead an alter-ego who bears his name. By killing Venichka at the end, Erofeev kills off the 'writer-visionary' in himself, as he makes clear through Venichka in an obliquely self-referential passage concerning Goethe:

> 'But why did he [Goethe] make Werther put a bullet into his forehead? Because – there's evidence – he was himself on the brink of suicide, but in order to remove himself from the temptation, he made Werther do it instead. Do you understand? He remained alive, but in a sense committed suicide. And he was entirely satisfied. It's even worse than straightforward suicide. In this there is more cowardice and egotism, and creative baseness.'
>
> (Erofeev 1995: 84)

The implication of the whole of Russian culture, understood as the bearer of ultimate authority and ideology, in the brutality of Stalinism, a notion also fundamental to Sorokin's writing, discussed in Chapter 6, recalls the position taken by Theodor Adorno in his essay 'Cultural Criticism and Society'. Adorno writes:

> The more total society becomes, the greater the reification of the mind and the more paradoxical its effort to escape reification on its own. Even the most extreme consciousness of doom threatens to degenerate into idle chatter. Cultural criticism finds itself faced with the final stage of the dialectic of culture and barbarism. To write poetry after Auschwitz is barbaric. And this corrodes even the knowledge of why it has become impossible to write poetry today. Absolute reification, which presupposed intellectual progress as one of its elements, is now preparing to absorb the mind entirely.
>
> (O'Connor 2000: 210)

As Lipovetskii points out, *Moskva–Petushki* constitutes a coincidental dramatization of Roland Barthes's 'death of the author', in which the writer no longer represents a source of truth, but a weaver of texts (see Lipovetsky 1999a: 81–2). In his essay, first published in 1968, Barthes writes:

> a text is made up of multiple writings, drawn from many cultures and entering into mutual relations of dialogue, parody, contestation, but there is one place where this multiplicity is focused and that place is the reader, not, as was hitherto said, the author.
>
> (Barthes 1977: 148)

Barthes's essay greatly influenced Russian and Slovak writers discussed later in this study, but the expression of similar ideas by the writers discussed here appears more a coincidence of cultural mood than a deliberate act of reinterpretation. Whereas for Barthes, the 'death of the author' is an act of liberation, in *Moskva–Petushki* it is accompanied by the end of literature, which Erofeev, with nostalgic melancholy, suggests cannot now recover its innocence. This position is reiterated more caustically in another patchwork text, Viktor Erofeev's *Russkaia krasavitsa* (A Russian beauty, 1990, dated as written 1980–2), which describes a high-class prostitute, Irina Tarakanova (Irene Cockroach), whose name alludes to the Princess Tarakanova, a pretender to Catherine's throne whom Catherine had thrown into prison, where she died. Erofeev's Tarakanova, who has had countless abortions, but still considers herself the saviour of Russia, may be seen as a metaphor for the traditional Russian understanding of literature as leading the people to salvation. Her abortions represent the many failed ideas of how salvation might be achieved, of which Marxism-Leninism is the last, since at the end of the novel she commits suicide.[9]

In *Příliš hlučná samota*, by contrast, books are not implicated in the positivist march of progress, but rather represent for Haňt'a not only a refuge from it, but a source of resistance, a constant reminder of the gap between the aspirations and capabilities of human beings. Books in *Příliš hlučná samota* embody the search for the meaning of existence, which will always be curtailed by death. Milan Jankovič links this 'asking questions about oneself', which he considers the overarching theme of the novel, back to the end of *Obsluhoval jsem anglického krále*, when Dítě has abandoned his quest for social acceptance and begun, stumblingly, to show concern for his soul:

> in fact in that pub I always found that the essence of life is in asking questions about death [...] that actually death, or rather, that asking questions of oneself is a conversation from the perspective of infinity and eternity, that just the examination of death is the beginning of thinking in the sublime and about the sublime, because to taste the meaninglessness of one's path, which will in any case end in premature departure, that enjoyment and experience of one's ruin fills the human being with bitterness, and therefore beauty.
> (Hrabal 2000: 223)

From *Taneční hodiny* to *Příliš hlučná samota*, the work of the imagination shifts from being an externally directed to an internally directed activity. *Taneční hodiny* exemplifies Mikhail Bakhtin's conception of the relationship between self and other in his essay 'Avtor i geroi v esteticheskoi deiatel'nosti', in which he argues that because the self experiences itself as 'unconsummated', constantly moving forward in space and time, it is only the other, from its privileged position outside the self, that can give the self form and wholeness. Since the other is also a self seeking 'consummation', the relationship is reciprocal (see Bakhtin 1990: 12–13). This 'consummation' does not, however, result in the imprisonment of the self, which continues to move forward. Richterová writes: 'All of Hrabal's "natterers" (*pábitelé*) may be seen as people who create themselves in speech in such a way that they cannot be contained within any known and established system' (Richterová 1991: 68).[10] However, writing on *Příliš hlučná samota*, Roth comments: 'In the external world, in the world of history, Haňťa would be reduced to an object, whereas in his "loud solitude" he remains a creative subject, defending the remains of his freedom' (Rothová 1993: 151). Seeking acknowledgement of the self carries too great a risk that the self will be trapped in an externally imposed definition, in Richterová's terms, 'become transformed into a sign'. The experience of the self as dynamic, existing, must be acquired without recourse to the external world. This implicitly endless internal self-creation underpins key works of unsanctioned fiction in the 1980s like Brabcová's *Daleko od stromu* (Far from the tree, Cologne 1987, Prague 1991), Placák's *Medorek* (Little Medor, 1990), and Kremlička's *Lodní deník* (Ship's log, 1990).

In *Příliš hlučná samota*, however, this attempt at self-preservation results in another form of objectification. Near the beginning of his monologue, Haňťa declares: 'I've been educated against my will, and so I don't really know which ideas are mine and from inside me and which I got from something I read'

(Hrabal 1994b: 9). Instead of seeking the meaning of life in communication with the benevolent other described by Bakhtin, Haňťa seeks it in books, and thus, like Venichka or Vilikovský's spy, becomes an amalgam of the texts he has read, the embodiment of their futility, identical to the packages he carefully puts together for pulping. Towards the end of the work Haňťa comments: 'The books conspired against me and I didn't receive even a single message from Heaven' (ibid.: 63). Roth places the blame for Haňťa's fate on a society bent on eradicating its soul, a society which had itself come to perceive him as a book no longer wanted. In this context, while Venichka's death may be seen as a form of divine punishment, Haňťa's dream of his own death at the end of *Příliš hlučná samota* represents martyrdom. As *Taneční hodiny* indicates, for Hrabal the writer was always a humble weaver of texts, endlessly hoping, in Hodrová's phrase, for a 'glimpse of being' (Hodrová 2001: 780). It is this type of author whom the world above ground has declared dead. Roth writes of Haňťa: 'His last message is not without hope, but is bequeathed to another time, which will perhaps have more understanding for this message' (Rothová 1993: 156). That time could perhaps be the Changes, when Czech writers, as discussed in Chapter 5, sought to reassert the writer-as-seeker, precariously positioned between solipsism and absorption in a hostile other, and between the terrestrial and the celestial. Unlike their Russian counterparts, these writers retain Hrabal's perception of the innocence of literary creation, and the guilt of human beings who misuse it.

The tragic fates of the narrators of *Moskva–Petushki* and *Příliš hlučná samota* contrast with the absurdity of the fate of the listener at the end of *Večne je zelený...*, which reflects Vilikovský's altogether less melodramatic perception of the plight of the intellectual. Like Venedikt Erofeev, he suggests that the intellectual is to blame for his own predicament. Vladimír Petrík writes:

> We have got used to formulating (literature has got used to formulating) very unequivocally what is ambiguous, indefinite and difficult to grasp; we make absolute what is relative and has only limited validity. The criticism of language [in *Večne je zelený...*] is a criticism of the superficial acquisition of knowledge.
>
> (Petrík 1991: 16)

However, where Erofeev suggests that the intellectual should fall silent, allowing the herd instinct to take over, as happens in *Příliš hlučná samota*, Vilikovský seeks in his novel to overcome this conventional distinction between the intelligentsia and the masses in culture, by showing both narrator and listener to be tied up in the relativity of signs and the impossibility of absolute knowledge. As Darovec writes, this 'understanding of the impossibility of speaking wholly and objectively does not, however, mean scepticism and resignation, but is, paradoxically, encouraging' (Darovec 1996: 35). The ending of *Večne je zelený...* asserts the futility of conformity, of which both narrator and listener are guilty, opening up the possibility that the whole of each human being's life might be a private, unique process of creating a version of the world (see Beasley-Murray 1998: 276). At the end of the novel, the narrator, perhaps speaking in unison with the implied author, says:

> I'll leave you now to your fate. Soon you'll realize that the process of acquiring knowledge is not a tram which you can enter and exit as you please. Don't take this as a threat. Exciting times await you. You'll expand your horizons with new experiences, you'll be amused, you'll learn… And if the process of acquiring knowledge does not take the direction you supposed, don't let yourself be discouraged, because it still always applies […] that theory is grey and ever green is… '…the horse of life!' cried the colonel, opening the doors of the wardrobe wide, and when he had stretched his stiffened limbs, neighed joyfully.
>
> (Vilikovský 1989a: 86)

The sudden interjection of the Colonel may be read as a device designed to distract the reader, undermining the seriousness of the preceding message to prevent it too becoming a dogma. At the same time it reflects the travestying of high-flown notions about the nature of human existence – like Goethe's 'golden tree' – that takes place in the work.

Večne je zelený... is ultimately closer than either *Moskva–Petushki* or *Příliš hlučná samota* to the spirit of Barthes's declaration of the 'death of the author', since Vilikovský, like Barthes, perceives that death to be accompanied by the birth of all human beings as reader-creators of their own lives. In his short novel *Kôň na poschodí, slepec vo Vrabl'och* (A horse upstairs, a blind man in Vrabľe), also published for the first time in 1989, Vilikovský writes: 'The only freedom we have is to preserve our idea about things and not allow anyone else to mess with it' (quoted in Pynsent 1990: 125). This view in different ways may be said to inspire the works of each of the three writers discussed in the next chapter.

3 Giving a shape to one's fate

Evgenii Popov, Petr Placák, Peter Pišťanek

In her study of the novel, *Hledání románu*, Hodrová identifies two essentially teleological models for the novel. In the earlier type, the 'novel of initiation', the protagonist abandons his social, terrestrial identity to seek knowledge of the divine. This model is reversed in the later 'novels of lost illusions', in which the protagonist, his identity as yet unformed, seeks knowledge of the ways of the world in order to find his or her place in it. In conventional Socialist Realism, the underlying belief in a future paradise on earth leads to a blurring of the distinction between these types, with the central character's initiation into the Marxist-Leninist 'mystery' simultaneously symbolizing, in Nadya Peterson's phrase, the 'ultimate reconciliation of the individual and society' (Peterson 1997: 2).

A lasting effect of the Thaw in Russian, Czech and Slovak fiction was the attempt to depict the path to social assimilation in a Realist context, restoring the dominance of the 'novel of lost illusions'. Hodrová's use of this negative-sounding term, in contrast to *Bildungsroman* or *Erziehungsroman*, reflects an increasingly widespread perception in fiction of the 1970s and 1980s that social assimilation represented a form of defeat. The emphasis palpably shifted from the ending to the potentially life-long quest for the right path. Describing Soviet fiction of the late 1970s in terms which might equally be applied to Czech and Slovak sanctioned fiction of the same period, Geoffrey Hosking writes:

> [the] process of self-discovery (or failure in self-discovery) has something in common with the quest for inner meaning traversed by many Socialist Realist heroes: only now there is no certainty and no social utopia at the end of the path. Modern Soviet man must be content with fragmentary insights, must renounce any ultimate goal, and must become accustomed to the idea that the way is more important than the Purpose, the spirit than the result.
>
> (Hosking 1980: 201)

Hosking's account recalls the sentiments of Albert Camus's essay 'Le mythe de Sisyphe', one of Haňťa's favourite works, in which Camus argues that the human being, liberated from the 'illusion of another world', is, like Sisyphus pushing his rock up the mountain, no longer concerned about the outcome of his efforts, but about how the efforts themselves 'give a shape to one's fate' (Camus 1988: 106). In effect, fiction thus moves towards the third type of novel identified by Hodrová, the 'novel about a misfit' (*román o bloudovi*), exemplified for Hodrová by works including Sterne's *Tristram Shandy* and Dostoevsky's *Notes from Underground* (1864). According to Hodrová,

> [the misfit] does not himself change [...], nor does he abandon the world, but he lives in a state of constant tension with it because, unlike the practically-minded character, he is unable or unwilling to adapt to it, but at the same time does not seek to escape it through mystical initiation.
>
> (Hodrová 1989: 215)

Hodrová points out that the word *bloud*, which denotes an 'unreasonable, foolish, preposterous person unable to adapt to reality', has the same root as *bloudění*, meaning 'aimless wandering'. While the protagonist in the 'novel of initiation' or 'novel of lost illusions' pursues forms of self-definition, the 'misfit' strives to keep himself undefined.

The re-emergence of this type may already be observed in sanctioned fiction from the 1960s onwards; however, its expression in the fiction of the Changes is not simply more extreme, as Epshtein's glib notion of the shift from Shukshin's 'weirdoes' (*chudiki*) to the 'wankers' (*mudaki*) of 'other fiction' suggests. Sanctioned and dissident fiction of the 1970s and 1980s, preoccupied with morality, suggests that one 'gives a shape to one's fate' through one's actions, therefore the outcome is not completely forgotten. By contrast, in the fiction of the Changes, the focus is on words. A 'literature' after 'Literature' is thus conceived as writing which, rather than seeking to give a final, ideal shape to the world, seeks endlessly only to give shape to the self. This view, already seen in *Večne je zelený...*, is epitomized by Popov's *Dusha patriota*, Placák's *Medorek* and the fiction of Peter Pišťanek, which form the focus of this chapter.

Like the works discussed in the first chapter, *Dusha patriota* was published for the first time in 1989 and constituted a defining example of the emerging critical category of 'other fiction' (see, for example, Lipovetskii 1989, Potapov 1989, and Shtokman 1989). *Dusha patriota* takes the form of a monologue made up of individually dated missives to a certain Ferfichkin, written in the period before and immediately after Brezhnev's death in the autumn of 1982. In the foreword, Popov explains that, although he and the author of the missives have the same name, 'I am not him' (Popov 1994: 8). As Porter points out, the narrator's rambling style owes much to Sterne (see Porter 1994b: 114–16), and is used to assert the aimlessness of life in the face of the conviction, arising from the ideologization of living, that life must have a purpose. Whereas, however, in *Moskva–Petushki* and *Příliš hlučná samota*, the quest for a meaning to life results in tragedy, and in *Večne je zelený...* in absurdity, in *Dusha patriota* Popov presents as banal not only the inevitable failure of such quests, but also the restatement of their futility in literature.

This banality is encapsulated in the single-word epigraph, '...garden...', the last word of Voltaire's *Candide*. Through this epigraph, Popov seeks to bring writers and literature down from the pedestal of authority they occupy in Soviet and mainstream dissident culture, implying that the only wisdom that literature is capable of imparting about the world is that asserted at the end of *Candide*: that human beings, rather than pursuing the 'best of all possible worlds', would do better to devote themselves, as Haňťa does, to a lifetime of self-cultivation for its own sake. Indeed, Popov's own version of the message lacks even this high-minded dimension, seeking instead to demystify the spiritual wanderings of the intellectual, most obviously in the second part of the novel, when he and the poet Dmitrii Prigov roam around Moscow on the day of Brezhnev's funeral, trying to get close to where the body is lying in state.

Just as Vilikovský gives only half of the quotation from Goethe in the title of *Večne je zelený...*, Popov uses only the last word of the quotation from Voltaire to indicate that the message of the novel is well-known, but adds an ellipsis after the word 'garden' to reflect that people none the less still go looking for some other, more uplifting message. For Popov, however, as for Voltaire at the end of *Candide*, the only uplifting aspect of life is that the process of preserving one's humble, private individual existence may be conducted with a few good friends. The work contains frequent, playfully disguised references to Popov's friends in the Moscow underground of the 1970s and 1980s, including Prigov and Viktor Erofeev, and while Skoropanova grandly describes the novel as a 'postmodernist hymn to the fraternity of non-conformists (*inakomysliashchikh*), the creators of unofficial culture, those wandering stars of the national underground' (Skoropanova 1999: 235), it is as much a straightforward celebration of friendships formed between these 'wandering stars'.[1]

Throughout the novel, Popov's narrator parodies the attempt to make existence meaningful by repeatedly setting himself objectives which he fails to realize. In the second part of the work, Popov satirizes the Soviet planned economy as a model of progress. The narrator commits himself to writing a certain number of pages by a set date, adopting the rhetoric of Andropov's 'discipline at work' drive, which called upon workers to show greater enterprise and initiative and 'fight slackness' (Popov 1994: 147). The narrator panics whenever he falls behind and has to recalculate his plan, all of which becomes part of the word count, leading the narrator to refer to his own text as 'self-multiplying, ever increasing nonsense' (ibid.: 86). Popov here implicitly satirizes those writers, frequently senior members of the Writers' Union, who expressed their commitment to the Soviet goal, particularly in the 1970s and 1980s, by writing enormous works of fiction, usually on historical or Second World War themes, which Popov playfully implies must be the result of a personal production plan.

His failure to meet his target mirrors the collapse of his attempts in the first part of the novel to preserve the memory of deceased relatives by committing his recollections of them to paper, which founder not only because Brezhnev's death interrupts them, but also because he has no memories of certain relatives and therefore cannot complete the task. In frustration he demands of his reader: 'Must we resurrect our fathers, Ferfichkin?' (ibid.: 44), a reference to the philosopher Nikolai Fedorov's ambition to resurrect the dead and create an immortal fraternity of human beings. Fedorov's 'common task', which aimed to tame the physical world through science, serves as a metaphor for all the 'grand plans' devised by human beings, all of which in Popov's view, rather like his own attempt to deny the transience of human life by 'resurrecting' his ancestors in text, go totally against the nature and capabilities of the human being. Vladimir Sharov (b.1952) makes a similar point in his novel *Do i vo vremia* (Before and during, 1993), in which he asserts the kinship between Fedorov's grand design and Stalinism by suggesting that Stalin was the illegitimate child of Fedorov and Madame de Staël.

Popov's satirization of the pursuit of perfection culminates in an apparent outburst of optimism prompted by Brezhnev's death which, according to Porter, Popov considers 'perhaps the most important moment in the book' (quoted in Porter 1994b: 126). The passage concludes:

> and we'll be able to think about [...] the immortality of the soul, about how all people, like brothers, will begin to worry about each other and will forget how to shove with their elbows, and a diamond age will come, and flesh will unite with spirit, and new forms of 'somatopsyche' will be consolidated, the origin of new species will take root, and yes, yes, we will all be happy, happy, happy. Let's all finally BECOME HAPPY, let's forget discord and apply all our liberated strengths to the common defence against THE DARK, against the devil, entropy, disappearance. And if we do disappear, then in such way that somehow we'll also simultaneously remain. Come on, eh? I'm ready to do it. I'm ready to become the brother of anyone who at least occasionally looks in the direction of happiness, peace and quiet.
>
> (Popov 1994: 121)

The whole passage, quoted by Porter in full, places Popov's own hopes, which somewhat resemble Venichka's call for 'universal faint-heartedness' in *Moskva–Petushki*, at the end of a chaotic catalogue of 'grand narratives', including Marxism-Leninism, Freudism, Darwinism, Pan-Slavism and Fedorov, all of which have sustained a teleological model of history as progress towards the ideal. In this way, Popov casts doubt on the innocence of his own optimism, suggesting that any form of hope for the future, however banal, is ultimately a delusion of grandeur.

In his afterword to the first publication, Sergei Chuprinin associates the narrator's lack of a sense of purpose with the particular relationship (or lack of relationship) between the individual and the state in Brezhnev's Soviet Union, arguing that *Dusha patriota* 'principally speaks about the alienation of the human being, the citizen, from politics and ideology and from the history of his native country' (Chuprinin 1989b: 79).

The relationship between the individual and the state is exemplified for Chuprinin in a scene in the second half of the work in which, in another example of a purposeful venture thwarted, the narrator and Prigov are turned back with a friendly smile by a policeman close to the place where Brezhnev is lying in state. The narrator is amazed:

> after all, if he were really *not letting us through*, he would have answered rudely, heavily, visibly, sharply, precisely, but in fact he *wasn't letting us through as though he were letting us through*. It seemed that at any moment he might just let us through. But in fact he really didn't let us through at all as though he were letting us through, that is, politely, almost indulgently.
>
> (Popov 1994: 193)[2]

Chuprinin comments:

> we would dearly love to be citizens in the full sense of the word, but they won't let us, they shuffle us off into side-streets, a little further away from the activities of the state machine. They politely but unbendingly remove us from participation – even through the right to a consultative voice or the 'bird-seed' [ptich'ikh] rights of an eye-witness – in the resolution of problems which are not without interest to all of us.
>
> (Chuprinin 1989b: 79)

Chuprinin's interpretation suggests that life might become more meaningful under a different system, betraying not only the tendency among readers and critics to regard works of literature as social commentary, but also the social democratic aspirations of liberal critics in the period. Popov's narrator does express a sense of having been unjustly excluded for political reasons; he makes frequent references to the *Metropol'* affair, to editors who have rejected Popov's work and to theatres which will not perform his plays. However, when the narrator plaintively remarks: 'I really want to fulfil some sort of function on earth, but there is absolutely no point of application' (Popov 1994: 71), he expresses an existential, rather than a political problem, echoing in effect the Oblomov-type 'superfluous man', whom he parodically resembles.

In *Dusha patriota*, as in his next novel, *Prekrasnost' zhizni* (The splendour of life, 1990), whenever state power has intervened in someone's life, Popov uses the phrase 'through circumstances not dependent on anyone', presenting the event as a stroke of misfortune interrupting the normal situation, in which the two exist independently of each other. The scene with the policeman is not portrayed as a confrontation either between oppressor and victim or between the absurd and the reasonable, but as a meeting of the equally absurd (or equally reasonable); the state feigns friendliness to the individual just as the individual feigns obedience to the state, but both are conducting a private existence to which the other has no access. In contradiction to Chuprinin's statement that 'one cannot live in a society and be free of society' (Chuprinin 1989b: 79), Popov shows in the work how he and his acquaintances take from the state what they need to survive and then retire to their private activity.[3]

The understanding of literature expounded in *Dusha patriota* casts further doubt on Chuprinin's interpretation of the work as an expression of socio-political protest. In an attempt to dissociate his novel from precisely this sort of reading, the narrator declares:

> My missives to Ferfichkin are of a private, peaceful nature and do not pursue political, ideological, religious or any other aims. They are entirely distant from literature, these missives of mine, as distant as they are, in their turn, from real life. They are in general as distant from everything as I am myself.
> (Popov 1994: 90)

According to the narrator, just as the human being loses 'something crucially and originally human' by becoming absorbed in an ideological model of existence, as suggested by the novels discussed in the first chapter, so literature is damaged by becoming the means by which such a model is propounded. Popov's narrator complains:

> It's stupid, Ferfichkin, when ideology places its bets on literature, taking it seriously. After all, literature is fragile and tender, and unable to bear the weight, it breaks and withers, but then all the same sprouts, having spitefully strengthened itself with terrible weals and thorns, as a result of which it becomes dangerous, insolent and poisonous. What do we have such a nasty tradition for?
> (Ibid.:119)

The weakness of literature corresponds to the weakness of the human being; placing unrealistic expectations on either results in their deformation.

At one point the narrator asserts that the only purpose of writing is 'self-characterization' (*avtokharakteristika*) (ibid.: 70). In *Dusha patriota*, the narrator's self becomes the plot, defined by Peter Brooks as

> a kind of arabesque or squiggle toward the end [...] that suggests the arbitrary, transgressive, gratuitous line of narrative, its deviance from the straight line, the shortest distance between beginning and end, which would be the collapse of one into the other, of life into immediate death.
> (Brooks 1984: 104)

Brooks takes the notion of the plot as arabesque from Balzac, who took it from *Tristram Shandy*. In *Dusha patriota*, Popov implicitly suggests that the text, instead of attempting to move ahead of the self, ordaining its destination, in the manner of the Socialist Realist teleology, should, as in Sterne's novel, strive to follow the self, tracing the unique twists and turns of its passage through life, 'giving a shape to its fate'. In this way, the text is transformed from being a metaphor for the end of life, its final goal, to a metaphor for life in progress, understood as constant resistance to the end. This resistance is reflected in the narrator's dislike of change, which recalls Haňťa's Taoist assertion of inaction in *Příliš hlučná samota*: 'I have, perhaps, decided to become a CONSERVATIVE, or perhaps I have already become one [...] or perhaps I always was' (Popov 1994: 158). By opposing change, he hopes to 'conserve' life, an ambition reflected in his efforts to resurrect the memory of his ancestors in the first part of the novel.

This notion of narration as endless self-creation, the constant assertion of the independence of the narrating self from a final, externally imposed definition, recalls *Notes from Underground*, a connection suggested by the name of Popov's addressee, Ferfichkin, which is the same as that of the smirking social climber in the second part of Dostoevsky's novel, whom the Underground Man challenges to a duel. Critics like Porter, Lipovetskii and Skoropanova have perhaps been too hasty in declining to read much into the link between the two works, which arises initially from a pun on the word 'underground' (see Porter 1994a: vi, Lipovetskii 1989: 35 and Skoropanova 1999: 228). Like Dostoevsky's Underground Man, Popov's narrator has rejected the rationalist model of human existence dominating society and therefore finds himself in the literary 'underground', rather like Haňťa in his cellar. Whereas, however, Haňťa retreats further and further from the external world until his physical existence becomes irrelevant, Popov's narrator asserts his independence from the external world through his meandering narrative.

Mikhail Bakhtin argues that the Underground Man uses narration to resist final definition by what he experiences as a hostile external world, distancing his present self from any earlier selves which his readers may have defined, hence his frequent claims that he has just been lying or joking, or that he does not believe what he has just said. Bakhtin writes:

> There is literally nothing we can say about the hero of *Notes from Underground* that he does not already know himself: his typicality for his time and social group, the sober psychological or even psycho-pathological delineation of his internal profile, the category of character to which his consciousness belongs, his comic as well as his tragic side, all possible moral definitions of his personality, and so on – all of this, in keeping with Dostoevsky's design, the hero knows perfectly well himself, and he stubbornly and agonisingly soaks up all these definitions from within. Any point of view from without is rendered powerless in advance and denied the finalising word.
>
> (Bakhtin 1984a: 52)

Dusha patriota exemplifies the 'struggle against a reification of man' (ibid.: 62) which Bakhtin perceived in Dostoevsky's work. Popov's narrator lacks the self-pity or malevolence of Dostoevsky's Underground Man, and he regards his Ferfichkin with considerably more affection. However, he does become irritated when he suspects Ferfichkin of seeking aims or imposing definitions on his text: 'I'm not forcing you to read; the last thing I need is a reader like you, who secretly frowns because…I write what I want to write, the way I want, the way I know how' (Popov 1994: 53). For Popov, as for Vilikovský, all that the literary text can express is the enduring, charming but ultimately futile freedom of the human being to create his own version of himself and the world.

Popov's humbling of literature's pretensions in *Dusha patriota* contrasts with the re-definition of literature's purpose in the fiction of Liudmila Petrushevskaia (b.1938), who is mentioned in *Dusha patriota* and who also echoes *Notes from Underground* in her work, both in the opening lines of her short story 'Svoi krug' (A closed circle, 1987), and in the subtitle of her short novel *Vremia-noch'* (The time is night, 1992), 'Zapiski s kraia stola' (Notes from the edge of the table). Like Dostoevsky's Underground Man, the cold, aggressive narrative voices of these works are products of a society founded on rationalism, residents of anonymous blocks of flats in which individuality is being steadily effaced, as Petrushevskaia indicates through the absent, unmemorable or easily confused names of her characters. The title of *Vremia-noch'* is, however, ambiguous, since it not only suggests the 'twilight' of humanity, but also the time when the narrator has time and space to write. Her account of the cycle of psychological tyranny she plays out with her daughter may be seen as a confession, the expression of a sinner's longing for redemption seen also in the Underground Man. The editor's note which prefaces the main text, explaining that the notes were brought to her by a woman who found them among her mother's things after she had died, indicates that the narrator at least won the forgiveness of her daughter. In Petrushevskaia's fiction, the literary text is not reduced to words, as in the work of so many of her contemporaries, but rather acquires the power to reconcile and perhaps redeem.

The influence of *Notes from Underground* may also be seen in Placák's *Medorek*, one of the most widely discussed works of fiction to emerge from the 1980s generation of Czech underground writers. In the novel, Placák distinguishes between the conformist language of clichés, formulae and slogans, used by society to impose external limits on the self, and the language of literary creation, through which the self constantly resists 'normalization'. In his linguistic study of the distribution of literary and non-literary Czech in the novel, Ondřej Hausenblas writes: 'literary Czech here is unambiguously associated with higher values, spiritual or creative activity, whereas non-literary Czech belongs to the everyday reality of work' (Hausenblas 1994: 12). The collision of these two types of language is brought about by the basic plot of the novel, which František Kočka suggests is essentially autobiographical (see Kočka 1987: 1) and describes two years in the life of the central character, Karel Medor, from the time when, aged sixteen, he starts work in a factory. Medorek – the diminutive is discussed below – fears becoming absorbed by society. Eva Kantůrková describes Medorek as 'alive and ineffable in his lifelike-ness, an artistic likeness of the quiet, inward defence of an entirely unprotected human being against destructive power' (Kantůrková 1988: 50). A paradigmatic 'misfit', he at the same time fears either being identified as a sick animal that must be culled in the interests of the herd, or going mad, that is to say, becoming lost in the language of his own imagination. As I discuss in Chapter 5, this struggle to preserve an intermediate position, absorbed in neither type of language, recurs in the Czech fiction of the Changes.

In the case of *Medorek*, which appeared in various *samizdat* versions between 1985 and 1989, this struggle was generally understood by critics in its political context, as an account of the psychological turmoil experienced by the individual under extreme social pressure to assimilate. Karin Pohánková describes *Medorek*, along with Brabcová's *Daleko od stromu* and Kremlička's *Lodní deník*, as an 'irreplaceable confession about the formation of part of a generation which felt itself pushed to one side and limited by the political system, a generation which grew up surrounded by barbed wire, a generation without a future' (Pohánková 1996: 181). However, as the diminutive in the title suggests, it may also be seen as the account of the passage of the child from the fluid world of its own imagination to the fixed notion of the world asserted by adults. Writers like Tolstaia, Pelevin, Hodrová and Kahuda repeatedly assert the preferability of the child's way of perceiving reality, which they seek or yearn to restore through their writing. In *Medorek*, however, Placák appears to favour adolescence, understood as the time of initiation, and a state in which one is simultaneously aware of the child's and the adult's way of seeing while wholly possessing neither.[4] Finally, Medorek's struggle may be seen as that of the writer, characterized by Hodrová as precariously engaged in an implicitly unending movement between the stable, accepted model of the world and the chaos of the unstable and unknown (see Hodrová 2001: 129).

The style of Medorek's refusal to fit in is encapsulated in the opening passage of the chapter entitled 'Medorek, nový soudruh' (Medorek, a new comrade), which satirically describes how society anticipates his first day at the factory:

> The evening before Mummy ironed his clothes, in the morning she put a packed lunch in his bag and her little darling set off by himself into a new, unknown world, into the labyrinth of adults, into the world of real worries, serious faces without frivolous chatter, into a world where he himself would forever be responsible for everything, would take care of everything himself, would deal with the others as an equal with equals and together with them would solve important problems. [...] A new citizen, a new comrade is entering the world, who with full responsibility is coming to build his fatherland and the happy and joyful future of all mankind. Enormous fields of golden corn, newly painted combine harvesters, there will be no hunger, no war, just joyous work. A little soldier with his red scarf round his neck, marching triumphantly over all the roads of the world. The whole universe,

> to meet the sun! Little Medorek happily smiling to welcome those millions of kind-hearted people! Watch out, Medorek's coming.
>
> He was ill and started at the factory a month later.
>
> (Placák 1997: 7)

Placák's ironic crescendo of Socialist imagery and rhetoric culminates not in a grand gesture of revolt from Medorek, but in a bathetic 'wrong note' which also reflects the contrast between the great expectations that Marxism-Leninism has of human beings and their actual physical weakness.

Throughout the novel, Medorek strives to prevent his responses to the external world becoming predictable, thereby sustaining the state of confusion on which his survival depends. In a scene comparable to the encounter between Popov, Prigov and the policeman in *Dusha patriota*, Medorek is asked by the factory's personnel officer why he refuses to join the Party youth movement. Medorek explains: '"since time began, no Red Indian has ever been in any youth movement"' (ibid.: 15). After a moment's amazement, the personnel officer decides it must be a joke and bursts out laughing. Medorek is in turn stunned by his reaction: '"What's that idiot laughing at?" scowled Medor. "Does he think I was kidding?"' (ibid.: 16). Whereas the scene in *Dusha patriota* depicts the chance meeting of two worlds, in *Medorek* it constitutes the confrontation of two different games. The mutual confusion which results indicates that Medorek has won. His victory is emphasized when a fellow-worker subsequently advises him to sign up just to get the bosses off his back, in terms of Hodrová's analysis of the 'misfit', to reduce the 'state of constant tension' and begin to 'fit in'. Medorek's furious reaction to this suggestion provokes a twinge of guilt in the fellow-worker, the realization that he has become part of someone else's game.

In his 1978 essay 'Moc bezmocných' (The power of the powerless), Václav Havel (b.1936) describes the Czech who tolerates the approved 'rituals' of the Normalization power structure as 'living in falsehood', since he has 'accepted "appearance" as reality and acceded to the given "rules of the game"' (Havel 1990: 64). In Havel's view, the path to 'living in truth' begins in rebellion against such rituals and exposure of the game as a game, and continues in working towards the creation of a society in which all may 'live in truth'. However, like the Underground Man, Medorek resists not in the hope of bringing about a better society, but for its own sake.[5] The narrator comments that in fact Medorek was quite happy to join the youth movement, but just could not be bothered to fill in the form. He wipes his bottom with the form during a visit to the lavatory not in protest, but because it was the nearest paper to hand. Placák reveals here how the external world imposes its own interpretations on the actions of individual human beings in an attempt to pigeon-hole them. Medorek's refusal to join the youth movement reflects his refusal to be part of any crowd, whether pro- or anti-regime; this is the only consistent aspect of his behaviour. For example, he likes the 'Internationale' precisely because no one else does. In an outburst in a pub which strongly recalls *Notes from Underground*, he argues: '"Maybe someone would like to argue, some wily old fox, that 1+1=2! I, on the other hand, wouldn't see it like that, I wouldn't see it like that at all, just because that's the way everyone sees it and quantity, that's just stupidity and dim-wittedness"' (Placák 1997: 34). For Medorek, as Vilikovský also implies in *Večne je zelený...*, there is no alternative to the 'game', only the choice between submitting to the rules of others, or striving endlessly to retain the freedom to make one's own rules. Medorek's struggle to preserve his adolescent perception of social relations as a game bears comparison with the controversial sanctioned novel *Hra na slepo* (Playing blind, 1982) by Ludvík Němec (b.1957), in which the central character, a gifted chess player, is treated for schizophrenia apparently brought on by the pressure to commit himself to the responsibilities of adult life.

For Placák, the game is above all linguistic. Karel Vaca comments: 'at the centre [of *Medorek*] is not the description of the event itself, but its literary experience, how it is captured in language, how it appears in "codes"' (Vaca 1988: 56). In the novel, Placák presents the world as a chaos of these codes. In her detailed linguistic analysis of *Medorek*, Karen Gammelgaard comments: 'Tending towards diversity, uncertainty and chaos, [the text] blends a multitude of narrative modes. Moreover, the borderlines between these modes are regularly blurred, or at least heterogeneously signalled' (Gammelgaard 1997: 115). The individual must strive constantly to slip between these codes in order to preserve his subjectivity, defined as the continued capacity of the mind to project 'red herring' selves upon the external world. The novel may be described as an account of the mind of Medorek as he observes the various selves he projects in the company of others. Throughout the novel, the reader, like those who encounter Medorek, cannot pin down to a single definable self the sullen factory worker who is also an aggressive loner in pubs, a fervent lover of literature and writer of poetry, an obsessive football fan and a mysterious underground activist. Kantůrková writes that the latter part of the work merely contains 'variations on Medorek' (Kantůrková 1988: 50), though such an interpretation would require an identifiable 'original Medorek' earlier in the work. Placák thus presents the disintegrated personality as the consequence not merely of particular political circumstances, but of social existence in general.

The awareness of this disintegration in *Medorek* is not a source of horror, but on the contrary, evidence of the continued mental health of the individual. Medorek's ability to perceive life, understood as one's social existence, as a linguistic game of identities implicitly renders him superior to the other characters in the novel. His behaviour recalls the description by the Czech Decadent Arthur Breisky (1885–1910) of the dandy as a 'victor over life', 'an artist of life, a lover of artificial paradises and new, personally differentiated sensations, and a despiser of all that is natural, self-evident and general' (Breisky 1996: 128). The narrator repeatedly notes how the world fascinates and amuses Medorek, who, like Breisky's dandy, or Popov's *flâneur* in *Dusha patriota*, observes the life around him as though he were not involved. For Medorek, the mind absorbed in the external world adopts an active relationship with all that surrounds it, seeking to explain, understand or supply causality; in contrast, Medorek's mind takes a passive, descriptive role:

> You go along describing things. You observe them and let them fall without an echo, without comment. You throw them just like that into the depths of the swamp of your soul. You go along sucking in everything around you with your senses like enormous ladles, while considered reactions sleep.
>
> (Placák 1997: 104)

The ease with which Medorek becomes bored by physical and social reality and drifts into vivid and intense daydreams reflects his refusal to be restricted by the physically manifest world, which for Medorek does not constitute the maximum space within which the mind can operate, as in Realism, but rather the minimum required for flights of fantasy. Towards the end of the work, prefiguring in particular the fiction of Václav Kahuda (b.1965), discussed in Chapter 7, Medorek appears able to separate himself from his body, which learns to conform to the work process, and abandon the notion of a discrete individual self altogether:

> He travelled around the little paths of the consciousness of people around him, without them suspecting anything. He travelled through the infinite spaces of things around him [...]. Everything constantly forked and headed off into infinity. Every new thought evoked a thousand others and those thousand a thousand times more.
>
> (Ibid.: 120)

In these moments, as Placák describes at the end of the work, Medorek escapes the 'anti-Christ' of Socialist industry-worship and becomes a 'knight of God':

> He looked back at the factory for the last time. It stood there, huge, grey, with a fading star on its brow. [...] Medorek urged on his horse. His sword glittered gold in the light of the rising sun. Eagles circled in the heights of the kingdom of heaven and lions greeted him with a welcoming roar. Medor's song floated among the cliffs and rose to the heavens.
>
> (Ibid.: 162)

In imitation of the bathetic finale to the novel's opening rhapsody, quoted above, the reader is returned abruptly from Medorek's fantasy to an image of him sleeping soundly on the bus home from work. On this occasion, however, the preceding passage is not undermined; rather, through the juxtaposition of the spiritual and physical worlds, Placák indicates the continuing success of Medorek's battle not only to survive, but above all to preserve the freedom of his imagination, and therefore, implicitly, his soul.

In *Dusha patriota*, writing is presented as endless self-characterization, and in *Medorek* as a means of endless self-preservation. In Pišťanek's fiction, however, it represents endless self-aggrandisement, the ever more extravagant exploitation of the capacity of the self to impose itself upon reality through writing. In his best-known work, the *Rivers of Babylon* trilogy, his ironic celebration of the excess and total disregard for limits which marked the amoral, barbaric world of post-Communist gangster capitalism mirrors the utterly unironic celebration of the ferocious, limitless ambition of the imagination. Vilikovský wrote in one review:

> Our life, says Pišťanek, is banal and rests on the principle of crass pleasure. Luckily, we still know how to suffer and dream; it's a pity, though, that our suffering is narcissistic and sterile [...] and our dreams are vulgar and without imagination [...]. However, as long as a human being is capable of writing this sort of fiction, the situation cannot be completely hopeless.
>
> (Vilikovský 1993: 19)

Rivers of Babylon, Pišťanek's first novel, described by Igor Otčenáš as a 'breakthrough work' in contemporary Slovak literature (Otčenáš 1992: 40), signalled that Pišťanek's intention was not merely *épater le bourgeois*, but also, above all, *épater l'intelligent* by ironically glorifying all that the intelligentsia reject, and degrading all they hold dear. Daniel Ucháli called Pišťanek the 'murderer of national literature' (Ucháli 1992: 43). A parody rags-to-riches tale, the novel recounts how Rácz, cheated of his inheritance and bride, leaves his village to seek his fortune in Bratislava, where he rises from apprentice boiler-man at a city-centre hotel to become head of his own business empire centred on the same hotel. According to Marta Součková, Pišťanek's description of an amoral cartoon world in which every character is motivated only by personal gain relieved Slovak literature of its seriousness, hyperbolically breaking taboos on sexual motifs, restoring parody, black humour and the grotesque and introducing characters about whom it had previously not been possible to write, including 'prostitutes, lesbians, homosexuals, greedy intellectuals and venal female students' (Součková 1994: 63). Moreover, like Topol in his novel *Sestra*, discussed in Chapter 5, Pišťanek does not so much replicate as embellish the vernacular of the world he portrays. In his fiction, Pišťanek also uses, for example, highly literary Slovak, urban and rural non-literary Slovak, the Americanized Slovak of a returning émigré, archaic Slovak and grammatically and idiomatically correct Czech not for verisimilitude, but to claim these different 'languages' as his own.

Pišťanek's use of 'low' registers and literary forms, repeatedly noted by critics, represents a rare example in Russian, Czech or Slovak fiction of the Changes of a successful attempt, in Leslie Fiedler's phrase, to 'cross the border, close the gap'. In his 1970 essay, which has come to be seen in both West and East as a core text of postmodernist theory, Fiedler essentially attacks the élitism present in contemporary literature, which appears divided between experimental works that critics praise and analyse and books that people actually want to read. He notes from his then recent reading that writers are turning to 'pop forms' like the Western, science-fiction or pornography, producing works which are 'less serious, more frivolous, a form of *entertainment*' (Fiedler 1971: 466). The result is a 'closing of the Gap which aristocratic conceptions of art have opened between what fulfils us at eight or ten or twelve and what satisfies at forty or fifty or sixty' (ibid.: 472).

A Fiedler-esque, anti-élitist 'postmodernism' took time to emerge in 1990s Russian, Czech and Slovak fiction. Perhaps as a reaction to the perceived homogeneity of sanctioned fiction under Communism, when fiction was expected to be accessible to a wide readership, the writers of the Changes sought, in essence, to diversify contemporary literature by restoring rather than overcoming an uncompromising élitism. Of the writers discussed here, Pišťanek's combined commercial and critical impact in Slovak literature was matched only by the reception that greeted the fiction of Viktor Pelevin (b. 1962) in Russia in the early 1990s (see Chapter 7). In 1990s Czech literature this double impact was most sought by Michal Viewegh (b.1962), whose fiction combines contemporary social satire with trendy literary allusion and self-reflexivity, but reinforces rather than challenges stereotypes, and has proved far more successful with readers than with critics.

Of crucial importance for Fiedler was the closing of the gap between critic and audience, 'if by critic one understands "leader of taste" and by audience "follower"' (ibid.: 478). In the case of Pišťanek's fiction, these roles are reversed, to the evident discomfort of some critics. Stanislava Chrobáková wrote:

> The thematicization of the decay of values, also reflected in lowness of genre and language, raises too many questions (and indeed too much violence) for the cultivated reader to be able to submit unequivocally to the talents of the author as observer and story-teller.
>
> (Chrobáková 1992: 75)

Rather as Chuprinin's afterword to the first publication of *Dusha patriota* sought to delineate the 'moral message' of the work, Chrobáková's lukewarm review of *Rivers of Babylon*, together with that of Ladislav Čúzy in the same issue of *Romboid*, revealed Slovak critics' enduring expectation of clear implied authorial guidance, on which their enjoyment of a literary work apparently depended. While Chrobáková is dissatisfied with Pišťanek's 'incompletely defined position [resulting from] pre-meditated semantic ambiguity' (ibid.), Čúzy writes: 'aesthetically it did nothing for me, and philosophically it told me almost nothing' (Čúzy 1992: 74).

Pynsent writes: 'If Pišťanek does have a [morally self-conscious] goal, he manages to hide it, whatever we as readers impose on the white between the lines' (Pynsent 2000: 90). The world portrayed in the *Rivers of Babylon* trilogy bears such a teasingly close relationship to the reality of the gangster capitalism which overtook former Communist countries after 1989 that the reader cannot but interpret the novels as a comment on the period. Pišťanek, however, uses hyperbole not to force the reader's moral judgement, but to demonstrate the immutably absurd nature of the human being and make the reader laugh. Pynsent writes:

> [Pišťanek] enjoys what he abhors and seeks to lead his readers to the same enjoyment, at the safe distance of literariness [...]. The human race is risible for Pišťanek; he enjoys, perhaps even secretly admires, the species for its very risibility.
>
> (Ibid.: 91)

In this way, Pišťanek fundamentally rejects the conventional understanding in Slovak culture, of which the Marxist-Leninist period represented only an example, that literature should 'improve' the human being, both by seeking to educate and by providing examples of 'better' human beings. Součková argues that *Rivers of Babylon* did not represent the 'culmination of all previous literature, but rather its radical denial. Herein lies its greatest value' (Součková 1994: 63). For her, this radical denial is epitomized by Pišťanek's short story 'Mladý Dônč' (Young Dônč, 1993), which, like most classic Slovak literature, is set in the countryside. Součková writes, however:

> [Pišťanek] does not find charm in the family idyll, he is not moved by social misery in the village or town, caused, after all, by dim-wittedness and stupidity. He looks on the common people with neither benevolent humour nor affectionate distance, but rather parodies the sentimentality of previous fiction on this theme.
>
> (Ibid.)

Zoltán Rédey describes 'Mladý Dônč' as a 'morbid caricature' of one of the best-known literary treatments of the modernization of Slovak rural life, *T'apákovci* (The T'apákov family, 1914) by Timrava (pseudonym of Božena Slančíková, 1867–1951) (see Rédey 1994: 56).

In the story, a parody *Bildungsroman*, Dônč, a naive, sensitive youth from a mountain village, is sent by his mentally deficient and physically deformed family to work in the nearby factory to earn money for alcohol, which in the story appears to be the last requirement for keeping a Slovak peasant biologically alive. At the factory, Dônč hears rumours about prostitutes in the 'City' and begins to contemplate going there, to the horror of the other men from his village, for whom the very mention of the City is apparently taboo. Dônč, however, attacks them for not having first-hand experience of what they are talking about: '"We just sit here on our backsides and all the time it's 'they say', 'they say'! And we don't know anything for sure [...] Maybe somewhere in the world it's even better, and we only have to go there."' The response of one, Nagy, is scathing: '"Better?" asked Nagy scornfully, "It can only be better elsewhere for those…free-thinkers! Nothing ties them to the village"' (Pišťanek 1998: 68).

Nagy embodies the crass Slovak chauvinism which dominated the early post-independence period under the government of Vladimír Mečiar. However, Pišťanek's satire is not simply that of the urban intellectual, mocking rural backwardness. In his reference to 'free-thinkers', Nagy already identifies Dônč with the cosmopolitan intellectuals who betray all that is good and Slovak. After their argument, Dônč reflects how he has become estranged from his family, and he sets off for the City, where, however, he can only afford manual relief from a prostitute who takes pity on him. On his return home, he finds his father declaring that time has stopped, and exhibits his greater knowledge of the world by pointing out that in fact only the kitchen clock has stopped. Unable to stomach the stagnation, Dônč sets off once again. At the end of the story, Dante's metaphor for sinful existence, a 'dark wood', looms before him, Pišťanek's ironic indication that he has abandoned the Slovak nationalist Eden of the village for the venal, alien City.

Though the reader who knows *Rivers of Babylon* may infer from the conclusion that Dônč will become another Rácz, Dônč is a different type. Through Dônč's 'sentimental education' and his chastening return to his family, Pišťanek satirically documents the transformation of the dim-witted, self-absorbed village boy into the apparently equally dim-witted, self-absorbed urban intellectual who will write about his roots, any criticism suffused with nostalgia. In the context of the period, Pišťanek may be understood here to be attacking the writers who lent support to Mečiarite nationalism, but the satire is much broader, as indicated by the subtitle of *Rivers of Babylon 2 alebo Drevená dedina* (1994), a reference to the Socialist Realist novel, *Drevená dedina* (A wooden village, 1951) by František Hečko (1905–1960). In *Rivers of Babylon 2*, the 'wooden village' refers to what Pišťanek implicitly suggests is the new national symbol of Slovakness, the grim buffet-bar outside Rácz's hotel, run by Rácz's former sweetheart and the man who stole her from him, now wretchedly aspiring to match Rácz's wealth. In Pišťanek's view, writers like Hečko, but also Timrava and the contemporary nationalists, whose fiction implicitly or explicitly subscribed to a belief in the human being's capacity to redeem and be redeemed, simply lost sight of what Součková terms the 'biological' in the human being, which in Pišťanek's work carries none of the positive connotations of the 'natural' or 'authentic'. In encouraging his readers, as Pynsent suggests, to share his enjoyment of the innate ridiculousness of human beings, Pišťanek seeks, with irony, to make the intellectual reader love the physical human being from whom he or she recoils.

Rather as Peter Zajac interprets Vilikovský's narrator in *Večne je zelený…*, Otčenáš suggests that the 'moral devastation' of Pišťanek's characters, reflected in his choice of literary form and language, represents the outcome of intellectuals' imposing their ideas on human beings: 'Rácz and so on are the real product of this historical flatulence: an over-sensitive intelligentsia, bastardized workers, a corrupted nation. Long live non-literature! A non-period cannot be written about otherwise!' (Otčenáš 1992: 40). Defending Pišťanek's use of vulgarisms and low literary forms, Rudolf Sloboda writes: 'the most vile people were heroes who in fine literary Slovak, without disgusting words, hanged, tortured, blackmailed and tormented the Slovak nation' (Sloboda 1992: 40). Pišťanek, however, does not even credit literature with the ability to deform the human being, suggesting instead that human beings are immune to efforts to tamper with them. Whereas writers like Popov and both Erofeevs, and also Prigov and Sorokin, perceive ideas and ideals as inherently dangerous, Pišťanek, in common with other Slovak writers of the Changes like Vilikovský and Kolenič, considers them as ineffectual as the people who conceive them.

The weakness of Slovak writers, according to Pišťanek, derives from the fact that they have worked only to perpetuate a particular notion of the human being, imposing illusory limits not so much on human beings in general (as Russian and Czech writers imply), but on themselves. Throughout his fiction, Pišťanek portrays characters who invent arbitrary psychological limits for themselves, essentially by seeking to limit their aspirations, an approach which is often reflected in their attempts to secure a circumscribed autonomous physical space. For example, in *Rivers of Babylon*, that space corresponds for the head boiler-man, Donáth, to the confines of the boiler-room. Donáth preserves this space by being a reliable provider of heat, thus retaining the good-will of those who work in the hotel complex, and by accepting the restrictions placed on him by the hotel manager, excluding him from public areas of the hotel. The modest dimensions of the space are reflected by his aspirations in life: 'it's enough for him, Donáth, to have a little love and a little chat' (Pišťanek 1991: 14). His apprentice, Rácz, however, reflects: 'Donáth was a nobody. Not like him, Rácz. Rácz lives life to the full' (ibid.: 100). His remark recalls the comment of the narrator in Vilikovský's *Večne je zelený...*: 'Everything I've done in life, I've done to the full' (Vilikovský 1989a: 47). In contrast to Donáth, Rácz marches straight into the hotel foyer and, when his pay is docked for this offence, he turns off the heating, extorting money from hotel guests and local tradesmen and forcing a striptease dancer to sleep with him in return for restoring the heat. Only the hotel manager refuses to comply with Rácz's demands, but the limits of his power have been exposed, and those formerly in his power transfer their allegiance to Rácz: 'They know that Rácz hates the manager, and so everyone avoids him. Or they pretend not to see him. No one wants to compromise himself through contact with a condemned man' (Pišťanek 1991: 75). The hotel manager, trapped in his freezing office, slowly becomes convinced that he really belongs among the Eskimo, and eventually flees the hotel on a sledge pulled by kidnapped dogs perhaps to join the oppressed Slovaks in the Arctic Circle, described in *Rivers of Babylon 3 alebo Fredyho koniec* (Rivers of Babylon 3 or Fredy's end, 1999).[6]

Characters who seek to enclose their existence within fixed limits are motivated by self-preservation in the face of the daunting, apparent limitlessness of the world around them. They perceive that they can best shield themselves by accepting their humble position in a social, spatial hierarchy and being complicit in whichever power is most likely to maintain that hierarchy undisturbed. This willingness to collaborate is given an explicit political context in Pišťanek's *Skazky o Vladovi* (Tales of Vlado, 1995), a buoyant satire on the Mečiar period, in which Pišťanek playfully conceals prominent figures like Mečiar's Minister of Culture, Dušan Slobodník, and the Speaker of Parliament, Ivan Gašparovič, behind epithets such as 'slobodník z Vladovej stráže' (The Lance-Corporal of Vlado's Guard) or 'Vladov gašpar' (Vlado's Clown). The collection, followed by further volumes in 1997 and 2002, parodies the tradition of exemplars, describing episodes from the lives of saints or folk heroes or, indeed, as Pavel Matejovič points out, Lenin (see Matejovič 1996: 68). However, the target of Pišťanek's satire is not Mečiar himself, but those who protect his position in order to preserve their own including, as Pišťanek makes clear, supposed opponents of Vlado, notably leaders of opposition parties like Ján Čarnogurský or Peter Weiss, and the Czech president, Václav Havel. The narrator frequently reveals that Vlado's followers have not understood his teachings, but none the less fall to their knees in the presence of such wisdom. In their eyes, the logic is not that of meaning, but of power. Vlado and his followers appear to do nothing but tour the country making speeches, while Vlado's one heroic act is to fix his official car, yet the reader, like Vlado's followers, accepts the reality of his power, which, like that of the Emperor in Hans Christian Andersen's story, is based on nothing but the complicity of others.

Pišťanek rejects the complicity and compromise inherent not only in the socio-political collective, but also in literary circles, which become beholden to their collective theories. In *Rivers of Babylon 2*, Pišťanek explicitly expresses his disdain for the self-styled Barbarians, Bielik, Litvák, Turan and Zbruž, depicting them as drunken long-haired hooligans who spend their summers cleaning lavatories in the West, before returning to make an exhibition of themselves in the Writers' Club until their hard currency runs out. Pynsent argues that, in *Rivers of Babylon 3*, Pišťanek also responds to the Genitalists, commenting: 'The vulgarity of the action had by then intensified, the breadth of Pišťanek's satire extended – like the penis of one of the "characters", Zongora, which is thirty-two centimetres long when erect. Probably consciously, Pišťanek had out-genitalized the Genitalists' (Pynsent 2000: 89). Above all an ardent individualist, Pišťanek seeks in this way to dissociate himself from any identification with what he implicitly presents as the mediocrity of the 'herd' of post-1989 writers.

Pišťanek may also have had in mind Viliam Klimáček, whose fiction shares elements of his approach, but is more obviously self-centred and self-reflexive, and therefore, in Pišťanek's terms, limited. Like Ivan Kolenič, Klimáček first came to attention as a poet in the late Communist period. His first collection of stories, *Ďalekohladenie* (Telescoping, 1991) uses apparently personal experiences – mainly from military service – as the basis for various games with language. Somewhat comparable to Berková's approach in *Knížka s červeným obalem*, Klimáček's collection focuses less on creating an individual voice and more on foregrounding artifice, bringing his fiction closer to that by writers like Kolenič or the Barbarians. His first novel, *Panic v podzemí*, in which the narrator has a permanent erection from birth, misleadingly suggests a link between Klimáček and the Genitalists. According to Čúzy, in the novel, which follows the narrator's personal history and the history of Slovakia from 1956 to the near-future (2003), Klimáček expresses his rejection not only of the Communist past, but also of the post-Communist present, in which, in Čúzy's view, 'all that is left is sexual instinct, which […] has lost, however, its acceptable form and become merely something unrealizable, incomprehensible and in fact totally uncontrollable' (Čúzy 1997: 88). Such moralizing is alien to the Genitalists. As in the Genitalists' writing, however, the penis in *Panic v podzemí* serves as a metaphor for writing, but as a symbol of potency; Čúzy's definition of sexual instinct could equally be applied to Klimáček's conception of the creative impulse. In *Panic v podzemí*, the narrator is effectively cast out of paradise and driven underground because of his condition, which represents the author's insistent need to stylize experience, to subjugate it to the imagination. This travestying of the *poet maudit* does not entirely undermine Klimáček's essential admiration of the ineffability of writing as a means of reflecting and contending with the absurdity of reality.

The lack of any overt reflection on the process of writing in Pišťanek's work underlines the fact that his understanding of the notion of literature as 'self-characterization' implies no sense of loss or weakness; on the contrary, Pišťanek's fiction expresses the energy and potency of liberation from obedience to any collective. In his fiction, Pišťanek seeks, like Rácz, to 'live life to the full', to expand constantly the limits of the imagination. In his review of *Rivers of Babylon*, Ucháli identifies Pišťanek with the wheedling, sexually perverted car park attendant Fredy Meštánek (see Ucháli 1992: 43); apart from the similarity in names, the plump, unshaven Fredy, wrapped in an anorak, physically resembles photos of the author on the cover. While for Fredy, Rácz represents a model of personal success to be emulated, for Pišťanek he represents a model of unfettered imagination.

Rácz features only sporadically in the sequels to the first *Rivers of Babylon*, but his constant presence in the reader's mind gives him the status of a muse. The sequels recount how not only Fredy, but also Pišťanek radically expands his horizons, culminating in his most spectacularly ambitious novel, *Rivers of Babylon 3*, which, comparable perhaps to Pelevin's *Chapaev i Pustota* (Chapaev and Pustota, 1996), undoubtedly achieves its aim to outstrip not only Pišťanek's own other work, but also all contemporaneous Slovak fiction. In the novel, written in a mixture of modern and archaic Slovak and Czech, Fredy is at first a tyrannical producer/director of hard-core pornographic films starring his wife, then a wanted sex pest. He flees to the Arctic Circle, where, through absurd good fortune and despite exceptional cowardice, he assists in liberating a Slovak minority in an oil-rich region from a Russian-backed khanate and is crowned their king. Significantly, however, at the end he remains the puppet of Rácz, indicating that the limits of the imagination can never be reached. In *Medorek* and other works by the Czech writers of the Changes, the desire to write is invested with a nobility that teeters on the brink of becoming a comical compulsion. In common with other Slovak writers whom he scorns, Pišťanek's portrayal of Fredy goes further, equating the unending process of self-characterization with a sort of vital deviance.

4 Subverting realism

Aleksandr Ivanchenko, Tat'iana Tolstaia, Dušan Mitana

The assertion of literature as 'self-characterization' epitomizes the desire of the writers of the Changes to abandon the 'collectivizing' voice which they consider to be inherent in Realist writing. In their view, Realist techniques seek to establish and perpetuate a fixed, shared version of the world into which the reader is drawn. In *...na okraji chaosu...*, Hodrová associates the rejection of Realism with the cooption of the style for political ends:

> [The 'open work'] does not suggest to the reader a single, undoubted meaning, but a radiating network or field of possible meanings. This conception of meaning is not only a general reaction to the conception of meaning aspiring to unambiguousness in works with a Realist poetics, still surviving and indeed dominant in the twentieth century, but sometimes (in Czech literature in the 1960s and subsequently in the 1990s) it has unquestionably also constituted a very concrete reaction to the single and unerring Meaning dictated to literary works by totalitarian ideology.
>
> (Hodrová 2001: 164)

This apparent synonymity of Realism and socio-political didacticism is also reflected in Viktor Erofeev's conflation of the two in a single paragraph of 'Pominki po sovetskoi literature'. According to Erofeev, 'hypermoralism', the defining feature of Russian literature, has all too often caused Russian writers to 'deviate from aesthetic tasks into the realm of unambiguous prophecy'. He continues:

> Literature has frequently been measured by the degree of acuteness and social significance of problems. I am not saying that there should not be social realism – let there be everything – but to imagine the national literature only as literature with a social bias is nothing short of hard labour and anguish.
>
> (Erofeev 1996: 431)

The pointedly over-simplified, often caricatured notion of Realism presented by writers like Hodrová and Erofeev undoubtedly arises from the particular literary situation pertaining in the Soviet Union and Communist Czechoslovakia. At the same time, however, it closely corresponds to the presentation of Realism in works by British and American 'metafictional' writers of the 1960s and 1970s, who also question the unselfconscious creation of a fictional illusion in Realist writing. Of these writers Patricia Waugh comments:

> Contemporary metafictional writing is both a response and a contribution to [a] thoroughgoing sense that reality or history are provisional: no longer a world of eternal verities but a series of constructions, artifices, impermanent structures. The materialist, positivist and empiricist world-view on which realistic fiction is premised no longer exists. It is hardly surprising, therefore, that more and more novelists have come to question and reject the forms that correspond to this ordered reality.
>
> (Waugh 1984: 7)

The Czech writers of the Changes, whose fiction I examine in the next chapter, equate the abandonment of Realism with the liberation of literature from ideologization. In this chapter, however, I shall discuss works by Ivanchenko, Mitana and Tolstaia, who present the Realist approach as a hubristic misdirection of human efforts, but consider the abandonment of Realism not liberation, but merely the acknowledgement of human impotence.

Tolstaia and Ivanchenko bridge the transition from Soviet to post-Soviet literature, rather as Mitana bridges the transition between pre- and post-Changes Slovak literature. Tolstaia had been publishing short stories in journals since 1983, and in 1987 brought out her first collection in book form, *Na zolotom kryl'tse sideli...* (On the golden porch were sitting…), the title of which refers to a children's nursery rhyme similar to 'Tinker, tailor, soldier, sailor' (see Vail and Genis 1988: 124). Ivanchenko's first novel *Avtoportret s dogom* (Self-portrait with a Great Dane, dated as written 1982) was published in *Ural* in 1985. The fiction of Tolstaia and Ivanchenko was therefore initially viewed as a continuation of the development of Soviet urban fiction in the 1970s and 1980s. Indeed, Evgenii Shklovskii's 1988 discussion of 'new' fiction by 'young' writers, including Tolstaia and Ivanchenko, begins with an expression of disappointment that it appears to offer nothing new (see Shklovskii 1988: 222). However, despite adopting the appearance of urban Realism, the fiction of both Tolstaia and Ivanchenko in fact seeks not only to subvert Realist techniques, but also to reject the principles perceived to underlie them. It thus typifies the approach of what critics in 1989 began to call 'other fiction'.

Ivanchenko's best-known work is probably the novel *Monogramma* (Monogram, 1992), which was nominated for the first Russian Booker Prize in 1992. However, writing that same year, Lipovetskii, also from Ekaterinburg, considered it inferior to *Avtoportret s dogom*, which he described in 1992 as 'still quite exceptional in the context of the "new wave"' (Lipovetskii 1992: 46). Perhaps because of its superficial resemblance to a typical work of urban Realism from the late Brezhnev period, the novel received less critical attention in the late 1980s than fiction that was more overtly 'other'. However, perhaps uniquely, through the contrast of two perceptions of the nature and purpose of art – one which seeks to absorb the human being completely into a fixed physical reality and one which strives to free the human being from that absorption – the novel encapsulates the transition from Soviet urban Realism to the rejection of that method.

The novel focuses on the relationship between the narrator, Robert Mameev, and his ex-wife, Alisa. The fact that they are divorced but still living together might suggest the standard urban Realist themes of marital breakdown (because of suspected infidelity) and the lack of living space. However, Ivanchenko does not use their unusual living arrangements as a means of expressing and exploring social and moral breakdown, but as a metaphor for the simultaneous detachment and dependence that mark the relationship between the self and other. This simultaneous detachment and dependence is reflected in a series of oppositions in the novel which suggest simultaneous identity and non-identity: the self and its mirror image, the object and its artistic representation and the word and what it names. When Mameev first hears Alisa's name, he is struck by how much it suits her:

> As in childhood, I experienced a familiar, joyous feeling, which I had never felt again, of the absolute synonymity of the audible and essential world, the correspondence of name and object, the total merging of the name of a thing and its appearance, of name and image, of essence and form.
>
> (Ivanchenko 1987: 47)

The tantalizing possibility of overcoming this intermediate state of detachment and dependence motivates both Mameev's and Alisa's use of artistic creation, Alisa by seeking total absorption in the external world, Mameev by seeking total detachment.

The contrast in their approaches is indicated by the fact that, while Mameev is an embittered outsider, hiding himself in a 'niche of demonstrative non-participation' (Lipovetskii 1989: 11), Alisa is a typical insider not only embodying the pretentiousness, pettiness and banality of provincial intellectual society so frequently satirized in sanctioned fiction of the 1970s and 1980s, but also conforming to the norms of that society, above all in the area of creative art. By setting Alisa's artistic approach against Mameev's in the novel, Ivanchenko in effect seeks to analyse the dominant understanding of the nature and purpose of art (Alisa's) from the 'other' perspective, represented by Mameev, who narrates. Throughout the work, Ivanchenko is concerned that the implied reader does not interpret Mameev's comments on Alisa's artistic method solely as an attack on politically motivated compromise and dissimulation, but rather as a criticism of a particular way of perceiving and representing the world in art. For this reason, Mameev comments of people like Alisa:

> They will never mention anything which has not been approved, noticed or sanctioned by someone else. It is not a question here of cowardice, or intellectual or aesthetic timidity, but simply of the fact that they do not see these things.
>
> (Ivanchenko 1987: 71)

The contrast between Mameev's and Alisa's approaches to art is encapsulated in their different occupations: as a successful journalist and photographer, Alisa does not doubt the capacity of her words and images to capture the reality they seek to represent, while as a portrait painter, Mameev's constant preoccupation is the discrepancy between the object and its artistic representation. Early in the work he criticizes the way in which words spoken by Alisa and her friends appear to consume the reality they describe: 'Words, I told her, should, as it were, quail before their own content, they should only come near to it. This especially applies to words which express the most significant concepts' (ibid.: 11). Alisa's use of words reflects her use of art to assert the substantial and lasting nature of the world and thus the substantial and lasting nature of her self within it. This artistic method is reflected in her constant accumulation of possessions. Ivanchenko here subverts the critical depiction of bourgeois consumerism in Soviet urban Realism, implicitly suggesting that the desire for a 'full', concrete, nameable world motivates and underpins the activity of Realism. Just as Alisa's purchases encroach further and further on the living space available to her, so the self becomes absorbed into and restricted by the 'already-named' world.

Mameev argues that, by allowing herself to be absorbed within an 'already-named' world, Alisa sacrifices not only the detachment necessary for artistic creation, but also her awareness of her self. By contrast, Mameev attempts through art to lose all attachment to the external world and thus to come to a perfect knowledge of himself: 'All my life, unconsciously or consciously, I have striven to destroy all kinds of connections with life, to straighten and smooth a way for myself, to find the straight line of my existence, not depending on anyone' (ibid.: 223).

In *Monogramma*, this use of art acquires an explicitly Buddhist meaning. Alla Latynina and Martin Dewhirst over-simplify *Monogramma* when they comment that 'despite its postmodernist devices, it rests firmly on the Realist tradition' (Latynina and Dewhirst 2001: 242), since, rather as Mameev's and Alisa's artistic methods oppose each other in *Avtoportret s dogom*, in *Monogramma* Ivanchenko mixes a densely written historical account of the accumulated suffering that has shaped the identity of the central character (and implicitly Russia) in the late twentieth century with descriptions of Buddhist meditation exercises in which the central character contemplates physical objects in order to rid herself of her attachment to them. The pursuit of emptiness in both *Avtoportret s dogom* and

Monogramma prefigures Pelevin's in his Buddhist-influenced novels, discussed in Chapter 7. Ivanchenko's intense theoretical expositions, however, contrast sharply with Pelevin's pop Buddhism.

The process of writing in *Avtoportret s dogom* may therefore be understood as Mameev's contemplation of Alisa in an attempt to rid himself of his attachment to her. His efforts, however, merely reveal the extent and intensity of his dependence on her. After giving an account of his life before and with Alisa, Mameev appends a short story describing an affair he has with a schizophrenic girl during a business trip to Moscow. He then tries to show the reader how this short story arose out of a real affair he had with a married woman, but this affair also turns out to be fictional, with the character of the married woman, like that of the schizophrenic girl, inspired by Alisa. Mameev wrote the stories while waiting in vain in a Moscow telegraph office for Alisa to contact him, convinced she was having an affair, when, in fact, she was having an abortion. The repeated, potentially endless re-contextualizing of sections of narrative from fact to fiction reflects the interminable, inescapable nature of the relationship between the self and other. As in Kolenič's *Mlčať* (Be silent, 1992), discussed in Chapter 6, it is the narrator's own inability to fall silent, to cease communicating with the external world, that prevents the attainment of silence. Mameev miserably declares: 'How can one be free, daily expelling so many words from oneself?' (Ivanchenko 1987: 223).

Mameev's experience of existence constitutes a negative version of Bakhtin's model of the relationship between the self and other and between author and hero, discussed in the context of Hrabal's fiction in Chapter 2. Bakhtin's essay, 'Author and hero in aesthetic activity', written in the 1920s, first appeared in the volume *Estetika slovesnogo tvorchestva* in 1979 and may well have directly influenced *Avtoportret s dogom*. In the essay, Bakhtin repeatedly returns to the difficulty of self-portrayal, on one occasion referring specifically to the problems of the artist creating his self-portrait from a mirror (see Bakhtin 1990: 34).[1] Bakhtin compares the relationship, in which the self repeatedly gives form to the other's self in an open-ended exchange, to an embrace and to the love between a mother and a child. However, for Mameev its infinite, inconclusive nature is intolerable, and he feels himself trapped. Alone in his studio at the end of the novel, Mameev smashes the mirror he has been using unsuccessfully to paint his own face into the self-portrait. The shattered reflection indicates the nature of self-knowledge without, in Bakhtin's terms, the form bestowed by the other. Bakhtin writes:

> The only thing left for me to do is to find refuge in the *other* and to assemble – out of the *other* – the scattered pieces of my own givenness, in order to produce from them a parasitically consummated unity in the *other's* soul using the *other's* resources.
>
> (Ibid.: 126)

Throughout the novel, Ivanchenko's satirization of Mameev as perhaps the most pretentious, obnoxious and feeble member of the suburban intelligentsia depicted in the work indicates that the character of Mameev is not to be identified entirely with the implied author, but serves as a vehicle for the implied author's message. Mameev fails not so much because he is unable to accept the 'unconsummated' nature of the self as the self perceives it, as in Bakhtin's account, but because he cannot stop clinging to the very notion of the discrete self, reflected in his continued preoccupation with the other. The desire for self-preservation thus results in the same artistic stagnancy which Mameev rejects in Alisa. Ivanchenko perceives this stagnancy in the way in which writers allow themselves to become identified with a particular style; in contrast, his own works differ radically from each other in style and content. Questioned by Kuritsyn about the lack of similarity between his works, Ivanchenko comments:

> Most writers mature stylistically ahead of their experience and artificially overtake it. That is, having developed a style in some externally determined way, they then impose it upon experience and thus experience is distorted by style […]. I try to write in another way, so that the seed and the water melon ripen together and are, in essence, inseparable from each other. For me, having many styles (*mnogostil'nost*) is a sign of spiritual movement, of spiritual self-definition.
>
> (Kuritsyn 2000: 616)

For Ivanchenko, the implied authorial self is a vessel to be emptied, rather than filled, through the process of writing, which is therefore not so much the accumulation of words, but the attainment of a new empty space, as he suggests at the end of *Monogramma*: 'Emptiness gazes at itself into Emptiness and thickens into a transparent darkness' (Ivanchenko 2000: 424). For Mameev, at the end of *Avtoportret s dogom*, this reconciliation with emptiness remains an impossible aspiration.

As with Ivanchenko's fiction published in the 1980s, it is perhaps not surprising that Tolstaia's stories were at first regarded as no more than a continuation of prevailing trends in Soviet urban fiction, given that they frequently exploit the topoi of *bytovaia proza*, including flat-swapping, marital infidelity, urban 'rabbit-hutch' squalor and the *embourgeoisement* of the suburban intelligentsia, represented by their pretentiousness, hypocrisy and social climbing. Although the implied authorial voice in contemporaneous urban fiction had become increasingly withdrawn and distant from the characters and events described, Tolstaia's work was repeatedly criticized for its apparent absence of implied judgement or sympathy, thus betraying the Soviet reader's ingrained expectation of implied authorial guidance (see, for example, Grekova 1988: 252–6, Spivak 1988: 201–3, Vasilevskii 1988: 256–8, Piskunova and Piskunov 1988: 188–98). While recognizing Tolstaia's rejection of all illusions about the nature and power of human beings, however, these early critics failed to see compassion in her abundant use of words, her assertion of the limitless possibilities of combination and meaning which sustain and enrich human existence even as they painfully remind human beings of the actual poverty and impotence of that existence.

Tolstaia in effect agrees with Popov's narrator in *Dusha patriota* that 'fragile and tender' literature has been deformed by the unreasonable expectations of human beings, above all by the belief that words can shape and change reality, that truths declared definitive in language may become so once and for all in fact. In *Dusha patriota*, Popov questions the importance of truth by juxtaposing Karamzin's account of a battle with the Tartars with an extract on defence spending from *Pravda*. As Robert Porter has pointed out, Karamzin's account once aspired to the status of truth, but is now read for its literary merits, while the implied reader does not expect to find the truth in *Pravda* (see Porter 1994b: 117). Popov thus shows the notion of truth not only to be relative, in the sense that different times and different people define what constitutes truth differently, but also to have no lasting importance in the assessment of a piece of writing. Tolstaia's stories encourage the reader to unlearn their expectations of language by warning of the consequences of believing in the reality of human fictions. At the same time, however, they retain a melancholy faith in the creative process, understood as a source of comfort, a gift to human beings rather like Hope at the bottom of Pandora's box.

Helena Goscilo, who published a monograph on Tolstaia in 1997, argues that the manipulation of perspective is essential to the rejection of didacticism in Tolstaia's writing: 'Tolstaia's narratives both embrace philosophically and offer a concrete instance of perspectivism, which presupposes that if there is an objective reality, humans lack the cognitive equipment to apprehend it accurately, without bias' (Goscilo 1988: 283). However, as Hosking points out in *Beyond Socialist Realism*, writers of post-'Thaw' Soviet literature in general, and urban fiction in particular, had long questioned the ability of human beings to discover the 'objective reality' of existence (see Hosking 1980: 201). By complicating narrative strategy, writers like Trifonov sought to create a plurality of perspective and suggest the subjectivity of truth. Character, implied author and reader were thus united in a quest for meaning which itself, as Hosking argues, implicitly defines the meaning of existence (see ibid.). Tolstaia's stories do not simply represent a continuation of this approach, but, on the contrary, present the use of fiction to articulate the meaning of existence as the corruption of art. The 'objective reality' of existence in her stories is represented by *byt* itself, understood as the circle of time from dust to dust which renders all human lives indistinguishable, banal and meaningless. Her use of the themes and settings of *bytovaia proza* parodically draws attention to the futility of writing that attempts to give an accurate portrayal of daily life in the hope of discovering its essence. The search for meaning is portrayed as the vain attempt to assert the truth of products of the imagination. Lipovetskii writes:

> Those illusions by which all [Tolstaia's] characters live are not at all designed for realization, but for another purpose entirely; so that the circle does not lead to despair, so that there is at least some kind of meaning in life. A theatre for oneself? Yes, if you like [...], but without it life in the circle conclusively becomes dust and decay.
>
> (Lipovetskii 1989: 9)

In this context, the 'perspectives' which Goscilo describes do not constitute relative or partial truths, hinting at a greater, as yet undiscovered meaning; rather, they are merely competing fictions which conceal, but cannot eradicate or replace the passage of time.

The image of the circle of time is encapsulated in the very structure of the story 'Krug' (The circle, 1987). The story begins with the depiction of a sixty-year-old man, Vasilii Mikhailovich, as he sets off on a walk round the block while his wife is at the hairdresser's, then passes retrospectively through accounts of Vasilii Mikhailovich's various extra-marital affairs before returning to him on his walk just before he suffers a heart attack and dies. Through Vasilii Mikhailovich, the narrator shows how the oppressive awareness of the inevitability of life provokes the search for a way out other than that for which he is destined: 'The three-dimensionality of being, the finale of which was coming closer and closer, was stifling Vasilii Mikhailovich. He tried to come off the rails, drill a hole in the horizon, leave through a door drawn in the air' (Tolstaia 1997: 46).

Vasilii Mikhailovich's domesticating and domesticated wife symbolizes his imprisonment in the circle of passing time, while his other women represent potential escape routes. Like the 'door drawn in the air', however, the 'escape routes' are created through the magic of imagination. Vasilii Mikhailovich finds one woman by transforming seven digits printed on a sheet at the launderette into a telephone number, but she turns out to be exactly the same as his wife. He is then drawn towards another woman for whom he begins creating personality traits from the moment he glimpses her at the market. Vasilii Mikhailovich even appears to have invented her name, Yseult, in his effort to elevate their affair to the status of timeless romance.[2] Yseult, however, bores him, and he returns to his wife, and to the circle. On his fortieth birthday he receives a poem from Yseult which reveals that, like him, she saw their affair as a potential way out of the circle. By this time, however, Vasilii Mikhailovich considers her dead; the attempt to merge his imaginary notion of her with reality destroyed her for him. However, the suggestion that the characters scarcely differ either in the way they live or in the way they attempt to deal with life emphasizes that the act of invention itself is vital, since it creates the impression of individuality. For Vasilii Mikhailovich, in his final moments, these invented episodes appear to be the most significant and the most 'real' in his life.

The distinction in 'Krug' between bleak, inevitable reality and the bright, endless possibilities of invention reflects the rejection of the pursuit of verisimilitude in favour of fictionalization in Tolstaia's work as a whole, and recalls the separation of Art and Life in Oscar Wilde's 'The Decay of Lying'. In her stories, Tolstaia implicitly shares the views of Vivian, Wilde's spokesman in the essay, that human life is 'poor, probable, uninteresting' (Wilde 1986: 72), and that the quest to depict it as accurately and realistically as possible is entirely unsuitable for art. Vivian's account of the nature of art is worth quoting at length because it closely resembles not only the view expressed in Tolstaia's fiction, but also her expansive descriptive style, which frequently exploits mythological and fairy-tale images and gives objects and natural phenomena lives of their own:

> Art finds her own perfection within, and not outside of, herself. She is not to be judged by any external standard of resemblance. She is a veil, rather than a mirror. She has flowers that no forest knows of, birds that no woodland possesses. She makes and unmakes many worlds, and can draw the moon from heaven with a scarlet thread. Hers are the 'forms more real than living man', and hers the great archetypes of which things that have existence are but unfinished copies. Nature has, in her eyes, no laws, no uniformity. She can work miracles at her will, and when she calls monsters from the deep they come. She can bid the almond-tree blossom in winter, and send the snow upon the ripe cornfield. At her word the frost lays its silver finger on the burning mouth of June, and the winged lions creep out from the hollows of the Lydian hills. The dryads peer from the thicket as she passes by, and the brown fauns smile strangely at her when she comes near them. She has hawk-faced gods that worship her, and the centaurs gallop at her side.
>
> (Ibid.: 73)

The contrast between Art and Life resembles the distinction in Venedikt Erofeev's *Moskva–Petushki* between the celestial paradise of Petushki and linear terrestrial existence, represented by Moscow. Just as Venichka's attempt to find Petushki on earth ends in disaster, so Tolstaia's stories repeatedly describe the dangers inherent in trying to realize one's inventions in life. Whereas the awl plunged into Venichka's throat at the end of *Moskva–Petushki* indicates the silencing of a literature forever tainted by its complicity in the pursuit of paradise on earth, in her stories Tolstaia posits the restoration of literature's innocence as a means of escape from reality.

In 'The Decay of Lying', Vivian describes how the attempt to bring Art and Life together destroys Art:

> Art begins with abstract decoration, with purely imaginative and pleasurable work dealing with what is unreal and non-existent. This is the first stage. Then Life becomes fascinated with this new wonder, and asks to be admitted into the charmed circle. Art takes life as part of her rough material, recreates it, and refashions it in fresh forms, is absolutely indifferent to fact, invents, imagines, dreams and keeps between herself and reality the impenetrable

> barrier of beautiful style, of decorative or ideal treatment. The third stage is when Life gets the upper hand, and drives Art out into the wilderness.
> (Wilde 1986: 68)

Tolstaia in effect dramatizes this process in the story 'Fakir' (The fakir, 1986), in which the 'fakir', Filin, represents Art. Filin holds impromptu parties in a bright, warm, fabulously decorated flat in the centre of Moscow, at which he serves unheard-of delicacies, shows off new objects he has acquired and new people he has discovered and recounts the stories which lie behind them all. Life is represented in the story by a married couple, Galia and Iura, who live with their daughter on a dingy, cold housing estate beside the Moscow ring road. Galia's desperate desire for an invitation to Filin's flat reflects what Goscilo terms her 'yearning for culture' (Goscilo 1993a: 82). Goscilo reveals the contrast between Art and Life when she writes: 'If Filin's domicile is a repository of art, culture and civilization, those far removed from its caressing lights dwell in the brutal darkness of ignorance' (ibid.).

Galia fails to recognize that the values of the everyday world do not apply in Filin's world; on the contrary, she believes she can be, in Vivian's terms, 'admitted to the charmed circle' of culture through social climbing. She curses the arbitrariness of Fate, which has placed Filin and his various women in a central flat and herself on the outskirts, and when Iura's efforts to find them a better flat fail, she decides to leave him and become Filin's mistress. At this point she unexpectedly sees Filin, almost unrecognizable in the setting of a crowded Metro station, small, anxious and in a hurry. That evening she learns that he is only renting the flat from a polar explorer and is in fact registered to live in a socially unacceptable suburb, even further from the centre than her own estate. When she goes to the flat for the last time, as Goscilo puts it, 'although Filin and his authorial practices remain unchanged, Galia's perspective has irrevocably altered, unavoidably affecting her reception of his work' (ibid.: 83).

What has changed is the intervention in Filin's world of the alien notion of truth, a category which is shown to belong to the everyday world through its close association in 'Fakir' with Galia's husband, Iura, who is unmoved by Filin's charms. Early in the story, Iura inadvertently exposes Filin when he points out that the pâté about which Filin has begun to tell a fabulous story may be bought in the nearby supermarket. Later, Filin recounts how he acquired his Wedgwood china from a peasant who had taken it as booty from a German aircraft he shot down during the Second World War. Iura at once exclaims that the peasant is a liar, but Filin is unhappy with Iura's response and comments: 'Of course, I don't exclude the possibility that he wasn't a partisan at all, but merely a vulgar little thief, but, you know… somehow I prefer to believe' (Tolstaia 1997: 213). Filin is taken aback not because he is afraid of being found out, but because the notions of true and false are absent from his world.

Galia seeks an art which will take the place of the existence she has; Filin, by contrast, does not assert the truth of his inventions, which merely serve to conceal the wretched reality of his life. It is Galia, not Filin, who is guilty of self-delusion, since self-delusion depends upon the notion of truth. By questioning the truth of Filin's world, she causes it to vanish, but she is left with the 'wilderness' of reality:

> Ahead a new winter, new hopes, new songs. Well then, let's sing in praise of the outskirts, of the rain, of houses gone somewhat grey, of long evenings on the threshold of darkness. Let's sing in praise of waste ground, brown grass, the chill of layers of earth beneath a nervous foot, let's sing in praise of the slow autumn dawn.
>
> (Ibid.: 226)[3]

As Galia's experience of Filin's flat indicates, 'pure' art conceals the passage of time, creating a radiant eternal present. Once contaminated by the notion of truth, it loses this power and the bleak reality of existence is exposed. The distinction between 'pure' and 'impure' art is reflected in the two types of invention contrasted by Tolstaia in 'Plamen' nebesnyi' (Heavenly flame, 1987). In the story, a humbler version of the 'fakir', Korobeinikov, who is recovering from an ulcer at a convalescent home, pays regular visits to a certain Ol'ga Mikhailovna and her husband at their nearby *dacha*, bearing tales of extra-terrestrial aliens and the supernatural. As the narrator indicates, the notions of true and false initially bear no relevance to Korobeinikov's stories: 'Ol'ga Mikhailovna both believes and does not believe' (ibid.: 117). This happy equilibrium is, however, disturbed by the arrival from the city of Dmitrii Il'ich, a sculptor who tells Ol'ga Mikhailovna and her husband that years previously, while Dmitrii Il'ich was in prison, Korobeinikov apparently published some of his poems under his own name. Dmitrii Il'ich asks Ol'ga Mikhailovna not to judge, lest she be judged, but she is unable to comply: 'Well, let her be judged, but at the same time she will herself condemn. She loves the truth, nothing can be done about that now, her organism has been made that way' (ibid.: 121). On his subsequent visits, Korobeinikov is treated with barely concealed hostility, while Ol'ga Mikhailovna and Dmitrii Il'ich begin an affair. When Dmitrii Il'ich at last confesses to having made up the story, Ol'ga Mikhailovna's search for truth is shown to be pointless; faced with a choice between two fiction-makers, she opts for Dmitrii Il'ich, reflecting that Korobeinikov bored her with his patently ridiculous tales. Tolstaia's conclusion is therefore anti-moralizing, since Ol'ga does not choose the morally pure man who had been slandered, but the man who appears more suited to the world in which she lives.

In 'The Decay of Lying', Vivian comments: 'the only form of lying that is absolutely beyond reproach is lying for its own sake, and the highest development of this is, as we have already pointed out, Lying in Art' (Wilde 1986: 85). Deliberately or subconsciously, Dmitrii Il'ich seeks to usurp Korobeinikov's place in Ol'ga Mikhailovna's affections. His story is therefore not 'lying for its own sake', but can only have its desired effect if it is believed. The implication of Dmitrii Il'ich's story is that he was a political prisoner, while Korobeinikov attempted to gain by deception. In fact, the reverse is true; Dmitrii Il'ich gains by deception, while Korobeinikov is imprisoned by the imposition of truth. Dmitrii Il'ich effectively subjects Korobeinikov to a show-trial, and Tolstaia thus implicates Soviet power in the destruction of 'pure' art. The innocence of Korobeinikov's inventions is reflected in the image of a 'heavenly flame' which, he says, once came down from the sky over Petrozavodsk, and to which he is repeatedly linked. Once the notion of truth has intervened, however, the 'heavenly flame' is extinguished and the act of invention, embodied in the story by Korobeinikov's tales, cannot regain its purity and power. Instead, Korobeinikov's celestial purity is replaced by the terrestrial notion of innocence, which merely heightens Ol'ga Mikhailovna's feeling of guilt. Just as Galia is left with the bleak inevitability of *byt* when she destroys Filin's world, so Ol'ga Mikhailovna is left only with the awareness of her sinful, mortal state.

The notion of truth creates a discrepancy between reality and invention which children in Tolstaia's work do not know and which adults seek to erase. As Lipovetskii points out, Tolstaia's child characters do not differentiate between real and make-believe, but inhabit a 'play reality' (Lipovetskii 1989: 12), confident in what Mikhail Zolotonosov calls 'their potential as demiurges' (Zolotonosov 1987: 60). Referring to J.M. Barrie's *Peter Pan*, Petr Vail' and Aleksandr Genis comment: 'the author is a person who refuses to grow up. It is for this reason that her main enemy is the unstoppable course of time' (Vail' and Genis 1988: 126). The implied author in Tolstaia's stories wishes in vain that she could restore this child-like perception, itself a victim of the passage of time. While child characters are unaware of time passing, adult characters attempt to use their creations to bring its passage to an end, in other words, to give their creations the status of truth. Just as, in *Peter Pan*, whenever a child says it does not believe in fairies, a fairy dies, when the notion of truth is imposed on a human invention, its magic is destroyed, and characters such as Galia and Ol'ga Mikhailovna are abruptly returned to the everyday, mortal world.

Art can only sustain the illusion of an eternal present when a character makes no distinction between real and make-believe, as Tolstaia demonstrates in the story 'Sonia' (1984), which contrasts the effect of a single act of invention on two characters. The story recounts events which take place in Leningrad before and during the Second World War, framed by the narrator's reflection on the insatiability of time, which absorbs human lives, leaving almost no traces. The first two sentences establish the contrast between the transience of human existence and the timelessness of Art: 'There once lived a person, and now she's no more. Only a name remains – Sonia' (Tolstaia 1997: 4). Tolstaia implicitly presents the very giving of a name as an act of invention which draws an individual life out of the homogeneity of human existence and the passage of time. In the 1997 complete edition of Tolstaia's stories from 1983 to 1992, the first lines of 'Sonia' acquire particular resonance because they are the first lines in the volume.

Sonia, an unattractive spinster, falls victim to a practical joke played on her by a group of friends, led by a certain Ada Adol'fovna, who begin sending her letters which purport to come from a secret admirer. The joke gets out of hand; Sonia unwittingly becomes part of her own epistolary novel, while Ada Adol'fovna, who is eventually left to continue the correspondence alone, fears the likely effect on Sonia of bringing the exchange of letters to an end either by telling Sonia the truth or by killing off the admirer. Ada Adol'fovna is closely associated with the besieging Germans through her name as well as her patronymic (*ad* is the Russian for 'hell'). Like the German blockade, the correspondence represents a vain struggle to hold back time, which is moving relentlessly towards the moment when the truth will be discovered. Consequently, continuing the correspondence appears to exhaust Ada Adol'fovna as much as the privations of the period, with the hellish connotations of her name ultimately an allusion to the Sisyphean nature of the task she has set herself. By contrast, for Sonia, endlessly rejuvenated by this love affair so reminiscent of her favourite type of literature, the exchange of letters constitutes an infinite cycle sustaining her in a joyful, eternal present. At the end of the story, the narrator speculates that Sonia may eventually have gone to the address to which she had been writing and found Ada Adol'fovna lying semi-conscious in bed. For Sonia, the power of Art holds, and she sees not Ada, but her beloved. She then goes out to fetch water and is killed in an air raid. The passage of time is suspended in Art, but none the less continues in the everyday world.[4]

Tolstaia gives her most comprehensive explication of her perception of the nature and limitations of human beings and their creations in one of her later, longer stories, 'Somnambula v tumane' (Sleepwalker in the fog, 1988), in which she satirically portrays the hubris inherent in the attempt to bring an end to the passage of time. The central character in the story, Denisov, is haunted by the memory of how, as a child, he sold a glass powder compact belonging to his Aunt Rita, who died in the siege of Leningrad, and thus caused her to be forgotten. Moved by this feeling of guilt, which constitutes a displaced fear that he will also be forgotten when he dies, he seeks a way of achieving immortality and at the same time forgiveness from his dead aunt. Tolstaia demonstrates the absurdity of Denisov's ambition through her comical account of his increasingly furious efforts to rearrange the map of the world, an attempt to impose his own inventions upon existing reality which parallels his pursuit of immortality. Her description of how he uproots Australia dramatically demonstrates how the products of the human imagination acquire a far greater appearance of reality than everyday existence ever could:

> Denisov abolished Australia, tearing it out by the root like a molar. He leant with one leg on Africa and the end broke off. He leant more firmly – that was fine. With the other leg he leant on Antarctica; cliffs crumbled, snow filled

> his boot, he should stand up more firmly. He grasped the errant continent more firmly and shook it this way and that. Australia sat firmly in its sea nest, his fingers slipped in the underwater slime, corals scratched his knuckles. Oomph! Again – there! He tore it out and broke out in a sweat. He held it in both hands and wiped his brow with his elbow. Water dripped from the root, from the top trickled sand – some kind of desert. The sides were cold and slippery – it had been completely embedded.
>
> (Ibid.: 344–5)[5]

Denisov decides to secure his reputation for all time through the apparently selfless act of establishing a monument to a certain Makov, who froze to death while climbing a mountain. The monument shows the human being to be substantial and lasting; it removes him from the ordinary passage of time and places him in an eternal present, turning him into a god. Given the Soviet passion for building monuments, Tolstaia's portrayal of Denisov clearly represents a satirization of the eschatological pretensions of Marxism-Leninism. A similar association occurs in *Avtoportret s dogom*, in which Mameev claims that the 'organizing idea' of Alisa's creative work is a belief in the 'monumentality' (*monumental'nost'*) of human beings, their creations and their achievements. Mameev rejects this as a delusion that conceals what he calls 'the imperfection of the human being [...] indeed, I wouldn't even call it insignificance and imperfection, but just the humanness of the human being' (Ivanchenko 1987: 80). Through the implicit equation of Denisov's monument with Makov's body, still petrified on the mountainside, Tolstaia suggests that the desire to preserve oneself permanently is morbid and unnatural. Unable to participate in the normal process of decay, the monument becomes a grotesque anachronism which time gradually buries without trace:

> There, in the mountains, the snow piled up, thicker and thicker, throwing up snowdrifts, covering Makov, his sprawled legs, his face turned to eternity. He is not decomposing, he is not rotting, not rusting, not decaying! ... The snowdrifts rose higher and higher; the mountain crackled under the weight of snow; it moaned and snapped, then with the thunder of an engine, an avalanche came down, and nothing remained on the summit. A snowy puff of smoke floated up and settled on the crags.
>
> (Tolstaia 1997: 365)

The monument typifies the static images which characters like Denisov conjure up and then expect to exist in reality. When he goes to discover more about Makov from his family, he is disappointed not to find them in a *tableau vivant* of mourning and remembrance. Makov's family take the view that life goes on – exactly what Denisov fears – and are rather bemused by his plans. Makov's mother suggests that if Denisov would like to help them, he could try to acquire a certain type of wardrobe which Makov's sister has long wanted. This request signals the collapse of Denisov's proud scheme into farce, culminating in his public humiliation by a Party bigwig and his friends in a restaurant named 'Skazka' (Fairy-tale) in recognition of the unreality of his plan. Hiding beneath the table under which he has been forced to crawl, Denisov finally recognizes the extent of his self-delusion: 'What stupidity to torture yourself with memories of nothing, to ask forgiveness from a dead person for something of which, by human reckoning, you aren't guilty, to try to grasp handfuls of fog' (ibid.: 367). The image of clutching at fog recalls the vain attempts of the title character in the story 'Peters' (1986) to conjugate the verb 'to conquer' (*pobedit'*) in the first person singular, which epitomizes his failure to force life to match up to his imaginary worlds. As John R. Givens points out, this verb has no first person singular form in Russian (see Givens 1993: 260). Tolstaia appears here to show that the inability of human beings to have any impact on life is not only expressed, but also ordained by language itself.

Goscilo suggests that the title of the story constitutes a metaphor for modern humanity 'roaming in a fog of metaphysical uncertainty, groping for clues that will shed light on the meaning and goal of life' (Goscilo 1997: 149). However, Denisov's remark suggests that the fog signifies the inventions of the human mind.[6] In 'Somnambula v tumane', scientific research, witchcraft, Oriental religion and, implicitly, Marxism-Leninism are all relativized as human creations, which are designed to give life a meaning other than the certainty of oblivion, but which cumulatively form nothing more than an elaborate overlay to the banal reality of existence. Tolstaia's stories themselves mirror this model of human existence through her technique of submerging self-consciously ordinary plots in an abundance of imagery and detail, as Vail' and Genis point out:

> Upon the fleetingly sketched out, minor *siuzhet* [the author] sews countless arabesques, until suddenly, amid the ornamental twists, capricious patterns and whimsical flourishes, the simple and rather unimportant story of the hero which Tolstaia had apparently intended to tell cannot be found.
>
> (Vail' and Genis, 1988: 125)

Human beings cannot quarrel with the inevitable circle shaping their lives, only with each other's inventions.

In this situation, the quest to discover or assert the truth undertaken by many of Tolstaia's characters, including Denisov, equates with 'sleepwalking in the fog' of competing fictions. Denisov's father-in-law, to whom the title of the story ostensibly refers, appears in his sleepwalking to be trying to re-discover a truth he once knew. His nocturnal world seems rather less dream-like than the world of natural history in which he writes his articles for popular magazines and which soothes rather than disturbs, in other words concealing rather than exposing the truth. His daughter calls him her 'Turgenev', not realizing that this implicit reduction of scientific research to the status of *belles-lettres* reminds him of his own defeat. As a zoologist, he once gave a paper proposing a link between birds and reptiles, which was taken as an insult by a certain Ptitsyn (the name derives from *ptitsa*, meaning ‘bird’), and he was sacked. Tolstaia’s particular choice of theory is mischievous because the evolutionary relationship between birds and reptiles has been scientifically proven; her point is to assert that all products of the human mind are inventions, upon which various interpretations may be imposed, and all or none may attain the status of truth. The subsequent writings of Denisov’s father-in-law are read rather as the stories of Filin and Korobeinikov are heard, without their truth being an issue. His flight into the forest at the end of ‘Somnambula v tumane’ will not, as the narrator playfully suggests, take him to the light he has been seeking for so long; it merely reflects his inability to live any longer in a world given over to absolute relativism.

In Tolstaia’s conception of the world, the inability of human beings to make their inventions substantial and lasting removes all possibility of a meaningful way of living. The only alternative to the futile pursuit of truth represented by Denisov and other ‘truth-loving’ characters is the story-telling of Filin, like Venichka in *Moskva–Petushki*, the embodiment of the exhaustion of literature. Filin’s creations are not equivalent to the illusory utopia constructed by Soviet ideology, as Natal’ia Ivanova suggests (see Ivanova 1991), but rather stand in opposition to it. In ‘totalitarian’ art, typified by Denisov’s monument, the notion of truth is central to the work of art; to ideologize is to seek to merge Art with Life. In contrast, the notion of truth is alien to the ‘absolute’ art practised by Filin, who perceives the world as a surface of competing fictions to be constantly rearranged and decorated anew. Lipovetskii writes: ‘Filin proves to be an exemplary postmodernist, who perceives culture as an endless series of simulacra, and who constantly pokes fun at their conventionality’ (Lipovetskii 1999a: 133). The work of literature is judged no longer on its verisimilitude, but on its capacity to divert the reader, as Goscilo indicates when she comments, referring to Barthes: ‘Tolstaia, like Pushkin, makes her readers luxuriate in “the pleasure of the text”’ (Goscilo 1997: 119). However, despite, or indeed because of the extravagant verbal colour of Tolstaia’s fiction, the feebleness of words provokes an air of disappointment deriving from the apparent defeat of grander ambitions for literature and the human being. This disappointment, which recalls the more overt grief and nostalgia expressed in Venedikt Erofeev’s *Moskva–Petushki* and is implicit also in the feigned nonchalance of Popov’s narrator in *Dusha patriota*, dominates the Russian fiction of the Changes.

Like other writers of ‘other fiction’, Tolstaia seeks in her work to liberate literature from the Russian cultural tradition, which Goscilo, opening her discussion of ‘Fakir’, describes as

> a myth that rescues art, and especially literature, from the jaws of inconsequentiality by restoring it to its medieval stature; that of literature as a sacred phenomenon, of its production as epiphanic process and voluntary self-abnegation, and of the writer as prophet, martyr, rebel, and hero.
>
> (Goscilo 1997: 100)

Like Denisov's monument, the myth, at least in its Soviet incarnation, asserts the potency of human beings, while its deflation in Tolstaia's writing corresponds to the reduction of Denisov's monument to a piece of popular furniture. As Aunt Rita's glass powder compact also indicates, the individual human life is better symbolized by something apparently insignificant than by something as grandiose as a monument.

Such items appear insignificant, however, only from the perspective which expects deeds of substance, significance and longevity from human beings, the same perspective which led some critics to describe Tolstaia's characters as contemporary manifestations of the Gogolian 'little man'. Tolstaia, however, indignantly responded: 'I write not about the little, but about the normal man' (quoted in Vasilevskii 1988: 257). The value of such items rests in the fact that, like a name or a story, they create the impression of an individual life which would otherwise be swallowed up by time. In her analysis of the enamel dove in 'Sonia', which is all that survives of the title character, Svetlana Boym comments 'Sonia's little brooch suggests the infinite powers of poetic metamorphosis' (Boym 1993: 72), in other words, the transformation of Life in Art.

Boym's article examines Tolstaia's role in the restoration in contemporary Russian culture of *poshlost'*, best translated in this context as 'kitsch', which also forms the theme of an article by Natal'ia Ivanova named after Sonia's 'inflammable little dove' (see Ivanova 1991: 211–23). Both critics detail the history of the notion of *poshlost'*, in particular the early Soviet campaign against what was perceived as bourgeois vulgarity, and the converse attack of the 1960s intelligentsia on what they perceived as Soviet *poshlost'*. The incorporation of kitsch into Tolstaia's writing, as Boym suggests, 'challenges cultural hierarchies' (Boym 1993: 81), reflecting an attempt to, in Fiedler's phrase, 'cross the border, close the gap', to end the cycle which turns yesterday's high culture into today's kitsch by relativizing all human creations.

The presentation of art in Tolstaia's stories as deliberate fictionalization which appears to suspend the passage of time and thus hide the meaninglessness of existence closely resembles Matei Calinescu's description of kitsch as a 'specifically aesthetic form of lying', 'a pleasurable escape from the drabness of modern quotidian life', 'a reaction against [...] the meaninglessness of chronological time' and an attempt to assuage the 'fear of emptiness' (Calinescu 1987: 229, 248, 251). This understanding of art in Tolstaia's stories is set against an understanding of art which, like Soviet art, seeks not to conceal, but to replace the bleak reality of human existence. Thus contaminated with the notion of truth, it is no longer capable of resisting the passage of time and, in keeping with Nabokov's equation of *poshlost'* with a tin of lobster that has been left open, starts to smell (quoted in ibid.: 261).

The human preoccupation with truth has been a central theme of Mitana's fiction since his first collection of stories, *Psie dni* (Dog days, 1970), in which he continued the questioning of the principles behind the Realist mode that emerged in Slovak fiction in the 1960s. Comparing Mitana's methods of subverting Realist techniques with those found in the slightly earlier fiction of Johanides and Jaroš, Tomáš Horváth argues that, while the latter instantly unmask the 'reality effect' of fiction as illusory, Mitana exposes that illusion more gradually and ambiguously. According to Horváth:

> On a thematic level, Mitana's unvarying prose model rests in escalating *everyday* situations to absurd ends using elements of deviation. This escalation requires that the text *first of all* attains the 'effect of reality', of monotonous mundanity, and *then* re-encodes it or causes it to come to a head.
>
> (Horváth 2000: 9)

These remarks might also be applied to Evgenii Popov's short fiction from a similar period.

The novel *Hľadanie strateného autora (Rozhovory s Luciferom)* (In search of the lost author: Conversations with Lucifer, 1991), Mitana's first publication following the fall of Communism, marked a new stage in his work, in which he moves away from what Horváth describes as the 'classical epic structure' of his earlier writing in favour of the 'textual collage' (Horváth 2000: 146). Horváth quotes an interview in which Mitana declares that 'traditional *belles-lettres*, the traditional story has said nothing to me for a long time' (ibid.). The interview, given in *Dotyky*, a journal devoted mainly to new writing, not only demonstrates Mitana's enduring relevance to younger Slovak writers, indicated by Horváth's monograph, but also perhaps his desire to assert that relevance by indicating his long-standing interest in fashionable theoretical positions much loved by Horváth and his contemporaries (see Chapter 7).[7] Like the rejection of Realism in Ivanchenko and Tolstaia, Mitana's abandonment of the story structure expresses scepticism about the human being's claims to be able to impose order on the world. However, whereas Tolstaia characterizes the writer as the melancholy 'fakir', Mitana implicitly defines the writer as an 'editor', devoid of any illusion of magic. The novel thus foreshadows the assertion of the redundancy of writing in much 1990s Slovak fiction.

As the subtitle indicates, Mitana's novel shares with Vilikovský's *Večne je zelený...* a central allusion to Faust's encounter with Mephistopheles, parodically re-enacted in a series of dialogues between Lucifer and a writer, Tomáš Eliáš, whose name (Thomas Elijah) reflects the writer's contradictory desires to be a doubter and a prophet. The ironic tone of the opening, however, indicates the sheer banality of the writer's desire for knowledge, and Lucifer's weariness with these encounters, establishing the theme of the exhaustion of literature that dominates the novel (Lucifer speaks first):

> – What is your desire?
> – To know the truth and reveal it … to people. In words … a writer …
> – You don't ask for much, do you?
>
> (Mitana 1991: 11)

In the pursuit of knowledge, the writer in both *Hľadanie strateného autora* and *Večne je zelený...* becomes tangled up in the texts of others, previous attempts to discover the truth which appear to block the way. In his conversations with Lucifer, Eliáš attempts to discover the truth about the origins of human existence, but each time he is merely told another version drawn from the history of literature on the subject. For Vilikovský, the existence of potentially infinite versions affords the self-creator infinite possibilities of individual expression, a means of endlessly resisting absorption into the dogma of others. In *Hľadanie strateného autora*, however, the weight of existing versions on the contrary devalues the process of writing, which becomes a process not of self-discovery, but of self-dissolution in the texts of others.

The novel purports to be a collection of Eliáš's unpublished papers, put together following his disappearance, and is therefore composed of diary entries, notes, fragments of works-in-progress, interviews, correspondence, medical reports from his time in a psychiatric hospital, a curriculum vitae, letters written by his wife, extracts from reviews of his work, passages quoted from fiction, philosophy, religious texts and various works of specialist literature, and the commentary of the editor of the papers. Guided by the title, the reader may expect that these texts will somehow provide clues to Eliáš's disappearance and lead to his re-discovery. However, the reader in fact merely repeats Eliáš's quest for self-discovery to the point where he disappeared, to be replaced by an editor. In effect, Mitana enacts in the novel a version of Barthes's 'death of the author', as a result of which the writer, no longer able in good conscience to put his name to a text produced from an infinite body of pre-existing texts, becomes instead an arbitrary editor of the world-as-text. The editor of Eliáš's notes suggests that they be prefaced with a quotation from Jorge Luis Borges's story, 'The Utopia of a Tired Man': '"We have nothing else left now except quotations. Language is a system of quotations"' (ibid.: 23). Mitana demonstrates this in the very title, which merges Proust and Pirandello and alludes to Barthes, Foucault and perhaps even Hodrová's *Hledání románu*.

The title may also be interpreted as referring to the search for God. Throughout the work, Mitana encourages the parallel between the 'death of the author' and Nietzche's 'death of God', both of which, Mitana suggests, underpin the contemporary crisis of identity, represented in his novel by the textual collage, a counterpart to Mameev's shattered mirror at the end of *Avtoportret s dogom*. In *Hľadanie strateného autora*, the notion of personal identity in general and the identity of Eliáš in particular, stable at the beginning, becomes increasingly problematic as the work progresses. Rather as Tolstaia foregrounds in 'Sonia' the way in which the 'illusion' of the individual self is created by a name, Mitana suggests that the arbitrariness of the name, which may be adopted and discarded at random, indicates the arbitrariness of the notion of the self. Early in *Hľadanie strateného autora*, the reader learns that Eliáš writes under the pseudonym Dušan Mitana, on the one hand rendering the work implicitly autobiographical, and on the other destabilizing the identity of the biographical author. The publication of

Eliáš's first story under this pseudonym (Mitana's short story 'Oáza s jabloňami' (An oasis with apple trees), which appeared in the journal *Mladá tvorba* in 1965) had the effect of 'killing' a man called Dušan Mitana, who had begun to seek himself through writing, but, after he discovered that a writer called Dušan Mitana already existed, was hospitalized suffering from an identity crisis.

With more rueful irony, resembling the tone of Popov's satirical references to his problems after the *Metropol'* affair in *Dusha patriota*, Mitana implies that he has come to this understanding of identity because of the way it could be granted and taken away in the Normalization period. Eliáš's writer-friend, Pišta Abraham, 'dies' as an author and becomes a non-person when he is prevented from publishing in the 1970s and 1980s because of his association with the reformers in 1968. His 'non-existence' is sealed when, in an episode coincidentally reminiscent of Tolstaia's 'Plamen' nebesnyi', his book is published by his friend, Nikolai Mojžíš, who disingenuously claims that ultimately the text itself, and not its author, is more important. Through the two writers' names, Mitana suggests that this activity has been going on in Judeo-Christian culture at least since, Mitana playfully implies, Moses 'usurped' Abraham. Eliáš's own disappearance may have come about because his identity has been changed by the fall of Communism; readers no longer see him as a heroic writer, striving to write 'truthfully' in oppressive times, and have begun to suspect him of collaboration.

Typically of the writers of the Changes, Mitana's central preoccupation in *Hľadanie strateného autora* is to understand the enduring human need to create. Like his Russian counterparts, he associates with a desire for knowledge of the truth 'at once ennobling and disturbing' (Mitana 1991: 158). As his relativization of accounts drawn from Christian and Gnostic mysticism, Buddhism and Hinduism demonstrates, for Mitana, what purports to be a search for God is in fact an act of recreation, through which each generation reinvents God – and the author – for its times. Consequently the God discovered in *Hľadanie strateného autora* is not the ultimate authority whose death, Mitana implies, pre-figured the 'death of the author', but rather a God who created the human being out of a desire to escape loneliness and know Himself:

> He found himself faced with a dilemma: how can I be alone and not be lonely, when nothing else exists around me. [...] Yes, God had to create the human being if he wanted to be born, if he wanted to emerge from Nothingness, if he wanted to Live.
>
> (Ibid.: 176)

The writer, made in the image of God, cannot help but strive to imitate him, writing in a vain attempt to fill the void of existence and come to self-knowledge.

The resulting notion of writing as a form of private mysticism coupled with ostentatious dilettantism recurs in much of Mitana's subsequent fiction and poetry and in the work of the Barbarians and the Genitalists. Whereas Ivanchenko and Tolstaia argue that literature has been misunderstood by those with too high expectations for human beings, Mitana endeavours to be reconciled with the current notion of the ‘exhaustion of literature’, in which many of the new Slovak writer-theorists of the post-Changes period, discussed in Chapters 6 and 7, luxuriate. Their approach contrasts sharply with that of their Czech counterparts, whose fiction forms the subject of the next chapter.

5 Writing as being

Jiří Kratochvil, Zuzana Brabcová, Daniela Hodrová, Michal Ajvaz, Jáchym Topol

In his 1993 short story 'Má lásko, Postmoderno' (Postmoderna, my love), Jiří Kratochvil describes how a middle-aged writer frees Postmoderna, the little girl he loved when he was a little boy at school, from a prison where she has been kept for forty years, and carries her out into the world on his shoulders. The story serves as an allegory of how, according to Kratochvil, writers like himself, published for the first time after November 1989, liberated literature from its perceived manipulation for ideological purposes during the forty-one years of Communist rule. His use of 'postmoderna' is ironic, suggesting that what fashionable contemporary critics like to call 'postmodernism' is simply literature, released from the 'extra-literary' functions imposed on it by human beings. Whereas, however, in the versions of this liberation given by writers like Popov, Ivanchenko, Tolstaia and Mitana, literature emerges somehow diminished, Kratochvil portrays literature as eternally young and innocent, despite what human beings have tried to do to it.

The Russian and Slovak writers discussed in Chapters 4 and 6 emphasize the weakness of literature, which fails when asked to assert and defend fixed notions of the nature and limits of the world essentially because language is incapable of naming definitively, of conquering time. By contrast, the Czech writers of the Changes perceive this inability as the essential virtue of language, since in this way it resists fixedness and finality, permitting a dynamic perception of the nature of existence. Writing in their fiction thus comes to represent being itself, the vigorous preservation of what Bakhtin terms the 'loophole' in each definition that enables the self to resist 'reification'. In the Czech fiction of the Changes, Popov's notion of literature as 'self-characterization', presented in *Dusha patriota* as the doggedly aimless spouting of words, thus becomes an earnest and vital function. These contrasting notions of the potency and impotence of literature are encapsulated in a passage from Hodrová's *...na okraji chaosu...*:

> the [twentieth-century] novel is created through a number or a whole series of lines, which run in parallel or become interwoven and merge (polyperspectivism or polyphony). Though this type of composition may be linked to a destructive relativism that rejects the significance of cognition,

> this need not be the case at all. On the contrary, this type of composition frequently serves as an instrument of cognition from many perspectives, through which the author attempts to 'capture *being* in all its internal complexity and ambiguity'.
>
> (Hodrová 2001: 166)[1]

It is to the latter that writers like Hodrová, Kratochvil, Brabcová, Ajvaz and Topol aspire.

In the works by Ivanchenko and Tolstaia discussed in the previous chapter, the contrast between the bleak suburban landscapes and the feverish inner mental activity of the central characters, and the mood of melancholy and despair which repeatedly triumphs, unmistakably constitute an attempt to characterize the atmosphere of the Brezhnev period. The association, however, remains essentially implicit, a minor theme in both writers' works, in keeping with the attempt to break away from the urban realism most associated with the examination of that experience. By contrast, however, in the Czech fiction of the Changes, resistance to fixedness and the pursuit of openness is repeatedly linked to the experience of the Normalization period, which, unlike in Russian and Slovak fiction, has remained a painful, urgent subject in Czech fiction even in the late 1990s.[2]

The problem of the relationship between the form of expression and experience arose above all in Czech fiction of the Changes in the context of Kratochvil's first novel, *Medvědí román*, which, in Milan Jungmann's euphemistic terms, 'through its narrative experimentation provoked a great deal of unease among critics and readers' (Jungmann 1993b: 6). In the novel's epilogue, in terms subsequently borrowed by Hodrová in *...na okraji chaosu...*, Kratochvil describes the work as

> a novel as an open system, a novel as a living organism, growing, living and moving before the reader's eyes, and its modes of expression are, for example, story variants and some kind of – how to call it? – finely chiselled improvisations.
>
> (Kratochvil 1990: 264)

In response to Antonín Brousek's assertion that the work could be of interest only to literary theorists (see Brousek 1991: 4), Kratochvil argues:

> [I wrote in this way] to compensate for the anxious experience of the closed world of a totalitarian society in which I lived. So you may ask: is it a novel that emerged from the consolatory formal idea of creating an open literary space capable of resisting the oppressive experience of the closed systems which surrounded me, or did it emerge as a story depicting that oppression and the search for a way out of it? [...] And I would say that, with the best

> will in the world, it really is impossible to excise either content or form from my novel.
>
> (Kratochvil 1995: 192)

The question of whether the structure of *Medvědí román* seeks to mirror or to offer an escape from the social experience from which it arises is symptomatic of the general ambiguity underpinning the novel and Kratochvil's work in general. In the context of the fiction discussed in this chapter, *Medvědí román* serves as a point of transition where the pessimism about writing expressed in Ivanchenko and Tolstaia meets the optimism which characterizes their Czech counterparts. Moreover, as Klára Lukavská has pointed out, *Medvědí román*, which forms the first part of a trilogy of novels published by Kratochvil in the early 1990s, is also the 'key source novel for Kratochvil's fiction', establishing the themes and techniques developed in his later work (Lukavská 2002: 13).

Kratochvil's exploration of the writing process in *Medvědí román* arises not so much from literary-theoretical concerns as from the specific problem of expressing his own life experience through writing. As Kratochvil outlines in his defence of *Medvědí román*, he grew up in Communist Czechoslovakia not only without a father, but ostracized because his father had emigrated after the Communist takeover. Having begun to gain acceptance as a writer and critic in the 1960s, he lost his job in the aftermath of August 1968 and spent the 1970s in unskilled manual jobs familiar to unsanctioned writers, once again alienated because he was not counted among the prominent political dissidents, and perhaps because of a letter sent to Brno dissidents from West Germany by his émigré uncle suggesting that he was a police informer.[3]

As Jungmann points out, the writer-narrator of *Medvědí román* resisted the temptation to write a 'great family novel' because the form did not seem adequate to his situation:

> I feel as if the reality in which I live has for some time now had two or three alternatives at once [...] *reality* has acquired the character of *arbitrariness*, or I have lost some sense which is essential in perceiving, differentiating and working with it.
>
> (Kratochvil 1990: 130–1)

Kratochvil comments of his childhood, 'I found myself at the centre of some unspeakable secret' (Kratochvil 1995: 192). In his fiction, he attempts to transform his personal experience of exclusion in the totalitarian period in Czechoslovakia into a metaphor for what he presents as the 'genuine' condition of the human being, denied absolute knowledge of or influence over reality. In this respect, he follows in the tradition of Ladislav Fuks, whose experiences as an adolescent during the German occupation shape his characters' comparable sense of exclusion from reality, most explicitly in the novel *Variace pro temnou strunu* (Variations for a dark string, 1966).

In *Medvědí román*, Kratochvil attempts to convey this experience of reality to the reader through what Patricia Waugh terms a 'Chinese-box structure' (Waugh 1984: 30–1), encapsulated by the writer-narrator's description of the work as a 'novel about how I am writing a novel about someone who is writing a novel' (Kratochvil 1990: 168). This layering of text is intensified by Kratochvil's dense use of literary allusion, which simultaneously implies both the positive and the negative interpretations of the notion of the 'world as text', on the one hand suggesting imprisonment in pre-existing text, as in *Moskva–Petushki* or *Příliš hlučná samota*, and on the other, release into the interconnectedness of text through the eradication of the borders established between them.

The work begins with a parody science fiction allegory of Czechoslovakia under Normalization which, in its images of an island-state surrounded by water and ecological themes, like *Medorek* recalls Egon Bondy's already parodic dystopian novel, *Invalidní sourozenci*. The parody in Kratochvil's allegory, as in Bondy's, derives from his failure to make any effort to conceal its source, through which Kratochvil satirizes the repeated use of such allegories by unsanctioned writers. This part, narrated by a Sancho Panza-like character called Ursinus (*sic*), turns out to be a novel being written by a certain Ondřej Beránek. Having lost his job in the aftermath of 1968, Beránek initially finds employment as a crane-operator through an old friend from military service, Ríša, who remains grateful for the love letters which, in the manner of Cyrano de Bergerac, Ondřej wrote for him to his wife, Helenka. This episode typifies Kratochvil's use of literary intertext throughout his writing. Ríša and Helenka are the names of the sweethearts in a classic work of Czech fiction, *Pohádka máje* (The fairy-tale of spring, 1897) by Vilém Mrštík (1863–1912). However, whereas in that novel, the Moravian countryside near Brno represents an idyllic escape from urban life, in *Medvědí román* it is portrayed as a stinking industrialized place of exile. At the end of this part, Beránek, now working as a night-watchman on a battery farm, realizes the extent to which his allegorical novel, its characters, setting, names, themes and motifs, have been influenced by his immediate environment, and in turn, the reader is encouraged to see Beránek's story as an allegory of Kratochvil's own. The name Beránek, meaning 'lamb' or 'young ram', not only casts Kratochvil as the scapegoat for the sins of his father, but also suggests that, unlike Isaac, he was sacrificed by his father when he went into exile.

At one point Beránek comments: 'it looks as though [...] I am only interested in a reality which is infested with similarities' (Kratochvil 1990: 157). Kratochvil here not only rejects the Realist mode as inadequate to the task of conveying his experience of reality, but also suggests that texts only ever function as metaphors for reality, and that a 'reality which is infested with similarities' is the only kind of reality which can be known. Kratochvil's experience of exclusion from full, unmediated knowledge of reality thus constitutes an initiation into how human beings 'know' reality, denied to those, like Alisa in Ivanchenko's *Avtoportret s dogom*, who prosper in the material world. Alena Vrbová suggests that the central characters of Kratochvil's trilogy are mere variants on a single figure, essentially an authorial self-characterization which implicitly becomes a definition of what it is to be a human being, a 'passive observer or even a victim of different external influences and events [...] a kind of closed spiritual island in an aggressive, superficial and "worldly" world' (Vrbová 2001: 53).

Rather as the authorial selves proliferate in *Hľadanie strateného autora*, a new narrator appears in the third part of *Medvědí román*, apparently the 'real' writer of both the first and second parts, and identified as 'Mr Kratochvil'. Having expressed his delight at finally being able to speak for himself in his own voice, however, he then casts doubt on this assertion:

> if it can be assumed that in Ursinus's fate is mirrored not only Beránek's fate, but perhaps also mine a little, just as Beránek's fate reflects not only Ursinus's fate, but again also mine a little, then I have to take into consideration that I, the narrator, as it were, now carry in myself something of Ursinus's fate, and perhaps also of Beránek's, and so from the three wefts arranged next to each other is now a web that cannot be disentangled, so which I? what I can there be? and why bother about this any longer?
>
> (Kratochvil 1990: 168)

The narrator's problem resembles that of the painter-narrator Mameev at the end of Ivanchenko's *Avtoportret s dogom*, trapped in an implicitly infinite series of texts which cannot be differentiated in terms of truth or fiction, and unable to break through to a discrete self. However, in place of the mirror shattered in despair, which serves as a metaphor for the self in Ivanchenko's novel, Kratochvil offers the patchwork of text, and in place of the impossibility of distinguishing between truth and fiction, Kratochvil offers the notion of 'story', a concept which recurs throughout his work.[4] In his 1994 essay 'Příběh přiběhu' (The story of the story), Kratochvil describes postwar Czech history as the undesirable exchange of reality for an 'improbable story', which has led people away from stories in the belief that reality is more exciting. He comments: 'Literature is not doing well, but because, despite everything, the human need for stories is undying, stories still remain here with us, only in their most degraded form, teeming like fish' (Kratochvil 1995: 23). Unlike Mitana, who rejects the story outright in *Hľadanie strateného autora*, Kratochvil's preoccupation with the story and story-telling in the 1990s appears to be motivated by a desire not only to represent stories in their contemporary form, indicated by his use of countless fragments and variants of stories and references to other stories, and his mixing of 'high' and 'low' forms of story, but also to protect and preserve the story as it goes through troubled times.

In effect, Kratochvil's conception of 'story' constitutes a more optimistic version of the comforting but ultimately vain activity of Tolstaia's writer-'fakir'. In a reproach to the reader similar to that made by Popov's narrator in *Dusha patriota*, the narrator of *Medvědí román* expresses sentiments implicit in Tolstaia's writing:

> Why on earth do you ask questions in advance and why do you want to grasp, comprehend everything so quickly? why do you put pressure on me? why are you so insistent and pushy? what's driving you where and what on earth's the hurry? after all, it's already clear now that what is awaiting us is ultimately always only catastrophe, but isn't the story here to delay that a bit? telling a story or listening to one, it's as if both took our life into comforting hands for a moment, the story is our last refuge, the last grace which has been left us by Him-who-takes-everything-away-in-the-end.
>
> (Kratochvil 1990: 118–19)

Květoslav Chvatík credits Kratochvil with reminding the reader that 'the epic is above all the art of time, the ability to allow the reader to feel the passage of time' and 'the art of slowness; it does not hurry, it can expand itself at each individual thing, it can recall, dream, rewind, return again and again and see the human being always from a new perspective' (Chvatík 1992: 6).Whereas Tolstaia emphasizes the illusoriness of stories, and their feebleness in the face of time, in his essay on the story, Kratochvil asserts not only the importance of the story as a means by which people can orientate themselves in their own history and thus defend themselves against existential angst, but also the importance of the author, who supplies the causality:

> Human life and the human world are not composed of stories, but only of situations connected by mere chronology. Structuring the sequence of situations into a story is only a matter of authorial invention, which does not, however, have any prototype in reality.
>
> (Kratochvil 1995: 21)

The potentially infinite number of stories – of variants, versions and narrators – indicated in *Medvědí román* is therefore a 'good infinity' for Kratochvil, as in *Dusha patriota*, since it demonstrates the continuation of life.

In the conclusion of 'Příběh s telefonem' (A story with a telephone, dated as written 1977), Kratochvil writes: 'All my stories are merely correspondences to better stories. So they are really *substitute* stories… Stories instead of the stories which I don't know how to – or don't want to? – write' (Kratochvil 1994a: 84). Like Venedikt Erofeev, who sends an alter-ego on the vain messianic journey of the writer, Kratochvil rejects the notion that human beings have the power to create paradise on earth, and therefore his stories are, like *Moskva–Petushki*, substitutes for that story. In his first three novels, Kratochvil plays with the longing of both writer and reader to restore wholeness, to re-discover Eden. Jungmann's description of *Medvědí román* as a 'dream about a father, some kind of anti-Oedipal quest for family roots and personal identity, a longing to overcome human incompleteness and the mystical paralysis caused by the loss of the paternal element' (Jungmann 1993b: 6), which applies even better to

Kratochvil's next two novels, where the paternal theme figures more strongly, fails to take account of the ironization of that search.

In *Uprostřed nocí zpěv* (Singing amid the nights, 1992) and *Avion*, the narrator's quest for reunion with his father parallels the reader's search for a unified explanation or single origin for the disparate layers of texts, encouraged by hints, clues, coincidences and similarities. This strategy operates at its simplest in *Uprostřed nocí zpěv*, of which Kratochvil writes:

> This time I decided to write a novel about the miserable fate of the children of post-February [1948] émigrés, and thus provide a testimony about them. In the thrall of this noble mission, I tried to write the novel in a way that would find it the greatest number of readers, and subordinated the means of literary expression to this communicative consideration, too.
>
> (Kratochvil 1995: 193)[5]

In *Uprostřed nocí zpěv*, the chapters alternate between ostensibly different boy-narrators seeking lost fathers, with the two narrators' stories and characters gradually coming closer until, in the final chapter, they appear to merge. Lukavská, noting the general disappointment among critics regarding this conclusion, comments that it seems to be a 'mere mechanical, unsurprising drawing-to-an-end of a method for which Kratochvil had decided in advance' (Lukavská 2002: 19). However, in the context of the structure of *Medvědí román*, and given the details drawn from Kratochvil's own biography shared between the narrators, the ending may be perceived not so much as a neat resolution, but rather as the emergence once again of the author from amid various versions of his story. At the end of the novel, the text is posted to an address in Rio de Janeiro where the father may be living, a sanitized echo of the ending of *Medvědí román*, in which the narrator urinates away the characters, demonstrating that that version is definitive. As in Ivanchenko's work, writing is shown as a process of emptying, in Kratochvil's case to create space for new stories, rather than an attempt to fill space once and for all. In this context, the title *Urmedvěd* (Ur-bear, 1999), for Kratochvil's publication of the unedited version of *Medvědí román*, is also ironic, since no 'original' or 'final' version can exist.

The reasons for Kratochvil's resistance to resolution become clearer at the end of *Avion*, when the narrator and his father, as adults, are apparently reconciled beside a giant watering can. The scene links back to one of the narrator's few memories of being with his father as a little child, when the watering can did appear enormous, but in fact subverts the sincerity of the search for reunion with the father in the latter two books of the trilogy, since it is equated with a longing to return to childhood, described in *Medvědí román* as 'the only perfectly unified universal, mythical world,' and equated there, as in Sorokin's writing, with the totalitarian state. In *Medvědí román*, Kratochvil includes an essay playfully attributed to one of the characters, a psychiatrist, in which he asserts that, on the one hand, totalitarianism is a form of collective schizophrenia and, on the other, schizophrenia is a form of individual totalitarianism. According to Kratochvil, both arise out of a 'fear of freedom understood as the variegated face of chaos and also a subconscious desire for infantile dependence', and manifest themselves through the creation of 'closed systems' which mean 'giving up on life and the world in the name of a unifying idea, and in practice therefore only total isolation and a reality built from a few thoroughly logically developed ideas' (Kratochvil 1990: 251).[6] The consequence, Kratochvil claims, is not, however, wholeness or stability, but the disintegration of the personality in schizophrenia and of society in totalitarianism.

Kratochvil's description of schizophrenia closely resembles a personality disorder described by R.D. Laing as the 'shut-up self', an 'attempt to create relationships to persons and things within the individual without recourse to the outer world of persons and things at all'. The consequence, however, according to Laing, is that:

> [The 'shut-up self'] is unable to be enriched by outer experience, and so the whole inner world comes to be more and more impoverished, until the individual may come to feel he is merely a vacuum. The sense of being able to do anything and the feeling of possessing everything then exist side by side with a feeling of impotence and emptiness.
>
> (Laing 1969: 74)

In the novels discussed in the previous chapter, both Ivanchenko and Mitana assert the need for the human being to lose his or her attachment to the notion of a discrete self, to be reconciled with the disintegration of the self. By contrast, in common with Czech contemporaries like Hodrová, Placák and Topol, Kratochvil retains a notion of the individual self which, in his view, is best preserved not by closing itself off, but by opening itself to interaction with the unknown, in which it finds its being.

As in Ivanchenko's portrayal of Alisa in *Avtoportret s dogom*, the attempt to preserve the self by enclosing it is associated in *Medvědí román* with materialism, and with characters who are utterly embedded in terrestrial existence and seek to impose their influence upon it. Kratochvil uses the image of the bear, trained to infiltrate the powers-that-be only to supplant them, as a metaphor for the desire for power which becomes oppressively normative. In the first part of the novel, Kratochvil describes how, during the change of power in the allegorical state of Ostrov, the symbol of the bear passes from the adherents of Kloboučník (Hatter), a reference to the shoe manufacturer and symbol of Czech First Republic capitalism, Tomáš Báťa, to those engaged in the 'reconstruction of the world', who start to write history with a 'bear's claw' (see Kratochvil 1990: 80). In this way, the desire to take control of history and bring it to a happy ending is directly connected with bear-like activity. The link between the bear and the Russians is inescapable.

In the novel, the motif of the bear is set against the motif of the lamb, reflected in Ondřej Beránek's name. In the third part of the novel, the narrator is given a lift by a prominent local Communist functionary with a secret fondness for Masaryk, whose name, Pes (Dog), indicates his evolutionary link with bears, and who apparently inspires the whole novel by mentioning a man called Beránek in conversation with the narrator. As a gift in return for the name, the narrator invents a story about a seventeenth-century religious sect called the Lambs, traces of whom remain in the surname Beránek, common in the area of southern Moravia where the sect lived. The narrator admits that his story derives from the depiction of a sect called the Abrahamites in *Děti čistého živého* (Children of pure living, 1909) by Teréza Nováková (1853–1912), a connection illuminated by Vladimír Forst's description of Nováková's sect:

> Though they want to live joyfully and usefully according to reason, they are actually incapable of bringing about anything, and even their most discerning head ultimately commits suicide for petty reasons. Though the story sounds pessimistic, a tension remains between characters striving for spiritual elevation and those who content themselves only with material prosperity.
>
> (Opelík (ed.) 2000: 587)[7]

In a burlesque version of the Abrahamites, the eccentric descendants of the Lambs are likewise incapable of dealing competently with the demands of everyday life, and repeatedly meet their ends tragi-comically, often through suicide. As a result of their incompetence, they are easily tyrannized by 'bears', to the point of turning into bears themselves, or made scapegoats – sacrificial lambs – like Ondřej's father František, who, in a comic passage intended to recall Jaroslav Hašek's *Osudy dobrého vojáka Švejka za světové války* (The fortunes of the good soldier Švejk during the Great War, 1921–3), is falsely accused of collaborating with the Germans during the Second World War and imprisoned in a barn. In one version of the outcome he is shot, and in the other he escapes to the West inside a stuffed Russian bear; in the context of the trilogy, these represent the first variants on the possible fate of Kratochvil's own 'vanished' father.

The narrator explicitly discourages the reader from perceiving the Lambs as an allegory of a nation like the Jews, while at the same time linking them with the Czechs, in particular in his description of the mass transformation of Lambs into bears in the late 1940s and 1950s. Indeed, in keeping with the Czech messianic myth, the Lambs, who as a religious sect perceive themselves as the collective embodiment of the Lamb in the Book of Revelation who rids the world of the Anti-Christ, aim to save the world through their suffering, underpinned by their 'nevýslovná pokora' (unspeakable humility). The simultaneous association of the Lambs with the nation as a whole and with only a tiny section of it, however, prevents the metaphor from becoming conclusively 'national'.

The Lambs, like the bears, perceive themselves as instruments of salvation, though passive rather than active. František's escape in the bear-skin, described in a chapter entitled 'Beránek v rouše medvědím' (Lamb in bear's clothing), indicates his refusal to be either an active or a passive instrument of salvation, a Communist bear or a Christian lamb, being instead an instrument of self-preservation through resistance to external definition. Kratochvil suggests that one must be a 'lamb in bear's clothing', like Ursinus in the first part of the novel, infiltrating the bear-like 'powers-that-be' only to undermine them, without oneself actually becoming a bear.

In the epigraph to the first part of the novel, which describes the types chosen to dress up as bears during the last three days of Lent, Kratochvil indicates that disguising oneself as a bear is connected with a time of carnival, a word which, like 'story', repeatedly appears in Kratochvil's writing. In his 1994 essay on Czech sanctioned fiction of the late 1940s and 1950s, 'Literatura karnevalu', he notes the similarity between Bakhtin's theory of carnival and the first manifesto of the Poetists, the Czech 1920s Avant-garde movement, written by its chief theorist, Karel Teige (1900–51), which presented life itself as carnival. According to Kratochvil, however, what happened during and after the Communist takeover of Czechoslovakia obliterated the symbolic nature of carnival as a substitute for reality, playing out 'for real' the carnival ritual of enthroning and then dethroning a 'king', described by Bakhtin, with what in *Medvědí román* would be described as the 'bear-like' objective of establishing a new order once and for all. Kratochvil writes:

> While carnival only plays at being reality, a theatricalization of reality with a strict time limit, the carnivalization of the 1950s was played out 'for all time'. Through a grotesque 'metaphor' brought to life, it was supposed to squeeze out reality and also to rid literature of all its life-giving functions.
>
> (Kratochvil 1995: 71)

In a literary context, Kratochvil's image of the 'lamb in bear's clothing' serves as a metaphor of the danger inherent in literary creation, however innocent its intentions, epitomized by the contrast between the Poetists' vision of revolution and its realization. Kratochvil writes:

> As the literature of a small nation, Czech literature has repeatedly been in danger, and perhaps continues to be in danger, of falling victim to its own messianism, just as soon as it is given the opportunity again to enter the suggestive space of 'playing at reality' [*hra na skutečnost*].
>
> (Ibid.)

At the same time, however, the image seeks to reassert the carnivalistic function of the story, understood as an act of rebellion by someone oppressed by authority that seeks only to assert the relativity of all authority. Chased away by Pes and his dogs, the narrator of the third part of *Medvědí román* comments:

> I felt how inside me it was slowly starting to raise its lamb's head (the bear's novel) and how it had woken up and come to life with all this running and shaking up, because the novel, you nitwit, is the lot of the spent and humiliated.
>
> (Kratochvil 1990: 166)

The story, suddenly bear-like, must aspire to supplant the tyrant, absorbing its audience and apparently taking it over, only to subvert itself, dissolving before it can become concrete and definitive, urinated or mailed away. In effect, Kratochvil's perception of story-telling coincides with that of Korobeinikov in Tolstaia's 'Plamen' nebesnyi', and counters the bear-like use of story-telling to gain advantage practised by Dmitrii Il'ich. At the end of *Avion*, the 'lamb-like' narrator, Hynek, merges with František, the central character in the science-fiction novel he is writing, who is a 'homunculus' produced from human pain by the mysterious embodiment of evil, Malý Muk. In this way, Kratochvil presents the story as a merging of good and evil, in which each neutralizes the other, allowing the self to continue to survive uninhibited, free to tell more stories about itself.

Kratochvil characterizes his own writing and that of his contemporaries as the rescue of the story – of literature – from its complicity in tyranny. The desire to neutralize the potential danger inherent in creating art, expressed in a more self-destructive way in *Moskva–Petushki* and the fiction of Sorokin, is also found in the first two novels by Zuzana Brabcová, which share with Kratochvil's fiction the quest for reconciliation with the father, the motif of schizophrenia and the ironized yearning for a messiah that recurs in Czech fiction of the Changes. Brabcová is the daughter of the academic and literary critic Jiří Brabec (b.1929), who lost his position in the Writers' Union in the 1970 purges and subsequently published prolifically on Czech literature and thought in *samizdat* and *tamizdat*. Unlike in Kratochvil's novels, however, the autobiographical identification of the father–child relationship in Brabcová's fiction is suppressed.

The title of *Daleko od stromu* alludes to the saying 'The apple never falls far from the tree'. In the novel, the narrator, Věra's father, a 1960s reformer turned dissident, cannot understand his daughter's inability to commit herself to any sort of cause or action. Her alienation from her father represents an alienation from meaning, a fear of surrendering her identity to an idea. She shares her sense of alienation with her grandfather, a fervent Communist after the war who, like Tolstaia's elderly naturalist in 'Somnambula v tumane', has retreated into his own private world, crippled by an awareness of the absolute relativity of human action and unable to understand his son. As a small child, Věra was asked by her father in front of a group of other children to draw a flash of lightning, but could not. Later that day, however, she covered the walls of his study with lightning flashes in a futile but vital act of rebellion not only against her father's authority, but also against the notion of civilization and progress for which he stands. The flash of lightning is, according to Věra's teacher, the oldest example of cave painting and therefore symbolizes the end of pre-history and the beginning of the process of civilization that, implicitly, has produced the society in which she finds herself. As in *Medorek*, her refusal to subscribe to his process requires the abandonment of the notion of the individual self:

> going mad was inevitable, because otherwise I would be sealed in a tank or broken in on a firing-range, which in this state is a strange initiation custom. And so, in this century of numbers, graphs, the anonymity of the masses, statistics, energy, the deranged subtleties of reason, monkeys in rockets and functions, I decided to stay for now somewhat outside, with the divine side of the coin, with the tiniest hem of illusion and with a handful of lines. I shall start again.
>
> (Brabcová 1991: 120)

As she suggests, the disintegration of the self in Brabcová is not, as in other writers of the Changes, an end in itself, but the beginning of a quest for a new wholeness. Věra sets herself the aim at the beginning of her narrative of writing a book and having a child. Her achievement of these ambitions at the end of the work marks the reintegration of herself and her reconciliation with her father, symbolized by her planting of a tree in his home village at the end of the novel.

Brabcová's second novel, *Zlodějina* (Thievilry, 1995; the title is explained below), is less neurotic and more playful, with a third-person narration that creates distance between the implied author and her two central characters. The two alternating narratives in the novel reflect the same split personality as in *Daleko od stromu*, in which one part seeks a way back to selfhood, while the other attempts to abandon selfhood completely. One narrative focuses on a woman, Matějů, trapped in a lift, whose yearning for a child gradually turns into awareness of a child growing inside her. The other features a man called Eman, who has a mental breakdown when asked what he did on 17 November 1989. On that day, rather than participate in the protests, he had tried to run away from a student demonstration and was beaten up by police, a reflection of his position 'outside' both opposing sides. The title of the novel is a neologism derived from *zlodějna* (thievery) and the notional singular of the plural noun *dějiny* (history) that reflects how a single historical event 'steals' Eman's fragile intermediate identity, causing its disintegration. The two characters are linked by their names; Matějů's alludes to Matthew the Evangelist, who was the first to report the Good News, and who also recalled the name Emmanuel, used by Isaiah for the Messiah. Eman, who epitomizes the travestied messianism that recurs in the Czech fiction of the Changes, reflects the 'holy-foolish' nobility of the social outsider similarly asserted by Venedikt Erofeev and Hrabal. The coming of Eman, however, does not so much mark the culmination of history as its erasure through a return to the beginning. Like Věra in *Daleko od stromu*, he yearns to return to a time before history, and at the end of the novel he flees from Prague with a Gipsy woman to a cave by a lake, perhaps in Romania, thereby reversing the journey once taken by his father from the 'prehistoric' Carpathians to 'civilized' Prague. In effect, while Věra – like Matějů – finds a way of writing herself into history, Eman writes himself out of it, thereby recovering silence.

The resolutions in Brabcová's novels distinguish them from other Czech fiction of the period, in which the preservation of intermediacy and open-endedness is vital. Her fiction, like Kratochvil's and Placák's, has a strong political subtext, expressing in effect a means of individual resistance against an oppressive external environment. By contrast, the fiction of both Hodrová and Ajvaz is more preoccupied with aesthetic approaches, opposing different 'ways of seeing' in art, and thereby placing their conflict with prevailing trends in the context of a long alternative tradition. In her fiction and theoretical writing, Hodrová explores and exploits themes and motifs from early Christian, Jewish, medieval, Renaissance and Baroque esoteric texts, and subsequent works which adopt the same approach. In this way, she seeks in unfavourable circumstances to sustain the memory of understandings of the nature and purpose of literature other than that not only propounded in doctrines like Marxism-Leninism, but also perceived in Western society as 'normal', or essential for facilitating the conduct of everyday life.

The close relationship between Hodrová's fiction and her research, which underpins the following discussion, has frequently been noted by critics: for example, Zdeněk Heřman describes her first novel, *Podobojí* (In both kinds, 1991, dated as written 1977–8 and 1984), as the 'artistic realization of what she declared in her theory' (Heřman 1992: 4), while Vladimír Macura comments on the particular pleasure derived from reading her novels and her theoretical work 'in one go' (Macura 1991: 5). Indeed, *Théta* (Theta, 1993, dated as written 1987–90), the third novel in her trilogy, also comprising *Podobojí* and *Kukly* (1991, dated as written 1981–3), described by Martin Ryšavý as the most 'anti-illusive' of Hodrová's novels (Ryšavý 1993: 18), reads as much as a commentary to the first two novels as a novel in its own right. In her analysis of the poetics of the twentieth-century literary work, Hodrová frequently uses images and metaphors taken from Ajvaz's fiction, reflecting not only the proximity of his approach to writing to her own, but also the didactic clarity of its articulation in his work. This section therefore also contains discussion of Ajvaz's fiction, in particular his first collection of prose pieces, *Návrat starého varana* (The return of the old Komodo dragon, 1991) and his first novel, *Druhé město* (The other city, 1992), as much to illuminate Hodrová's work as to provide a point of comparison.

In her study of literary topology, *Místa s tajemstvím* (Places with a mystery, 1994), Hodrová asserts the co-existence in Western literature of two approaches, one of which, broadly associated with types of Realism, strives to eradicate mystery, while the other, associated with the types of writing she prefers to study, endeavours to preserve it (see Hodrová 1994: 10–11). As Ryšavý points out, Hodrová's pointedly excessive shift away from Realism puts into practice her own assertion in *Hledání románu*, that the novel 'renews and reconstitutes itself' through the endless 'movement' between these two approaches. According to

Ryšavý, the study was originally called *Pohyb románu*, but Marxist editors objected to this notion of movement which was not dialectical, but rather implied cyclicality or oscillation. Hodrová's own fiction may be seen not only as a reflection of a temporary sense that Realism has exhausted itself, as Ryšavý suggests, but also as an attempt to restore the balance upset by the aggressive shift towards Realism to the exclusion of all other modes in the Communist period (see Ryšavý 1993: 18).

Hodrová dramatizes these two contrasting approaches in *Théta* through the characters of Comrade Midas and Mr Chaun, the leaders of a children's theatre group, whose preferred titles give the account an obvious political subtext:

> Mr Chaun loved secrets, he had a flair for all sorts of little surprises and games, with which he constantly enchanted us. Comrade Midas didn't like secrets; perhaps he used to see in them something of the devil, which, thus disguised, might creep into life and change it fundamentally.
>
> (Hodrová 1999: 392)

Hodrová's playful use of the name Midas links the character's approach to life with materialism, the desire to turn everything into gold recalling the yearning of Tolstaia's Denisov for a monument. At the same time, however, the name may allude to the myth about the music competition between Apollo and Marsyas, in which Midas declared Marsyas, rather than the god, the winner. In this case, Comrade Midas is associated with hubris and finding beauty in implicitly the wrong kind of art.

Midas eradicates mystery by making the children confess their secrets to him, rewarding them with chocolate. One day, however, Eliška Beránková (another Lamb), explicitly an implied authorial alter-ego, instead takes a piece of orange from Mr Chaun, which represents for her not only the exotic, linked to Mr Chaun, but also the forbidden: 'By taking the blood of Mr Chaun, and not the body of Comrade Midas, she becomes from that moment a follower of a different cult, one that is forbidden, pagan' (ibid.: 393). The communion metaphor reflects Eliška's rebellion and her desire, contrary to conservative Roman Catholicism, in which communion is received only 'in one kind', to live 'in both kinds', to participate fully in the 'sacred mysteries'. From this point, Hodrová implies, she will be a writer who seeks not to adapt reality to existing models, but to see it simultaneously from both points of view. Kratochvil found himself 'at the centre of an unspeakable secret'; Hodrová chooses to depict reality as a 'place with a mystery'.

In *...na okraji chaosu...*, Hodrová describes the activity of the writer as the 'movement between a recognized context, which is given the appearance of order, and all-consuming emptiness' (Hodrová 2001: 129). This activity is effectively dramatized by Ajvaz in *Návrat starého varana* in the story 'Sochař' (The sculptor), which Milan Exner considers, along with 'Nic' (Nothing) and 'Koncert' (The concert), the 'most successful expression of the author's poetics, text as meaningful as it is artistic' (Exner 1991: 14). In the story, the sculptor-narrator lives in a house built into a cliff, behind which bubbles an underground lake. The sculptor takes up a position on the threshold between the 'recognized context', the cosmos of the house, and 'all-consuming emptiness', the chaos of the lake, using a valve fitted into a crack in the back wall to fire into the room lumps of magma which he then sculpts. The sculptor does not try to make the material match a pre-conceived idea, which represents a movement back to cosmos, but rather allows himself to be led by the shapes of the lumps, 'realizing the strange underground dreams of matter, dreams which I don't understand'. He refutes, however, the suggestion that he is too passive, maintaining that what is usually considered 'active' is merely the 'comfortable assimilation of reality to a ready-made model'. In the same way, to those who claim to know from his sculptures what he was trying to say he remarks:

> To impose reality onto something, the design of which is ready in advance, in my view is to exchange a living organism for a withered shell of life. It means walking the path of death, sacrificing the future to the past and the subtle, imperceptibly dominant harmony-rhythm to a repressive notion of order.
>
> (Ajvaz 2000: 112)

In 'Nic', the narrator expresses ironic admiration for those people with ready-made opinions who take up writing in order to lend weight and permanence to these views. Having no opinions of his own, he tried borrowing those of others, but found that they dissolved into nothing in his hands, so he decided to work with this 'nothing' instead. He comments:

> Is nothing really nothing? How little we notice nothing. We see only that which we have patronizingly acknowledged as 'something', hardened, ready-made shapes; for us, 'nothing' is the dark sphere beyond the borders of that 'something'. But is this neglected sphere really emptiness? In these overlooked corners of being, in the backyards of existence with their wondrous, varied life, of which 'something' is merely a withered shell, do we not meet with a life which in the pulsation of its forces conceals a secret of something so forgotten that we do not even ask about it?'
>
> (Ibid.: 122)

The not altogether satisfying paradox of Ajvaz's fiction, however, is that the rejection of fixed opinions becomes itself in effect an *idée fixe*.

This characterization of the writer as a figure who moves constantly between two places also appears in Vladimir Makanin's Booker Prize-nominated short novel 'Laz' (The man-hole, 1992), which thus provides a useful point of contrast in approaches. Makanin's central character, Kliucharev, inhabits a desolate, ostensibly post-Soviet dystopia, where it is forever twilight, but is able to dig down through a man-hole into a brightly lit world of chattering intellectuals. In common with the desire to preserve openness in the fiction of the Changes, and typical of Makanin's fiction, the work resists one single interpretation. Makanin has suggested that the work was inspired by the image of a man stuck in an hour glass (see Laird 1999: 61). The underground world, whether it represents emigration or perhaps the 1960s, is a place of fixed views, like Makov on his mountain in 'Somnambula v tumane' gradually being buried by passing time. Though Kliucharev is attracted to the underground world, he is committed to the world above ground, where his family and the future, however bleak, endure. Throughout the work, he travels and digs with a dignified doggedness reminiscent of Solzhenitsyn's Ivan Denisovich, striving to keep lines of communication open even though it seems hopeless; when, in the twilight world, he finds a phone that works, he is careful to leave the door ajar for someone else to find it. At the end of the novel, he finds that the shelter he has been building has been vandalized and his tools stolen. Rather than giving way to despair, however, he regards the act as the beginning of a dialogue. In common with the description of the writer in much of the fiction of the Changes, Kliucharev's actions are eccentric and compulsive, but, unlike those of Ajvaz's sculptor, they are not for their own sake. Makanin's story constitutes a defence of the intellectual and an articulation of his continued important and noble social function in straitened circumstances. Kliucharev's name derives from the Russian for 'sacristan' and denotes him as the 'keeper of the keys', the constant facilitator of dialogue.

As Ajvaz's metaphor of the sculptor reflects, the essential characteristic of existence in 'reality with a secret' is a constant sense of intermediacy which cannot be overcome. To sustain this experience of reality, Hodrová repeatedly uses motifs and devices from mainly early Christian, medieval and Baroque literature which present terrestrial existence as a form of intermediate state from which the human being yearns to escape. In the trilogy, the sense of lost completeness or a lost chance to restore completeness is expressed through stories of unrequited love, unhappy marriages and aborted or miscarried children.[8] The pain (*trýzeň*) of this yearning is reflected in the title of the trilogy, *Trýznivé město*, an allusion to Dante's description of Florence in *Inferno* as 'città dolente', and is represented in Hodrová's fiction by Prague, the name of which, according to legend, derives from *práh*, meaning 'threshold', the embodiment of intermediacy.

Hodrová's references to Prague, or more specifically the Olšany cemetery and its surroundings which form the setting of her trilogy, as a labyrinth also recall *Labyrint světa a Ráj srdce* (The labyrinth of the world and The paradise of the heart, 1623) by Jan Amos Comenius (1592–1670), in which the labyrinth, as in Hodrová's fiction, is connected with 'a city-world in which all is marked with vanity and death' (Hodrová 1993b: 71). Comenius's labyrinth constitutes an example of the *theatrum mundi* convention, in which, as Hodrová writes in *Místa s tajemstvím*, 'the world and history are perceived as the product of illusion, an illusory manifestation [...], as an allegory of reality, a dream from which the pilgrim should awaken and see it for what it is' (Hodrová 1994: 14). According to Hodrová, *theatrum mundi* recurs through literary history as a motif in works written at times of sudden social change, when 'reality has acquired chaotic features and its visible boundaries have disappeared', and corresponds to a 'sense of *being in exile* (in a Neo-Platonist, Gnostic sense), a sense of unreal being which separates the individual on his journey from his spiritual mission, from finding his true identity' (ibid.: 18). Hodrová's own use of the device is parodic, most obviously in her fourth novel, *Perunův den* (Perun's day, 1993) which presents November 1989 and its aftermath as such a period of change, since she rejects the suggestion that the limits and nature of reality are 'normally' stable, and satirizes the majority who prefer to believe that they are.

In *Podobojí*, Hodrová suggests that the sense of intermediacy arises from the fact that terrestrial existence is governed by the number 'two':

> Where the number 'one', according to the numerical cabala of Cornelius Agrippa of Nettesheim, is the source and origin of all numbers, rules out any kind of multiplicity, is always the same and unchanging, multiplied by itself it gives only itself again, is without beginning and relates to God, the number 'two', which follows immediately after it, is the number of creation and the manifestation of the prime movement. All embodiment flows from 'two'; 'two' is the principle of division, multiplicity and difference, matter and metamorphosis, it is the number of science, memory and the world, the number of the human being, the number of discord and impurity.
>
> (Hodrová 1999: 125)

Implicitly, 'one' is associated with Edenic unity, while 'two' denotes post-Edenic existence, tormented by the awareness of paradise lost. In *Podobojí*, Mr Turek, an explicator of Hodrová's conception of the world in her first two novels, comments: 'There are two worlds: the pre-Olšany and the Olšany' (ibid.). The Olšany cemeteries were built on vineyards following an outbreak of plague, and thereafter, whoever touches their soil, like Diviš Paskal, the central character in *Podobojí*, is condemned to die. Hodrová's description of the Olšany earth as 'vinná země', meaning both 'viticultural' and 'guilty', links with Diviš's name, a merging of Dionysus with the Paschal Lamb, to reflect the duality of human existence, existing in both body and soul. This duality is mirrored in the name of the central character of *Kukly*, Sofie Syslová, combining the goddess Wisdom with *sysel*, meaning 'ground squirrel'. Through these plays-on-words, Hodrová indicates that her characterization of the world is not intended to depress, but rather represents a playful statement of what she perceives as the obvious. At the same time, the double meanings reflect how Hodrová's writing celebrates 'two', the number of creation and change, of continuing survival, but also of endless intermediacy, and resists 'one', the number of stasis, but also of the release from intermediacy into unity, which most human creative activity, in her view mistakenly, seeks to achieve.

As in Tolstaia's short fiction, characters in Hodrová's trilogy believe they can 'invent' or dream their way out of intermediacy. Whereas Tolstaia's characters make up stories to deny the passage of time, in Hodrová's trilogy, characters attempt to conceal their inherent sinfulness beneath 'skins' they stitch for themselves. The metaphor of skin for identity recurs in *Podobojí*, indicating that, for human beings, identity functions as a border which proves and protects their psychological individuation just as skin proves and protects their physical individuation. Skin remarks of itself in *Podobojí*:

> Were it not for me, the human being would, in his foolishness, be capable of letting his body dissolve into the world. I am the boundary which keeps the body in its corporeality. While I exist, the body endures; if I disintegrate, then the body is also condemned to disintegration.
>
> (Ibid.: 38)

In *Podobojí*, Jan Paskal becomes a Lutheran preacher to 'hide' his expulsion from a Catholic seminary for making a woman pregnant, 'proving' his Protestant credentials by claiming to be descended from a Huguenot aristocrat who escaped the Massacre of St Bartholomew and fled to Bohemia, where, significantly, his descendants became weavers, throughout Hodrová's fiction a metaphor for story-tellers.[9] However, the identity which he believes he has acquired for himself appears, on the contrary, to have acquired him. Paskal is terrified of being 'flayed of his skin', an allusion to the martyrdom of St Bartholomew, but within the novel a reference to a bloody sheepskin coat hidden in a wardrobe which will expose Paskal as the murderer of a local S.S. man. When Paskal's guilt is discovered, by two policemen from the station on Bartholomew Street, he acquires a new 'skin', that of a hero of the Liberation, though in fact he murdered the German for having an affair with his wife and conceiving Diviš, who is thus born 'in both kinds', an 'utraquist'. After the Communist take-over, Paskal is made to work in a factory cleaning and preparing fleeces, which he regards as penance for his crime, but which really constitutes the author's playful punishment for a character who has spent his life changing 'skins' to save his own. Similarly, in *Kukly*, Dr Sysel's itching eczema reflects his vain desire to change the course of events in April 1945, when, while his fellow students rushed to put out a fire at Prague Castle and were massacred by Germans burning documents there, Sysel was in the arms of his future wife.

In *Podobojí*, the intermediacy of existence governed by the number two is linked specifically to Czech historical experience through the 'in both kinds' motif, which refers to a key demand of the Hussites that all should receive communion in both kinds. In 1436, the Council of Basle gave this right to the Czechs, who therefore became unique within the Roman Church. This anomalous position 'on the border between orthodoxy and heresy', between an autonomous identity and absorption into a larger identity has, Hodrová implies, consistently defined the fate of the Czechs. As she indicates through characters like Mr Turek's friend, Mr Klečka, throughout their history, Czechs have oscillated endlessly between fervent optimism that this intermediacy might be escaped, and deep despair when every attempt fails.

In the latter part of *Podobojí*, the joyful atmosphere of the period of liberalization which culminated in the so-called 'Prague Spring' merges at the Olšany cemetery with the heyday of the Czech National Revival, with figures from that period emerging from their graves to share in the atmosphere of hope. In this passage, the Communist period, the Revival and the Hussites are linked through the 'utraquist' figure of Karel Sabina (1813–77), a political Revivalist imprisoned after 1848, who remained a nationalist writer on his release while working as a police informer for Vienna. The street in Prague named after him was originally named after the theologian of Hussitism, Jacobellus de Mies (d.1429), who called in his teaching for communion in both kinds, but was re-named by the Communists because Jacobellus, at least in later life, was not radical enough for them. Hodrová connects the Prague Spring and the National Revival through the epic poem *Máj* (1836), best translated as 'Spring', by Karel Hynek Mácha (1810–36), subsequently the most celebrated work of literature written during the Revival. *Máj*, however, describes the human being's exclusion from the annual rebirth of Nature, which in the context of Hodrová's novel reflects the futility of any attempts by human beings to 'regenerate' their existence. The cycle of attempted rebirths is, for Hodrová ironically, reflected in the fact that the title of Mácha's poem was later used for an almanac, first published in 1858, which effectively marked the renewal of Czech cultural freedom following the repressive period of 'neo-absolutism' under Interior Minister Alexander Bach in the 1850s. In Hodrová's depiction, that repression, which came in the wake of the suppression by Habsburg troops of the Prague Whitsun Troubles of June 1848, mirrors the Normalization that followed the Warsaw Pact military intervention of August 1968.

By blurring the distinction between the 'revolutions', or radical shifts in power, of 1939, 1945, 1948 and 1968, Hodrová indicates how the cycle of hope and despair simply repeats itself endlessly. Mr Turek, conspicuous in his refusal to join in the optimism, comments: 'Every time completes old allegories in its own way and in its own image. So, for example, even the allegory of the three young men in the fiery furnace has its own form today' (Hodrová 1999: 100). Mr Turek is referring here to Jan Palach, who publicly set himself on fire in January 1969 in protest at Czechoslovak acquiescence to the Soviet Union, and was imitated soon after by Jan Zajíc. Rumours of further imitators (there was another in the countryside) are lost amid the recurrence of another allegory, the captivity of the Israelites in Egypt, as the Normalization, overseen by foreign troops, sets in. Unperturbed by previous failures, however, the Olšany dead fleetingly invest their hopes of redemption from this captivity in the promising-sounding Benjamin of the 'House of David', the unborn child of Alice Davidovičová. This ironization of people's unrelenting search for a Messiah is echoed in Topol's *Sestra*, in which the characters similarly place their hope in the potential offspring of a character called David. In Hodrová's trilogy, the impossibility of escaping the agonizing duality of existence is symbolized by the recurring motif of a muff made from unborn lamb that passes from generation to generation. Whenever the hands of two different people meet inside the muff, they instantly recoil in pain, indicating that the unity for which they long is forbidden to them.

Podobojí deals more explicitly with the experience of the Normalization than any of Hodrová's other novels and is permeated with a mood of melancholy and despair indicative of the time of writing. The cyclical model of history depicted may therefore be interpreted as an attempt to comfort the implied reader, since, by disrupting the reader's sense of linear chronology, the experience of each period individually is tempered – without being belittled – while the suffering witnessed and endured by Prague in the twentieth century as a whole is emphasized. At the same time, however, Hodrová is also critical of the response of the majority, who, by closing their eyes to what is happening, appear more dead than the dead. The hope of overcoming intermediacy results not in a restored Eden, but in acquiescence to a fixed reality, equated with death. Hodrová more or less aligns herself with Mr Turek, who appears more alive than the living, never optimistic, but never reconciled, always trying to see further and differently:

> He had seen what others had not seen, and heard what others had not heard, for here in Olšany everything emerges with much clearer features, and whoever wants to, whoever has the courage, can become a visionary. The only thing is, there are many more of those who prefer to bury their heads in their little mole-hills, who dig in their cemetery plots and look neither left nor right. And herein lies the meaning of the Olšany consolidation: that everyone be just like this and take no interest in anything else.
>
> (Hodrová 1999: 128)

'Consolidation' was the original term used by the post-1969 regime for the Normalization. Hodrová thus in effect defends her own form of intellectual, as opposed to political, 'eternal dissidence', constantly resisting the imposition of a single, fixed model and asserting openness, multiplicity and fluidity, which in her fiction becomes the definition of the writer under any circumstances.[10]

Throughout her trilogy, Hodrová plays with the reader's desire to simplify or organize reality, not only, as Alena Vrbová points out, through the frequent references to locations in Prague which 'encourage the reader's desire to make reading easier by using a map' (Vrbová 2001: 14), but also through her disorientating depiction of several generations of families, which might inspire the reader to draw a family tree. The use of maps or family trees, however, merely further complicates the novels, highlighting Hodrová's rejection of the attempt to simplify through cognition. For Hodrová, the process of mapping should not simplify a place, but make it more mysterious, as she indicates in *Kukly* through her reference to the writer Karel Ladislav Kukla (1863–1930), who, according to František Kautman, is an ancestor of Hodrová's, and in the novel is an ancestor of Sofie Syslová (see Kautman 1993: 6). In the course of writing his tetralogy of novels, collectively titled *Praha neznámá* (Unknown Prague, 1894–1927), Kukla mapped the city's sewers, and in *Kukly* Hodrová implicitly suggests that his approach is hereditary.

In the fiction of both Hodrová and Ajvaz, however, the rejection of writing as mapping constitutes not an assertion of the futility or comic absurdity of writing, but rather the rejection of writing as a one-way act of definition in favour of writing as wandering.[11] The motif of wandering is not simply a metaphor for the aimlessness of existence and the impossibility of knowledge, as in Popov's *Dusha patriota*, but a non-positivist approach to cognition, corresponding to the movement of the pilgrim in the 'novel of initiation'. In *Kukly*, Mr Turek asserts: '"Some places [...] must be gone round in a circle for them to disclose their secrets, others must be gone across, criss-cross. And some must be ascended and then descended again"' (Hodrová 1999: 265). This movement is actualized in the wandering of the characters like Alice Davidovičová, Diviš Paskal, Sofie Syslová and Eliška Beránková. For example, in *Kukly*:

> Sofie Syslová leaves Comenius Square and goes into Rokycana Street. From Rokycana Street she turns into Sabina Street, which leads onto Havlíček Square. Then she goes up Lipany Street [...], cuts across Taborite Street and goes up Bořivoj Street. And then Sofie Syslová goes along Kubelík Street and then Tchaikovsky Street, from where it is only a stone's throw to Přemyslid Street, where Hynek Machovec lives.
>
> (Ibid.: 277)

Most of the street names here refer to heterodox figures who shaped the labyrinth of Czech history, within which Sofie finds herself and from which she (and implicitly the author) is formed: for example, the coming of Christianity under Bořivoj, Hussitism (Rokycana, the Utraquist archbishop of Prague, the defeat of the radical Hussites at the Battle of Lipany), and Comenius, Havlíček and the conductor Kubelík, all forced to leave under different regimes.

Each novel of the trilogy takes the form of a 'novel of initiation'. *Podobojí* opens with Alice Davidovičová throwing herself from her window, apparently because she failed to arrive in time for a rendezvous with her sweetheart and thus lost him forever. In her stylized guide to Prague, *Město vidím*... (I see a city..., 1992), which together with *Théta* lays bare the autobiographical elements of the trilogy, Hodrová indicates that Alice Davidovičová was a Jewish girl who had lived in the house where Hodrová spent her childhood, and who committed suicide after the imposition of the Nuremberg Laws. Like the fall of Lewis Carroll's Alice into the rabbit-hole at the beginning of *Alice in Wonderland*, Alice Davidovičová's fall marks the beginning of her initiation into another world, and the reader's initiation into Hodrová's way of seeing. *Podobojí* also describes

Diviš Paskal's coming of age, while *Kukly* describes Sofie Syslová's sexual awakening, and *Théta* the birth of a writer. The actual wandering of characters like Alice, Diviš, Sofie and Eliška mirrors not only the wandering of the reader through the work, but also the wandering of the writer through her memory. Character, reader and writer are thus united in an endless quest for meaning which, in keeping with the tradition of the novel of initiation, serves as a metaphor for terrestrial existence.

Ajvaz's first novel, *Druhé město*, also takes the form of a novel of initiation which transforms Prague into a labyrinth, and indeed bears out Hodrová's assertion in *Román zasvěcení* that in the twentieth-century initiation novel, 'the space of initiation becomes a library (publishing house) and the object of initiation a book' (Hodrová 1994: 133). The novel began as a poem, 'Město' (City), from Ajvaz's collection *Vražda v hotelu Intercontinental* (Murder at the Intercontinental Hotel, 1990), in which the narrator looks for the remnants of an ancient civilization on which Prague was built, but finds what he seeks only when he has ceased looking, in the place where he least expects it. In the novel, the narrator becomes aware of the 'other city', existing parallel to Prague, through the chance discovery in a second-hand bookshop of a book written in an outlandish alphabet. The book opens a crack in his previously solid, stable perception of the world, recalling the fissure in the cliff face in 'Sochař': 'It was still easy to pass by the crack from which a disturbing and seductive breath had wafted on me, to let the fissure become overgrown by a web of self-renewing connections' (Ajvaz 1992: 8). The narrator refers to the book as a 'door elsewhere', but unlike the 'door drawn in the air' in Tolstaia's story 'Krug', which offers an explicitly fictional, 'daydream' escape from the grey banality of everyday life, the crack opened by the book in *Druhé město* exposes the arbitrariness of what has been demarcated as the 'real world', revealing the equally real or unreal possibilities which such an act of definition seeks to exclude. Once the mysterious book has awoken the narrator to the partial nature of the reality in which he lives, this awareness spreads like an infection to all aspects of existence, including, for example, speech: 'Those few phonemes which we use are surrounded by an unknown jungle of sounds' (ibid.: 29). In an essay first published in 1995, Ajvaz retains this metaphor of the book as a 'tear in the web of meaning', a means not of perpetuating an existing understanding of the world, but, on the contrary, of undermining it and turning the world once again into a 'place with a secret' (Ajvaz 1997b: 29).

In *Druhé město*, the discovery of the book awakens in the narrator a dormant awareness that the world in which he lives – in 'Město' explicitly the 'timelessness of the seventies' (Ajvaz 2000: 4) – has become desacralized, a 'withered shell' that lacks the reality and vitality indicative of being. He therefore travels beyond the boundaries of his world into the 'other city' in search of the origin of his own civilization, which is simultaneously the key to its rebirth. In *Román zasvěcení*, Hodrová points out that the basis of the quest for initiation is 'the myth of rebirth – the rebirth of the pagan nature deity, of the Christian people or of the neophyte' (Hodrová 1994: 11). Jaroslav Kříž comments: 'Ajvaz's hero longs to penetrate to the centre of the world, which reveals something of itself to him, evidently because in his normal world there is no longer any centre, everything is merely periphery or surface' (Kříž 1993: 7).

The quest, however, does not lead to the discovery of the origin or centre as the narrator envisages. On the contrary, the 'other city', most prominently represented by a figure resembling an American television evangelist, proves as rigid as the 'first city' in its perpetuation and defence of its limits, treating the narrator with intense hostility since he appears to represent a greater threat to its order than he does to his own. The description of the narrator's encounter with the young man who is the principal deity of the 'other city' indicates not only the messianic nature of the narrator's mission, through his identification with the young man, but also the distinction between the eternal uncertainty of the wanderer, as in Hodrová, and the tyrannical rigidity of the cosmos he ordains:

> He was not the proud and cruel deity depicted by the statues. His face was the face of a stranger hounded to exhaustion, who wanders like me through the lands of exile. It seemed that his divine being was only one infinitely great suffering which could never end.
>
> (Ajvaz 1992: 135)

The initiation at the end of the narrator's quest in *Druhé město* consists in learning that what he seeks does not exist:

> No final centre exists, no face is concealed behind the masks, there is no first word in the game of Chinese whispers, no original of the translation. There is only the constantly winding string of metamorphoses giving birth to further metamorphoses.
>
> (Ibid.: 148)

In *...na okraji chaosu...*, Hodrová writes: 'in connection with the twentieth century work, rather than talking about the loss of the centre, we could talk more about a new centring. The essence of this new centring appears to be the idea of many centres' (Hodrová 2001: 133). The 'other city' is in fact only a 'second city' – both meanings are covered by the word *druhé* – after which a third, fourth and so on must be sought. With this outcome, Ajvaz asserts in place of the notion of the book as a means of circumscribing existence, and therefore, in Ajvaz's view, denying being, the notion of a book which contains all the possibilities of transformation and thus possesses the openness and uncertainty that guarantee being. In *Druhé město*, this shift in the perception of the book is represented by the jungle which is slowly enveloping the shelves of the library, and the outlandish alphabet which infests the narrator's other books, images of a chaos which grows, moves, lives and transforms.

As many critics have noted, Ajvaz's writing, like Kratochvil's, owes much to Borges. Jan Malura suggests that the two writers are fundamentally united by the notion of the book as 'an end in itself, an independent world' (Malura 1993: 21). Ajvaz, however, appears much more optimistic than Borges about the capacity of words and the book to communicate the experience of being. In the conclusion of *Druhé město*, Ajvaz implicitly links Borges's notion of the universe as a book in 'The Library of Babel' (1964) with Jacques Derrida's assertion that signifiers refer only to other signifiers, only to reject them both:

> I read somewhere that books speak only about other books, that signs refer to other signs, that the book has nothing in common with reality, that rather reality itself is a book because it is created by language. This theory was melancholy in that it let reality disappear beneath our signs.
>
> (Ajvaz 1992: 140)

Ajvaz develops this view in his 1995 essay disputing Derrida's theories of language, entitled *Znak a bytí* (The sign and being).

In *Druhé město*, Ajvaz suggests that reality, or the experience of being, symbolized by the burgeoning chaos of the ever expanding jungle in the library, has become closed off by the contemporary preoccupation with language's inability to represent reality, and the consequent assertion that what is called reality is only a product of language, leading to imprisonment in language as a 'withered shell'. For Ajvaz, however, the experience of being is conveyed in language by the 'movement between an established context' and the signifier which remains unincorporated in that context. Hodrová considers a typical example to be the title of Ajvaz's next work, *Tyrkysový orel* (The turquoise eagle, 1997), which contains two separately titled stories, in the second of which a character reads of a woman who owned a brooch in the form of a turquoise eagle, an object which has no apparent importance and does not reappear elsewhere in either story. Hodrová comments of such 'things' in Ajvaz's work:

> Even though they are found, their purpose is not discovered, or they are ultimately used in an entirely trivial way, as though they were here only in themselves and for themselves. It only seems like this, however; in reality, it is precisely in the thing that the character glimpses a flash of being and encounters that 'single shining and strange being' of which these things are a symbol.
>
> (Hodrová 2001: 716)

In this interpretation, the turquoise eagle brooch may be seen to function in the same way as the apparently inconsequential but indestructible enamel dove in Tolstaia's 'Sonia'.

As the narrator of *Druhé město* in effect points out, the tension between the context and the unincorporated signifier derives not from the imminent, inevitable incorporation of the signifier into the context, perceived as the substitution of being by language, but from the constant threat that being 'will once again swallow [our meanings] and dissolve them in itself' (Ajvaz 1992: 141). For Ajvaz, this threat constitutes a guarantee of continued change, continued being. As the title of the novel suggests, this continued being may be understood as a product of the relationship between the self and the other, which the narrator of *Druhé město*, unlike Mameev in *Avtoportret s dogom*, seeks not to overcome, but to sustain: 'A real conversation is possible only between those who have left and those who stay. Discussions with fellow-clansmen are never anything more than the tedious reception of the echo of one's own words' (ibid.: 157).[12] However, whereas Bakhtin, in his essay on the author and hero in aesthetic activity, emphasizes the other's role in completing the self, the other in Ajvaz's perception acts beneficently by constantly opening up the self, preventing the self from becoming a 'withered shell'.

In Hodrová's trilogy, this constant activity of opening-up is associated with the notion of writing as endless wandering. Unlike 'writing as mapping', a caricature of Realism as the deadening identification of sign and referent, an attempt to assert existence governed by the number 'one', writing as endless wandering leads to unstoppable proliferation, as in Ajvaz a motif of being, and the embodiment of existence governed by the number 'two'. In *Trýznivé město*, Hodrová wanders repeatedly over signifiers which gradually, each time they are encountered, reveal more of the simultaneously existing, shifting signifieds within them and thus, in effect, 'come to life'. At the same time, as the signifier 'acquires' signifieds, it loses substance, becoming increasingly abstract, or 'multi-centred', and decreasingly 'fixed'.

The most striking example of this is the signifier in the title *Kukly*, a reference to the family portrayed in the novel, descended from the writer Kukla, which denotes the passive, intermediate stage in the development of a larva into an adult insect, and thus serves as metaphor for terrestrial existence. The impotence inherent in that existence is reflected in the Russian meaning of *kukla* (puppet), which, as Kautman and Ryšavý both point out, must be taken into account given Sofie Syslová's job sewing puppets and Hodrová's specialization in Russian literary theory. Hodrová may even be drawing attention to a linguistic 'place with a mystery', the curious link between the Latin 'pupa', meaning 'doll', and the Slavonic 'kukla'. The transient, 'unreal' nature of human existence is reflected in another possible meaning of the title, 'masks', referring to the impermanence and illusoriness of terrestrial identity. The title also evokes *koukol*, meaning 'tare' or, metaphorically, 'goats', as in 'separating the sheep from the goats', a recurring motif in *Podobojí*. This motif refers both to the separation of those implicitly more spiritual characters, aware of living 'in both kinds', from those who seek to impose notions of existence 'under one kind', and the separation of the soul from the body, and its return to God. In Hodrová's conception, the writer roams the space between the signifier and signifieds and between these signifieds, resisting the coalescence of a particular signifier and signified as the substitution of a relativity for the absolute which the writer hopes to glimpse. Hodrová writes in *Théta*: 'I am interested precisely in that illumination, the vague reflection of reality which constantly escapes the text between its letters' (Hodrová 1999: 528).

Throughout the trilogy, this initiation into the nature of meaning is also reflected in the initiation into the nature of the self, which in Hodrová's fiction is possessed not only by human beings, but also by objects and places. The self, in effect, like the signifier, corresponds to the notion of 'space' in *Místa s tajemstvím*, defined as a 'complex or network of places, which, like an individual place, only begins to exist through subjects and events', where place corresponds to identity (Hodrová 1994: 10). Hodrová makes this correspondence all but explicit when she continues: '[The character] carries a place (places) within itself, it creates them for itself like a spider its web, or, put differently, the place comes to life through a particular character, it begins to exist through the character' (ibid.). In *Kukly*, Hodrová writes:

> Sofie Syslová is beginning to understand. Her consciousness is a place in which past and future events run together like the radii of a circle. And just as Sofie Syslová gradually absorbs into herself time in its metamorphoses and permanence, she comprises in herself different beings.
>
> (Hodrová 1999: 341)

Kateřina Sternbergová similarly defines time in Hodrová's work as a 'saturation of moments, of the world of one human being, more people or even a mixture of time planes from many novels' (Sternbergová 1993: 9).

In this context, Hodrová's Prague may be seen as an actualization of her self, understood as a place where different time periods, fates, mythologies, stories, works of literature, memories, the living and the dead come together and co-exist. In the same way as for space and the signifier, the limits of the self become increasingly vague, since the number of identities it may contain is notionally limitless. For example, in *Podobojí*, Hodrová describes how, at different points in history, the barricades go up on 'Foch Avenue (formerly Jungmann, later Schwerin, then Stalin and finally Vinohradská Avenue)' (Hodrová 1999: 33), these different 'identities' combining with infinite previous and future identities to form the 'self' of the location in question.

For Hodrová, being is experienced precisely through the constant passage of these identities through consciousness. Hodrová presents the formation of the self as an essentially carnivalistic process, in which identities are constantly acquired and shed, like the renewal of skin or the life cycle of insects. The provisional, 'mask-like' nature of identity, and its relationship to post-Edenic, sinful existence, is encapsulated in the name of the tailor's dummy in *Podobojí*, Kajn, apparently not only Cain, but also from the German 'kein', who 'looks as though he is, but at the same time isn't, or as though he isn't, but at the same time is' (ibid.: 16). The title of *Podobojí* may be understood as a pun on *podoba*, meaning 'identity', suggesting that the sense of eternal intermediacy derives from the fact that, at any moment, a character is 'between identities', the one being acquired and the one being shed, which becomes in effect a re-casting of the notion, fundamental to the Baroque worldview, that 'in the midst of life we are in death'. Hodrová actualizes this notion in *Kukly* in her description of each chapter as a *tableau vivant*, in which the actors appear static, but are in fact moving in time. Sternbergová comments: 'time and its passing are a vital prerequisite for constant metamorphosis; however, we appear only to "glimpse" a certain phase, that "ever present moment" in which the past and future cross and permeate each other' (Sternbergová 1993: 9).

Death, however, in Hodrová's fiction does not mean ceasing to exist, but rather becoming fixed, waiting for change. In a passage in *Kukly* which Macura considers crucial to Hodrová's writing, Mr Turek comments: 'In this world nothing ceases to exist. [...] Everything just constantly metamorphoses' (Hodrová 1999: 347). This observation reflects what Ryšavý describes as Hodrová's 'consideration of the world as a text' (Ryšavý 1993: 18), in which all words and combinations of words wait, cocooned, until the moment when they pass through a consciousness, bringing it to life and coming to life themselves. Words correspond in effect to the souls of the dead (*dušičky*), hovering in the ventilation shaft in *Podobojí*, who say of themselves:

> We are incarnated breath, our inhaling and exhaling gives rhythm to the course of the universe. In the opposition of life and death we are situated right on the border, on a border that is, alas, too vague. We are half-divine and half-human and in this composition of ours we resemble the heroes of myths, descending to earth to enlighten ignorant humanity. We are capable of endless metamorphoses and reincarnations in which we evade the prying eyes of mortals.
>
> (Hodrová 2001: 43)

While living characters in Hodrová's fiction experience themselves as an ever-changing text, like Jan Paskal, unsure whether they write the text or the text writes them, dead characters, in life in the midst of death, find themselves trapped in a text which endlessly repeats itself and cannot be changed, the memory of them retained by the living. Hodrová writes in *Podobojí*:

> Diviš Paskal is beginning to understand: the dead continue to live their ordinary lives amongst us, lives strangely divested of their trappings, lives as if limited to what was most fundamental about them, and this goes on and on repeating itself after death. As though the person had sat on a strange roundabout from which he could not then get off, and on which he had to continue spinning like a top.
>
> (Ibid.: 63)

What is most fundamental invariably proves to be each person's worst memory; for example, the 'utraquists' Sabina and Čurda, the co-conspirator in the

Heydrich assassination who then informed on his comrades, cannot but endlessly repeat their treachery. Like cocooned words, they wait for the writer who may fleetingly breathe life into them again.

At the same time, however, cocoons of words and selves feel threatened by the writer who knows too much about them, because they fear that they may dissolve completely. In *Podobojí*, Diviš Paskal, in a coincidental link with Kratochvil's metaphor, is described by the dead as a 'wolf in sheep's clothing', a reference not only to his German origin, hidden beneath his Paschal surname, but also to his position as one of the living moving among the dead. According to the souls in the ventilation shaft:

> The most dangerous of all [mortals] are zealots like Diviš Paskal, who in their foolishness and uncontrolled curiosity transgress established limits. […] We protect ourselves from him by cocooning ourselves in a concrete thing, in enduring, limited being.
>
> (Ibid.: 43)

The characterization of Diviš Paskal in *Podobojí* as clownish, irrepressibly curious and constantly in danger of over-reaching himself not only constitutes authorial autostylization, but also, as in Tolstaia's fiction, asserts the child-like nature of the writer, prepared to tolerate the co-existence of all kinds of explanations and contradictions and perceiving living 'souls' in all things, animate or inanimate, dead or alive. As his understanding of Mr Turek's perception of the world grows, however, Diviš becomes convinced that he can intervene to alter the text of memory and release Alice Davidovičová from imprisonment in her failure to meet and ultimately to marry the man she loved: 'And Diviš Paskal sees himself as Hercules, as Theseus, as Orpheus and as Christ, and also as the poet Dante. This conceit will be fateful for Diviš' (ibid.: 123). This temptation remains ever present for the writer; in *Théta*, Hodrová compares watching her own past to watching her father acting in Tennessee Williams's *Night of the Iguana*: 'In the same way I know in advance how it will turn out, and none the less a tiny flicker of hope still remains in me that I will be able one day to step into it and give it a different direction' (ibid: 449).

Diviš's fate resembles that of Venichka in *Moskva–Petushki*; in his attempt to cross the threshold into the realm of the dead in the last lines of the novel, he falls from the same window from which Alice jumped in the opening lines. Diviš can only release Alice from the text of his memory by cutting off the text of his own life, and thus brings the novel to an end which, like Alice's fall, may also be a beginning. The circular form thus acquired by *Podobojí*, like *Moskva–Petushki*, corresponds to Hodrová's description of Time in the novel of initiation in *Román zasvěcení* as 'governed by the notion of return, but the origin which is being returned to is no longer an origin, but an end,' recalling the image of the Uroboros, the snake swallowing its tail (Hodrová 1994: 211).

As a writer, Hodrová strives to remain on the threshold, from where she may trace the 'endless metamorphoses and reincarnations' taking place in her consciousness, hoping in vain not only to experience, but also to capture that instance of being. Like Venedikt Erofeev in *Moskva–Petushki*, Hodrová substitutes characters for herself in order to preserve herself and escape their fate, as she indicates in *Théta*:

> Something made me change the first person narration in the chapter in which I depict the meeting between Mr Chaun and the Creature into a third person narration. I write 'something' and immediately catch myself engaged in an evasive manoeuvre. It is, after all, clear to me that I deliberately hid myself behind Eliška Beránková, just as before I hid myself behind Sofie Syslová and before that behind Alice Davidovičová and also behind Diviš Paskal. I just have to cocoon myself in the novel again and again, hide myself in it from the world.
>
> (Hodrová 1999: 398)

Just as Diviš and Alice erase each other at the end of *Podobojí*, so towards the end of *Kukly*, Sofie Syslová becomes anxious about her next metamorphosis, suspecting that, like the puppets for whom she sews clothes and stories, she too is a puppet whose story is being sewn. In an attempt to perpetuate her existence, like the parasitic larva of the *Meloe violaceus* species with which Mr Turek compares her, she tries attaching herself to Diviš, but is rejected, and at the end of the work is left static, moaning softly, without the language that would prolong her metamorphoses.

In *Podobojí*, Hodrová implicitly characterizes the activity of the writer who strives to remain on the border between the 'fixed' world and chaos as comic, futile resistance to uniformity which nevertheless retains a certain heroism – 'Poor Mr Turek! Great Mr Turek!' (ibid.: 129). In *Théta*, however, the same activity becomes more a compulsive struggle for survival. Writing on *Théta*, Alice Jedličková comments: 'the narrator writes the novel to keep herself alive, but also to bring the past and the dead out of oblivion, to bring out of it herself' (Jedličková 1992: 19). The two objectives appear incompatible, since the first demands that she keep herself outside the text, unlike her characters in the first two novels apparently unthreatened by erasure, represented in the novel by the Greek letter 'theta', the literary editor's symbol for 'to be deleted', while the second demands that she become an actant in the text.

Hodrová resolves this incompatibility, as Jedličková suggests, by trying to work 'in both kinds'. In *Théta*, to adopt the motif of theatre which recurs in the work, she abandons the 'illusory' perspective of a member of the audience, who 'temporarily believes that what is being played out on the stage before his eyes is real life', in favour of the intermediate position in the wings, where she used to watch her father act, and where 'lines from the play, as though from reality, mix with the lines which the actors pronounce off stage' (Hodrová 1999: 449). This position is reflected in Hodrová's frequent analysis of her reasons for writing sentences that the reader has just read, and her repeated indication that episodes from her own life have been or are being fictionalized, which seek to counteract the reader's 'suspension of disbelief' and thereby prevent absorption in the text. Unlike Ajvaz, however, Hodrová fears that, just as she is writing her characters, so she herself is being written, and may at any moment be deleted. She none the less concludes that she can do nothing except write in the hope of slowing the process:

> I am writing a novel in order not to metamorphose – into a bird, a puppet, into someone's phantasmagoria [...] I am slowly metamorphosing. As long as I am writing, however, a tiny flicker of hope remains of a way back, a return to life and consciousness, to will, to a human face. As long as I am writing...
>
> (Ibid.: 492)

This equation of writing with being also occurs in Topol's first novel, *Sestra*, which followed two collections of poetry published in *samizdat* in the 1980s. Just as, in Hodrová's fiction, characters invent in the vain hope of escaping their sinful skin, in *Sestra* terrestrial existence is shown to be inherently the preserve of evil, and freedom is defined, as in Kratochvil's fiction, by the activity of resisting imprisonment in that existence. This freedom is represented not so much by the physical actions of the narrator, Potok, but, as his name, 'stream', indicates, by the incessant narration rushing out of him, a narration which, Daniel Vojtěch points out, 'does not lose its integrated character even when the speaker changes' (Vojtěch 1994: 6). The assonance between the names Potok and Topol indicates not so much the identity as the discrepancy between a circumscribed biographical figure and ever-developing being, as Topol playfully indicates through Potok's acquaintance, Jícha. As Antonín Alenka points out, Jícha is a self-parodic past incarnation of Topol (see Alenka 1994: 6), whose name not only suggests 'Jáchym', but also means 'slurry', a metaphor for the inferiority of the past compared with the fresh stream of the present:

> Jícha had already been performing as a prominent young poet for about ten years, but because he drowned his first works in *samizdat*, no one really knew what he wrote. He was only well-known thanks to his underground past. His only collection, 'I love you beneath the astronomical clock of madness', was bought up by stupid grammar-school girls and their perverted mistresses. Then he stopped writing poetry, having exhausted the romanticism of the former underground, and had to find something really bloody. In my head I dimly recalled journalistic articles about raids on lodging-houses for *Gastarbeiter*. Jícha based his career as a post-revolution journalist on them.
>
> (Topol 1994: 156)

The title of Jícha's collection is a distortion of Topol's *Miluju tě k zbláznění* (I love you to the point of madness, 1991), while the reference to journalism relates to Topol's founding in 1990 of the liberal weekly *Respekt*, and his work there publicizing the problems of Vietnamese immigrants in Bohemia, which also features as a theme in *Sestra*. In a 2002 interview, Topol expresses his embarrassment at the naivety of these articles, reflected in his satirization of Jícha through Potok (see Chuchma 2002: 8). In *Sestra*, Topol shows that he has moved on by having Jícha killed off.

Potok's narration, imbued with what Alenka aptly terms a 'feeling of superiority over its less feisty surroundings' (Alenka 1994: 6), absorbs within itself pre-existing accounts from sources as diverse as Jewish, Christian, Oriental and Native American mythologies, film, European Romantic literature and Czech children's fiction, in order not to become absorbed into any one of them. As critics like Vojtěch assert, the resulting chaos of incongruous types of narrative constitutes an attempt to reflect the social and psychological experience of the world after, in Potok's words, 'time exploded' in November 1989. At the same time, however, it expresses the rejection of Realist modes of portrayal, not only because they are inadequate to the situation, but also because they imprison writer and reader within a concrete, 'named' world. Writing on Topol's strategy in *Sestra* in the context of the shift in post-1989 Czech fiction away from the ideologically motivated requirement imposed by both official and dissident establishments in the preceding period to 'tell the truth', Pavel Janoušek comments:

> The 'mirror' held up to the present by the writer did not come into being through the ideological distortion of a smooth reflective surface, but by smashing the image of external reality into thousands of pieces and putting them back together in a mosaic whose deconstructive order is ordained by the implied author. This author gives precedence, ahead of the quest for great Truth, to a free literary game, which does not allow itself to be tied down by the limits of our everyday present.
>
> (Janoušek 1994: 3)

In Topol's conception, to sustain freedom, the writer must strive to keep the world as fluid and provisional as possible. Pavel Janáček writes:

> the fundamental punctuation mark in Topol's fractured discourse is the ellipsis: like everything else, not even the sentence can have a sharply defined contour, everything is connected, the text just like good and evil, everything floats away or trickles through our fingers.
>
> (Janáček 1994: iv)

The lack of 'sharply defined contours', the lack of clear distinctions between speakers, types of narrative, dream and reality all serve to convey the impermanence and consequent 'unreality' of the terrestrial world.

As Alenka and others have pointed out, *Sestra* also takes the form of a novel of initiation, in this case, specifically a travestying of the sinner's quest for absolution and redemption. Early in the novel, Potok is apparently abandoned by his childhood sweetheart, Malá Bílá Psice (Little White She-Dog) with the promise that she will send him a new 'sister', whom Potok subsequently takes to be a woman called Černá (Black). Potok's existence is thus located between the white and the black, between good and evil.[13] The circumstances of Psice's departure remain unclear: at one point Potok is accused by former police spies of raping and murdering Psice, which seems possible when she appears to him in a dream, forgiving him for the pain he caused her; equally, however, she may have simply emigrated, in which case Potok's pangs of conscience may derive from having deflowered her. In any event, her disappearance serves as a metaphor for Original Sin, awakening in Potok an awareness of guilt. Potok's trials in a world of gangsters, conspiracies and savage violence, his circular wanderings round eastern Slovakia and his final stay in the depths of the underworld on an enormous rubbish dump may be understood as the sinner's journey through the darkness of terrestrial life back to God. Throughout his journey, Potok wears a silver Our Lady of Częstochowa, a scarred statue of the icon of the Madonna that is said to bleed, perhaps a symbol of the sin he has committed against his 'sister', but also of her promise to lead him to salvation. Towards the end of the novel, in a merging of the *Omen* films, vampire legends and the Book of Revelation, Potok uses the silver Madonna to make a bullet with which he kills a demon child, apparently the Anti-Christ, and with this act, his own sin appears to be absolved. Soon afterwards, he awakens in a convent which now stands on the site where he murdered or deflowered his 'sister', and is restored to health by a nun.

The pun here on the word 'sister' recalls Potok's earlier attraction to the redemptive figure of Sonia in Dostoevsky's *Crime and Punishment*, whom Potok describes as Raskolnikov's sister. The link is, however, parodic, ironizing the linear path from fall to redemption portrayed by Dostoevsky, and thereby undermining Potok's apparent redemption in the novel. Like Hodrová in her fiction, Topol presents a cyclical model of terrestrial existence in which the 'wheel of the world' turns endlessly to favour first one, then another, and sin is followed by atonement.[14] In *Sestra*, Topol applies this model to national history, implicitly rejecting the perception of Czechs as victims of history, evident in the work of Hodrová and Kratochvil, and suggesting instead that tribes suffer for the suffering they cause to other tribes. Like the individual, the tribe is also born into sin; the Czechs are portrayed as the product of Samo's betrayal of his tribe, the Franks. Topol presents the Communist period as a punishment for Czech complicity in the mass murder of the Jews in the Second World War. Potok calls the average Czech, collaborating with the Communist regime in order to survive as he had with the Germans, 'Josef Vissarionovich Švejk', an amalgam of Jaroslav Hašek's amoral survivor and Stalin which has echoes of Vilikovský's narrator in *Večne je zelený....*[15]

Existence in Topol's fiction, as in Hodrová's, is governed by the number 'two', as Potok tells Černá in a passage which, like Hodrová's exposition on the same subject, paraphrases mystical Christian teaching, in this case that of the tenth-century Bogomil:

> The world is an embrace, always of two, of day and night, man and woman and so on, even of nonsense, and it is unknowable, like a dream…and you struggle against everything, but you are a part of it. And sometimes, only sometimes do you glimpse…just for a moment you glimpse the wheel of the world…and then you return to go through more snares and traps and delusions, you go through deceptions…and it's only a question of being free, by oneself, avoiding enslavement…and we who know the secret, you know, I really love you!, we love eagles, because they can see…they are still somewhere…and in this vale of tears it is a question of finding your being, that is, that other, so that you can be whole, at least for a moment!
>
> (Topol: 1994: 337–8)

Potok's pursuit of Černá essentially parodies this perception of existence, since several times in the novel they are reunited, only to lose each other again, as Potok himself observes, like the bridegroom and bride in the Song of Songs. The equation of Potok's yearning for Černá with Solomon's longing for unity with God is, however, pure burlesque; in one episode, he becomes stuck inside her during sexual intercourse, and only the ringing of the doorbell separates them, drawing them back into the sinful earthly world, where they once again lose each other. The ringing doorbell at the end of the novel, which they refuse to answer in bathetic acknowledgement of their promise never to become separated again, nevertheless indicates that the cycle will continue.

Parody and burlesque typify what Josef Vohryzek describes as the 'profanation, compulsive and all-consuming which […] functions here as a sorting and testing of values, the author's main theme' (Vohryzek 1995: 5). Profanation acts in Topol's fiction to prevent the problem that arises in Ajvaz's work, where the rejection of opinions as fixative becomes itself a fixed opinion, halting the dynamism which equates in Hodrová and Ajvaz to continued being and in Topol to continued freedom. Potok follows examples of his poetry with the remark: 'I mixed old and new words. Some things I meant seriously, so I hid them in further words' (ibid.: 429). Just as Hodrová perpetually resists the coalescence of a signifier with a particular signified in the hope of glimpsing an instant of being, so, in *Sestra*, Potok's endless subversion of formulaic language provides fleeting experiences of freedom, before he once again falls into the imprisonment of words, synonymous with the evil of terrestrial existence. For Potok, this struggle, though vain, must nevertheless be sustained: 'only wars lost in advance, only those are interesting' (ibid.: 452).

This characterization of the writer, constantly striving not to be pinned down, not to lose the possibility of movement, leaping free only to fall again to earth, is embodied in Potok's professional activity as a dancer, which links him to Arthur Rimbaud, who, according to Potok, had to be constantly on the move because the earth hurt his feet. In Potok's account, Rimbaud, who serves as a model for the understanding of the writer asserted in the novel, rejected work in a 'department of culture', where they apparently work only to make life comfortable by perpetuating existing versions of reality and meanings and combinations of words, and set about changing his language by inventing an alphabet. In *Sestra*, Topol attempts in effect to re-create Czech, mixing registers, dialects and languages, suggesting, however, that the process will never be completed, that language, like life, can never be mastered, but will always surprise and undermine those who possess it. Through this activity, the writer in fact serves his tribe, those who speak his language, by preventing them from becoming too embedded in their present existence and preparing them for the 'snares and traps' ahead.

Sestra represents the culmination of the artistic approach in Czech fiction of the Changes, in which the use of words to create and perpetuate a shared understanding of the nature of existence, equated with death, is replaced by the use of words constantly to undermine such shared understandings and thus sustain life; as Potok remarks: 'Anyone who thinks that they are already something suffers from a lack of imagination' (ibid.: 264). Writing on the eradication of Gnosticism from the early Christian Church, Robert Grant comments:

> The triumph of [Christian] orthodoxy meant the triumph of the created world over the aeons, of collective experience over individual freedom, of history over the freely creative imagination, of objectivity over subjectivity. The creative freedom of the religious imagination was more completely channelled in the service of an institution.
>
> (Grant 1959: 183)

In *Sestra*, Topol, like Ajvaz, Hodrová, Kratochvil and others, seeks to overturn the triumph of orthodoxy in the context of post-Communist Czech literature, to reassert the 'creative freedom of the religious imagination' as the essence of literature. For this reason, so many of Topol's characters are mystics and dreamers, recounting their own mythologies, which mingle in the work with numerous ancient and contemporary allegories of the nature of the world.

The 'death of the author', ordaining the nature and limits of the world, and the emergence of the writer-'fakir', weaving and re-weaving these allegories anew, is also accompanied by a 'birth of the reader'. The effect and perhaps even the objective of the work of writers like Topol and Hodrová has been to make reading difficult, and thus restore élitism to Czech literature. In *Sestra*, Potok criticizes contemporary attitudes to reading, nostalgically recalling more dangerous times when people had to read with a knife in their hands, and not only to cut open the pages:

> I always ask in the pub: Have you read *War and Peace* and *The Epic Gilgamesh*, or, for example, *A Man without Qualities* and *Eskimo Welzl*, you'll get through it in an evening… Well, […] you should see the faces they pull, everyone says: That's a fat one! I haven't got time for that… these days! Haven't they made a film of it? Like the Bible?
>
> (Topol 1994: 450)[16]

Whereas the Russian and Slovak writers of the Changes discussed in Chapters 4 and 6 fear or morbidly celebrate the defeat of literature as a spent force, the Czech writers of the Changes repeatedly express their love of literature, which in their view was a spent force only when it was an ideological tool, but in their hands has been restored to life.

6 Empty words

Vladimir Sorokin, Ján Litvák, Ivan Kolenič

In an unpublished paper presented in Oxford in 1999, Lipovetskii divided Russian postmodernist fiction into two tendencies, which he calls 'neo-Baroque' and 'conceptualist'. He writes:

> While conceptualism replaces the authorial persona [*litso*] with a system of language images, neo-Baroque cultivates the authorial myth.[…] While conceptualism features the deconstruction and demythologization of authoritative cultural signs and whole languages, neo-Baroque, on the contrary, is aimed at the re-mythologization of cultural ruins and fragments. While conceptualism stands on the border between art and ideology, performance and extra-aesthetic reality, the writers of neo-Baroque exhibit an insistent aestheticization of everything that comes into view.
>
> (Lipovetskii 1999b:1)

Lipovetskii borrows the notion of 'neo-Baroque' from the Italian cultural theorist Omar Calabrese, who proposes it as an alternative to 'postmodern' which, rather than expressing contemporary culture's relationship to 'modernism', would denote the formal qualities of certain phenomena in contrast to other phenomena considered 'classical', outside the specific historical periods to which the terms 'Classical' and 'Baroque' refer. Calabrese also describes an 'aesthetic of Nothingness', which might be considered synonymous with Lipovetskii's 'conceptualism', but which lies within, rather than alongside, his notion of 'neo-Baroque' (see Calabrese 1992: 169–70).

Lipovetskii's categories recall Mikhail Epshtein's earlier division of new Russian poetry in the 1980s into 'conceptualism' and 'metarealism'. Epshtein writes:

> metarealism endeavours to return to the word the fulness of its figurative and transcendent meanings. To the same degree, conceptualism tries to wrench out of the word any meaning whatsoever, leaving an empty, echoing shell: a senseless cliché which says nothing.
>
> (Epshtein 1995b: 19–20)

Without wishing to advocate the more widespread use of either Lipovetskii's or Epshtein's particular terms, the distinction they identify in Russian writing of the late Communist and early post-Communist period may also be observed in Czech and Slovak fiction of a comparable period. The characteristics of 'neo-Baroque' or 'metarealism', epitomized in fiction by Tolstaia and Venedikt Erofeev, may also be found in abundance in the works not only of Hodrová and Ajvaz, who frequently use Baroque themes and motifs, but also in the 'insistent aestheticization of everything' in Topol's *Sestra* or Pišťanek's fiction. Moreover, writers like Vilikovský, who implicitly shares Popov's notion in *Dusha patriota* of writing as 'self-characterization', and Kratochvil, who describes new Czech writing in the early 1990s as the creation of 'individual myths' (Kratochvil 1995: 84), may also be included.

More or less explicitly, these writers perceive literature itself as innocent, an expression of vain spiritual longing which may become corrupted, but may once again be freed from this corruption. Their preferred theorists are those like Bakhtin, Barthes or Umberto Eco, for whom writing, as an endless process, remains almost sentimentally meaningful precisely as an expression of the enduring intermediacy of human life, as opposed to the finality of death. In contrast, the writers who form the subject of this chapter, whom Lipovetskii and Epshtein describe as 'conceptualist', prefer the more hostile questioning of the innocence of writing and the possibility of meaning in, for example, the theory of Jacques Derrida, Jean Baudrillard or Jacques Lacan. Since their theories have found very little coincidental or conscious expression in Czech fiction of the Changes, this chapter focuses only on Russian and Slovak writers.

Lipovetskii expands the term 'conceptualism' from its conventional use in a Russian context to refer to the work produced by a group of underground poets and visual artists, including Prigov, Erik Bulatov (b.1933), Il'ia Kabakov (b.1933) and Lev Rubinshtein (b.1947), which emerged in Moscow in the early 1970s. In their so-called 'sots-art' (a 'socialist' version of 'pop art'), the Moscow Conceptualists played with the visual images and verbal formulae of Soviet Socialist Realism to expose them as signs without referents, products of language which aspire to the status of reality.[1] In his article 'The Origins and Meaning of Russian Postmodernism', Epshtein links their work with Jean Baudrillard's theory that, in Western capitalist society, reality has been replaced by simulacra to such an extent that the awareness of the non-simulated behind the simulated is lost. Citing the Conceptualist Il'ia Kabakov's essay 'On the Subject of the Void', Epshtein argues that the Conceptualists' work foregrounds the notion that Russian civilization has never amounted to more than a series of signs 'borrowed from the West' without the referents (see Epshtein 1995b: 208).

As Epshtein's comments indicate, the Conceptualists' work displays their interest in cultural theory and their own work as cultural theorists more explicitly than that of writers like Venedikt Erofeev or Tolstaia, whom Lipovetskii considers 'neo-Baroque'. For Epshtein, Baudrillard's theory constitutes the aspect of Western post-Structuralist theory most fundamental to understanding Russian postmodernism. However, as with the work of other French post-Structuralists, such as Derrida or Michel Foucault, it is difficult to know how much Moscow Conceptualism in the early 1970s was directly influenced by Baudrillard's writings (published at about the same time), and how much it arrived at similar conclusions independently. Boris Groys, one of the earliest critics to embrace the Conceptualists, while noting the influence of French post-Structuralist theory on Moscow Conceptualism, points out that, for example, Il'ia Kabakov arrived at a notion of the self-sufficient text similar to Derrida's notion of *écriture* before he had read Derrida's work (see Groys 1992: 87, 106). In their own theoretical remarks, Conceptualists such as Kabakov and Prigov implicitly present themselves as Russian counterparts of the French post-Structuralists of the 1960s and 1970s, formulating or adapting theory for the late Soviet cultural situation. By contrast, in Slovak literature, the influence of French post-Structuralism has manifested itself most overtly in the much younger Genitalists who, unlike the Russian Conceptualists, treat post-Structuralist theory rather as the 'sots-artists' treated Soviet ideology, by simultaneously asserting and subverting its models.

For the Russian writers whom Lipovetskii labels 'conceptualist', the aspiration to the status of absolute truth is inherent in the work of art, and cannot be eradicated, only acknowledged. Groys argues that the Moscow Conceptualists came to this conclusion not so much through their experience of traditional Socialist Realism, but through the art apparently conceived in opposition to it, of which Groys cites the rural nationalism of Aleksandr Solzhenitsyn (b.1918) and Village Fiction. Groys writes: 'the attentive observer of the Soviet cultural scene in the 1960s and 1970s gradually became aware that all attempts to overcome Stalin's project on either the individual or the collective level resulted in fateful reproductions of it' (ibid.: 79–80). Like the 'other fiction' of the late 1980s, Moscow Conceptualism used the Soviet cultural context to make a general statement about the nature of artistic creation, which Groys expresses thus:

> Russian postutopianism […] has its roots […] in the discovery of the will to power in the seemingly oppositional artistic project, and a realization of the role the artistic project plays in the strategy of political coercion. For Russian artists and intellectuals this discovery has represented a loss of artistic innocence […] The goal now is to analyse this aesthetico-political will to power, which artists acknowledge to be primary in all artistic projects, including their own.
>
> (Ibid.: 81–2)

Unlike writers such as Tolstaia and Hodrová, the Conceptualists repeatedly foreground the essential harmfulness of the text. As an expression of their fear of the consequences of the creative process, and a desire, in effect, to escape writing through writing, they retreat from the notion of the writer as 'weaver' of text into parody and simulation. As a result, their work frequently reflects Linda Hutcheon's shorthand definition of postmodernism as 'saying something whilst at the same time putting inverted commas around what is being said' (Hutcheon 1989: 1).

This retreat is mirrored in Slovak literature at the turn of the 1990s in the work of the Barbarians, Bielik, Litvák, Turan and Zbruž. Kolenič, once associated with the Barbarians, withdrew his contributions to their anthology of prose, poetry and interviews, *Barbar(u)ská ruleta* (Barbar(uss)ian roulette, 1998).[2] Although they have produced more prose fiction than the Moscow Conceptualists, they too prefer verse, while Bielik also paints. Zbruž's novel *Spitý imidž* (Pissed image, 1993) (a pun on the British television programme *Spitting Image*) is written in the style of comic strip, also revealing his leanings towards visual art, considered central to 1970s Russian Conceptualism.[3] Whereas, however, the older Russian Conceptualists, writing out of the memory of Stalinism and the failure of the Thaw, seek to empty signs of their capacity to signify in an attempt to disarm them, for the younger Barbarians, the emptiness of signs and the impossibility of making them signify marks the starting-point of their assertion of the utter meaninglessness of human existence. Their view of language produces in fiction like Litvák's *Samoreč* (Autospeak, 1992) and Kolenič's *Mlčať* a type of impotent, malevolent outsider reminiscent of Dostoevsky's Underground Man, subsequently parodied by Balla in his novel *Outsideria* (1997). It also leads them, particularly in their 1998 anthology, towards the assertion of Eastern notions of emptiness, somewhat as Conceptualist techniques merge with Buddhism in Viktor Pelevin's fiction, discussed in the next chapter. In this chapter, I shall focus on prose fiction by Litvák and Kolenič, but I begin with Sorokin, the most prolific and widely discussed fiction writer to emerge directly from Moscow Conceptualist circles (see Rasskazova 1992: 119).[4]

Sorokin's work first became known in underground circles in the early 1980s in *samizdat* and particularly through live or tape-recorded performances. The publication in Paris in 1985 of Sorokin's novel *Ochered'* (The queue, Paris 1985, Moscow 1998, dated as written 1982–3) aroused critical interest in his work in the West and prompted a moralizing attack on the writer in *Moskovskaia pravda* in 1986.[5] As Vladimir Novikov points out, Sorokin's works have rarely appeared first in periodicals (see Novikov 1997: 274), with the result that his first publication in Russia, a collection of stories written during the early 1980s, did not come out until 1992. The publication of Sorokin's work from the late Soviet period during the mid-1990s, culminating in the 1998 two-volume collected works that formally established the writing order of his works up till then, masked the fact that, for most of the 1990s, Sorokin abstained from writing fiction in favour of drama and screenplays. This shift in genre leads Mikhail Ryklin to suggest that there are two Sorokins, 'first of all the non-writer creating superbly structured literature, and then the writer trying to create non-literature' (Ryklin 1998: 748). It is the former who constitutes the focus of the following discussion.

The Conceptualist perception of the 'will to power' in any work of art, articulated by Groys, finds an echo in the interview with Sorokin that accompanies his first publication in Russia, in which he comments, citing Michel

Foucault: 'any text is totalitarian, since it pretends to authority over the human being. A text is a very powerful weapon. It can hypnotize, and sometimes it simply paralyses' (Rasskazova 1992: 121). Viacheslav Kuritsyn also notes Sorokin's quotation of Derrida in this context in *Mesiats v Dakhau* (A month in Dachau, 1994, dated as written 1990) (see Kuritsyn 1999: 63). In much of his writing from the late Soviet period, Sorokin attempts to draw the reader's attention to this activity of the text through the use of some form of incongruous intrusion, which disrupts the predictable course of the narration. This technique is firmly established in the early short story collection 'Pervyi subbotnik' (First voluntary Saturday, 1998, dated as written 1980–4).[6] Here, most of the stories begin as a simulation of a particular style of Soviet fiction, before the narrative is interrupted by a sudden, unmotivated act of violence, swearing, defecation, vomiting or analogous occurrences.

These interruptions correspond to what Patricia Waugh calls a 'frame-break', a device which 'draws attention to the fact that life, as well as novels, is constructed through frames' (Waugh 1984: 29), because they do not belong within the 'frame' established by the preceding narrative, and thus show the apparently whole, harmonious world contained within that narrative to be incomplete. Waugh contends that the analysis of frames in 'metafiction' has demonstrated that all knowledge of experience is 'framed', that 'there is ultimately no distinction between "framed" and "unframed". There are only levels of form. There is ultimately only "content" perhaps, but it will never be discovered in a "natural" unframed state' (ibid.: 31). In Sorokin's first novel, *Norma* (The norm, 1994, dated as written 1979–84), as Peter Deutschmann graphically shows in his plan of its structure (see Deutschmann 1999: 52), the reader passes through frame after frame in a novel made up of texts-within-texts, written in different styles and literary or extra-literary genres, which function as a metaphor for the chaos of relativity that constitutes human knowledge. The outer 'frame' is formed by an account of how the text of the novel is confiscated during a police raid and given to a teenage boy to read, in effect simultaneously with the reader, apparently to assess the appropriate level of punishment. Sorokin thus seeks to demonstrate how the 'frame' – the 'norm' – through which the world is perceived is created by the interaction of reader and text. At the end of the work, following the total disintegration of the text into incomprehensibility, the return to the teenage boy-reader amounts in effect to a parodic recasting of the comforting phrase from children's fiction, 'but it was only a dream' as 'but it was only a novel,' itself only a frame.

By dramatizing the process of reading in *Norma*, Sorokin indicates that, though his comments in interviews frequently refer to the activity of texts, it is in fact the activity of the reader that his work seeks to define and subvert. Sorokin uses the 'frame-break' in place of the incongruous juxtapositions of images and slogans employed by Conceptualist visual artists to disrupt the unquestioned identity of sign and referent in the preceding text, exposing its formulaic nature and creating a sense of emptiness – of absent referents – fundamental to the

Moscow Conceptualist aesthetic. The use of a single 'frame-break' in the stories in *'Pervyi subbotnik'* disrupts the reader's expectations, revealing how the reader becomes absorbed into the 'frame' of the text, establishing the limits of the reader's perception of the world.

In this collection, as Lipovetskii notes (Lipovetskii 1999a: 199), Sorokin uses variations on the teacher–pupil relationship not only to reflect how, in Socialist Realism, an older, ideologically 'conscious' representative of the collective facilitates the integration of the younger, inexperienced individual, but also to stand as a metaphor for the relationship between text and reader.[7] For example, in 'Sergei Andreevich', the first story in the definitive version of the collection,[8] Sorokin depicts a trip to the woods made by a group of teenagers with their favourite teacher, Sergei Andreevich, to mark the end of their secondary schooling. At one point, Sergei Andreevich goes off to fetch water, accompanied by Sokolov, his most earnest admirer. On the way back, having sent Sokolov on ahead, Sergei Andreevich pauses to defecate. Sokolov, however, watches secretly, and when Sergei Andreevich has gone, he creeps up and with greedy reverence eats the excrement. In his interpretation of 'Sergei Andreevich', Lipovetskii describes how Sorokin's short fiction exposes the rite of passage underpinning Socialist Realist texts: at a transitional stage, the end of secondary schooling, the neophytes are taken from their normal environment into the wild, where only one is permitted to undergo initiation. According to Lipovetskii, Sokolov's consumption of Sergei Andreevich's excrement corresponds to an act of 'ritual incorporation', symbolizing the integration of Sokolov into the collective (see Lipovetskii 1999a: 199–201). However, the ritual of initiation depicted within the text also stands as a metaphor for the reading process, understood as the reader's integration into the collective, with the text itself as the voice of collective authority.

The final act of coprophagy reflects the fact that, throughout Sorokin's writing, the human being is characterized as fundamentally a consumer seeking satiation, which in the case of the reader equates with becoming part of a world as full, rounded and comfortable as the stomach after a good meal. Ryklin, noting the prominence of food and eating in Sorokin's work, suggests that 'it is difficult to name a greater gastronomist among contemporary Russian writers than Sorokin' (Ryklin 1998: 750). Sorokin repeatedly uses the linear model of the pursuit of satiation within the text as a metaphor for the activity of the reader. For example, the novel *Tridtsataia liubov' Mariny* (Marina's thirtieth love, 1995, dated as written 1982–4) describes the heroine's quest for her first orgasm with a man. Sorokin here simulates the style of erotic fiction, going through each of Marina's sexual encounters in detail, building up literally to the climax, equating the process of writing with masturbation, and the process of reading with voyeurism. Sorokin claims that he refrained from sexual contact for a month while writing the work (see Shapoval 1998: 18). Reading and writing are similarly characterized by Koleničin his half-hearted pastiche of pornographic fiction, 'Diletant 1' (Dilettante 1) and 'Diletant 2' (Dilettante 2), in the collection

Porušenie raja (The violation of paradise, 1993). At the same time, however, Sorokin's novel is a parodic reassertion of the Socialist *Bildungsroman*; Marina has various failed liaisons with dissidents, satirically portrayed as embourgeoisés, impotent, effeminate types, before finally achieving her orgasm with a factory *partorg*, at which point she abandons her promiscuous 'cosmopolitan' lifestyle and becomes an enthusiastic worker, and the text acquires the style of a Soviet economic report. According to Sorokin, the model used is that of the Russian 'novel of salvation', understood in *Tridtsataia liubov' Mariny* as 'salvation from individualization' (Rasskazova 1992: 124), and depicted, as in 'Sergei Andreevich', as satiation through absorption into the collective.[9]

This model is reversed in *Ochered'*, in which collective existence is symbolized by the queue, described by Sorokin as a 'single gigantic organism' (Laird 1999: 149), where people are prepared to stand indefinitely despite not knowing what they will receive at the end. The soft-sign feminine noun *ochered'* effectively stands for another soft-sign feminine noun, *zhizn'* (life).The novel is written in dramatic dialogue, without character indications, in Sally Laird's description, 'as if [Sorokin has] simply hung a microphone round the neck of the central character and transcribed the recording, unedited' (ibid.: 150). The effect, as Laird points out, is to make the reader part of the queue, to turn queuing into a metaphor of the reading process. Just as those queuing receive sufficient intimation of the goods awaiting them to remain interested, so the reader becomes aware of a hero, Vadim, and a plot, which culminates in Vadim being taken in from the queue during a rainstorm by an unknown woman who not only copulates with him, but also has access to the goods for which he has been queuing. As Sorokin points out,

> [the novel] offers only an ironic kind of salvation, a pseudo-salvation if you like. Because even when the hero's been granted this wonderful thing – this woman, and the goods he's been dreaming of – he remains somehow pathetic and impoverished. He doesn't fundamentally change.
>
> (Ibid.: 148)

For the reader-queuer too, the outcome is also only an ironic reward; consumer satisfaction, material or sexual, is not a transformation, but a temporary satiation of a need. In Sorokin's work, the inevitable outcome of the process of consumption is not satiation, but excrement, representing a renewed emptiness needing to be filled. The first part of *Norma* consists of a series of short stories imitating different styles of Soviet fiction, all of which portray characters eating their daily packet of 'norm', some with varying degrees of enthusiasm or reluctance, most without thinking. The process of eating here becomes a metaphor for the process of reading; the reader easily consumes the bite-sized chunks of text, gradually coming to suspect the ingredients of what he is reading, before eventually being left in no doubt that the packets contain the faeces of small children.

By equating reading with coprophagy, Sorokin seeks to inspire revulsion in the reader towards the normative, collectivizing activity of culture. As Viacheslav Kuritsyn points out: 'poo [*kakashki*] is, after all, what unites us [...] excrement in Sorokin is warm and festive' (Kuritsyn 1999: 62), reflecting the comfort of satiation. In Sorokin's writing, the warmth of excrement is the warmth of the shared. For many critics, Sorokin's writing reflects the distortion of human psychology under Soviet autocracy, a view sustained by Sorokin's comments in his early interviews regarding the nature of 'homo sovieticus' (see, in particular, Laird 1999: 148–52).[10] David Gillespie, who considers Sorokin's work a 'testament to the degradation of a whole society and its people' (Gillespie 1997: 171), interprets the first part of *Norma* as a criticism of the way most people learned to accept Soviet propaganda: 'everyone is fed on shit, and the vast majority of people love it' (ibid.: 161).

This perspective is shared by Skoropanova, who suggests that the long list of nouns preceded by the adjective 'normal'nyi' which forms the second part of the novel works by analogy with the ubiquitous and often incongruous use of the adjective 'sovetskii' in the Soviet Union (see Skoropanova 1999: 269). Serafima Roll, who details many of the Soviet *topoi* used by Sorokin in the first short-story collection, argues that the collection is aimed at 'demystifying the Soviet myth of human happiness founded on one's belief in sublimating and repressing the existential for the political and ideological' (Roll 1996: 66). In her view, the 'frame-breaks' serve to subvert sentimental or self-glorifying clichés about the human being which Socialist Realism has created or adopted, 'exposing the "actual" life events hidden beneath the glossy pictures of social paradise' (ibid.). However, Roll's use of the contrast between 'public' and 'private', terms of particular importance in the analysis of the social realism of the Brezhnev period, where they implicitly corresponded to the distinction between 'pretence' and 'truth', misleadingly places Sorokin's fiction at the extreme of a spectrum of contemporary Russian realist writing. The sudden, intense physical images which mark the 'frame-break' in many of the stories in 'Pervyi subbotnik' may be seen to reverse the abrupt switches in conventional Socialist Realism, which Katerina Clark describes as 'sudden, unmotivated transitions from realistic discourse to the mythic or utopian' (quoted in Lipovetskii 1999a: 204). However, the switch is not from fiction to reality, but from metaphors of culture to metaphors of what culture excludes; as Lipovetskii points out in his analysis of 'Sergei Andreevich', 'the symbolic code is forced out by a naturalistic code, conditional signals are replaced by unconditional ones, "culture" by "nature"' (ibid.: 201).

The two parts of Sorokin's stories might be better understood as metaphors for the psychoanalytical model of the human mind with the first, simulated element representing the *Ich* and *Über-Ich*, and the collapse into the disorder of physical violence and sexual perversion representing the *Es*. Ryklin, among others, has drawn attention to the psychoanalytical interpretation of Sorokin's work, suggesting that the coprophagy in his work signifies regression to Freud's oral stage, indicative of the infantilism of collective obedience (see Ryklin 1998: 737.)

Sorokin, however, dismisses his interest in psychoanalysis as a fleeting adolescent fascination, and indeed pre-empts Ryklin's reading in the story 'Dorozhnoe proisshestvie' (An incident on the road), in which the narrator's recollection of pretending to be a sewage worker as a child is followed by a section marked 'Interpretation', where the narrator points out: 'It is well known that at a pre-pubertal age the main erotic experience of the child is connected with the act of defecation, hence the heightened interest of children in faeces as their source of pleasure' (Sorokin 1998: 561).

For Sorokin, Freud's model merely serves as a useful metaphor (see Laird 1999: 156). In an article entitled 'Cherez "Vtoroe nebo"' (Through the 'Second Heaven'), published in 1994, Sorokin writes:

> Twentieth-century psychology has opened up the sphere of the lower psyche before us as some kind of abyss which is ready at any moment to swallow our 'Ich' – that which we call our identity [*lichnost'*] and in which God lays the foundation of our likeness to Him. It is easy to step into the abyss, but this step marks the end of our identity and, consequently, our likeness to God, and together with this, a return to pre-history.
>
> (Quoted in Skoropanova 1999: 281)

This article indicates how Sorokin's original starting-point, Soviet 'official culture', represents not an exception, but a culmination of the notion of culture, understood as the means by which, over time, the human being is gradually civilized. The 'frame-breaking' element in his short stories highlights not only the feebleness of this process's achievements, the 'ease of stepping into the abyss', but also the barbarism which has been perpetrated in the name of the process.

Like Venedikt Erofeev in *Moskva–Petushki*, Sorokin presents Soviet culture as the logical culmination of Russian cultural development. In the third part of *Norma*, a young man uncovers a case containing evidence that he may be a descendant of the Romantic poet, Fedor Tiutchev (1803–73). His awe and reverence, reflecting the conventional perception and reception of Russia's literary canon, recall an episode in the first part of the novel in which two characters come across a packet of 'norm' (faeces) which had belonged to an uncle who fell at Stalingrad, and which had subsequently been returned to his wife by a close comrade-in-arms.[11] Skoropanova suggests that in the story of the young man, by simulating Soviet 'village fiction' of the 1960s and 1970s, Sorokin reveals the connection between that type of fiction, nineteenth-century Slavophilism and the literary styles of Ivan Turgenev (1818–83), Anton Chekhov (1860–1904) and Ivan Bunin (1870–1953), in effect placing all within the nineteenth-century 'pochvennik' ('native-soil') tradition (see Skoropanova 1999: 270–1). Sorokin then attempts to break free of this tradition by 'desecrating' it; the 'pochvennik' is transformed into a literal 'lover of the soil' through the depiction of the young man, overcome with his discovery, copulating with the ground.

By choosing Tiutchev as the figure to whom the young man is related, Sorokin indicates his sense of affinity with the poet, who is symbolically the first Russian writer to feel the burden of Russia's literary past, which in Tiutchev's case amounted to the figure of Alexander Pushkin (1799–1837). In Bitov's *Pushkinskii dom* (Pushkin House, Ann Arbor 1971, Moscow 1987), a novel which expresses the impossibility of breaking free of this burden, the author appends an academic article ostensibly written by the central character, but in fact published separately by Bitov himself (see Lipovetskii 1999: 57), which explores how Tiutchev and Mikhail Lermontov (1814–41) confronted the responsibility of following Pushkin (see Bitov 1989: 223–42). Through his account of Tiutchev's relationship with Pushkin – Tiutchev's resentment at Pushkin's apparent indifference to him, his sense that he was 'not allowed' to be a better writer – Bitov characterizes the relationship of Russian writers to the consecrated literary past. Bitov suggests that the final straw for Tiutchev was the fact that Pushkin had already written the story of their relationship in the dramatic fragment *Mozart and Salieri* (1830).

Unlike Bitov's novel, Sorokin's dispute with Russia's literary heritage derives not so much from a sense of disappointment at having been born 'too late', as from his perception of a link between the notion of a solid, continuous cultural heritage and the belief in progress towards the perfection of the human being. (Both these perspectives are effectively contained in the half-nostalgic, half-sarcastic treatment of literature in *Moskva–Petushki*.) The Tiutchev story in *Norma* is immediately followed by a discussion, ostensibly between the writer and his editor, about how the story might be made more interesting. The passage in which the young man discovers the suitcase is then repeated, except that this time, instead of Tiutchev's letter and signet ring, he finds a text which he and the reader in effect read together, describing the brutal collectivization of a village.

Like *Moskva–Petushki*, Sorokin's implication of the whole Russian literary culture in the violence of the Stalinist period may be seen as an attempt to apply Adorno's arguments about Western culture's complicity in Auschwitz to the Russian context. Ryklin argues that one of the most significant Russian cultural taboos broken by Sorokin is his equation of Russian atrocities in the twentieth century with those of the Germans, notably in his plays, but also in the prose piece *Mesiats v Dakhau*, the title of which parodies that of Turgenev's idyllic *Mesiats v derevne* (A month in the country, 1850). Ryklin writes:

> [Sorokin] questions the silently accepted uniqueness of 'German guilt', of German fascism as a conveyor-belt of crimes, the uniqueness of the racial vector of these crimes, and the necessity of passing the work of mourning on to subsequent generations. In all these aspects he has introduced important innovations: fascism as a system of violence is not unique; the work of mourning after the no less criminal Stalinist system has not yet even begun, but has been replaced by uninterrupted euphoria; and the racial vector of the crimes as such is in no way worse than the class vector.
>
> (Ryklin 1998: 744)[12]

Sorokin most explicitly shows the nineteenth-century Russian canon to be the agent of the notion of progress towards a better world in his simulation of the nineteenth- century novel, *Roman* (1995, dated as written 1985–9), the title of which may be translated as 'Novel', but is also the name of the main character. The work only supports an allegorical reading in a minor way; however, the ambiguity of the title is sustained within the text, with the epithet 'Roman' often appearing to refer simultaneously to the character and the novel form itself. For example, at the beginning of the work, Roman returns to his native village after some years in the city to find little changed, rather as the work itself revisits familiar faces and places, the *topoi* of the nineteenth-century novel: 'I'm here again. In this dear house. With these dear people' (Sorokin 1998: 19). The fact that other characters frequently compare Roman to past literary heroes suggests that Roman, rather like Pushkin's Onegin, embodies the whole preceding history of Western literature in his person; moreover, the characterization of Roman may be understood as a characterization of the novel itself. He is described as a dandy, dressed like an English lord, yet is said to be incapable of being indifferent to anything, and possesses an unusual desire to captivate his audience with stories:

> While still a child he had noticed that it gave him great pleasure to illuminate events which interested anyone in a way that would completely stun the listener, provoking in him the desired trepidation of the soul, at which he would start to tremble.
>
> (Ibid.: 51)

This desire for power is implicitly presented as the motivation for Realist writing, which, in its efforts to represent reality, tries to capture its subject and absorb it in words. As a painter, Roman is impressed by his own ability to recreate landscapes, yet this ability appears to be intrinsically linked with Roman's impulsive greed: 'Unable to restrain himself, Roman stretched out his hand and took an apple, which, despite its long, cramped wintering in the spicy brine, had remained firm, and took a bite' (ibid.: 22). At the beginning of the novel, Roman is thirty-two, at the end, thirty-three, and the frequent implicit identification of Roman with Christ reflects the attempted exploitation of the novel by, for example, Dostoevsky, Nikolai Gogol (1809–52) and Lev Tolstoy (1828–1910), as the means of leading human beings to salvation.

What is most essential for Roman, and therefore for the novel, as he repeatedly tells other characters during lengthy philosophical discussions about art, life and the existence of God, is uncompromised personal freedom. Yet, as Sorokin seeks to demonstrate in the gory conclusion of the work, this freedom is to be achieved through subjugation and destruction. *Roman* culminates in Roman's wedding feast, a typical novel ending and a symbol of the satiation of all desires. However, during a quiet interlude with his bride, Roman suddenly declares: '"I know what is to be done"' (ibid.: 289) and proceeds to kill the villagers one by one with an axe. In a novel which stylistically and thematically merges Turgenev,

Dostoevsky, Tolstoy and Ivan Goncharov (1812–91), this simultaneous allusion to *What is to be done?* by Nikolai Chernyshevsky (1828–89) and the Lenin essay it inspired demonstrates for Sorokin the complicity of Russian culture in the barbarism of the Soviet period. In effect, Sorokin suggests, Chernyshevsky's novel merely made explicit the question that all Russian nineteenth-century novels sought to answer. Novikov writes:

> In both the form of the [Cyrillic] letter 'P' [for *Roman*], and its disturbing, rolling rumble may be seen and heard that same axe to which the revolutionary democrats and powerful fiction, thirsting for a storm, summoned Russia; not for nothing did Heinrich Mann later call our literature of the last century 'revolution before the revolution'.
>
> (Novikov 1997: 276–7)

Novikov suggests that *Roman* takes place in 'Turgenevian-Goncharovian times', but the references to the landscape artist Isaak Levitan and French Impressionism indicate that the setting is the 1890s. The emphasis on images of decay and twilight in the opening description of the graveyard in which Roman is buried, establishes the atmosphere of decadence. When Roman first enters his childhood home, the reader is told: 'The floor onto which Roman stepped was rotten and buckled, promising at some time to fall in completely' (Sorokin 1998: 18). For Sorokin, it is not society which is disintegrating, but the novel form, the 'floor onto which Roman steps'. Roman's choice of weapon thus recalls not only the symbol of Raskol'nikov's rebellion, but also the end of Chekhov's *The Cherry Orchard* (1903). Just as the sound of axes cutting down the orchard signals the end of the gentry's way of life described in the play, so Roman's axe marks the end of a particular and, for Sorokin, baleful tradition of writing and reading.

Roman's subsequent ritual of cannibalism, vomiting, defecation and masturbation with the corpses of his victims in the village church shows how attempted liberation leads merely to mechanized brutality. This is reflected in the way in which the repetitive sentences become gradually simpler, from subject–verb–object to subject–verb by the end. At the same time, this stylistic change demonstrates the disintegration of the novel 'frame', with the visual appearance of the unparagraphed, repetitive text coming to match the semantic horror. In effect, the Romantic revolt against 'frames' carried out by successive Russian literary heroes culminates in Roman, who revolts against the 'frame' of the novel itself. As the final 'Roman died' (ibid.: 356) indicates, however, Roman cannot survive this process; in destroying the 'frame' of the novel, he destroys what Sorokin calls his 'I', his 'likeness to God', and ceases to exist.

In *Roman*, Sorokin seeks to demonstrate that the freedom Roman desires cannot be attained in life, which is dependent on 'frames' for its continuation. The 'frame-break' in Sorokin's work, which frequently appears in place of the moment of 'salvation', may thus be seen to reject the promise of liberation, to remind the reader not only that existence is always 'framed', but also that he or she is dependent on that 'frame'. On the other hand, however, by reversing the conventional linear path towards 'imprisonment' in the frame and exposing the absolute relativity of text, the 'frame-break' provides a *frisson* of the freedom that the individual desires but cannot possess. The reader's notional horror at the 'frame-break' thus corresponds, in effect, to the flight of the elderly naturalist from this relativity at the end of Tolstaia's 'Somnambula v tumane'. Prigov, the Conceptualists' most prominent spokesman, comments:

> the main task of art, its purpose in this world, is to show absolute freedom, a freedom with all its dangers. Through the example of art, the human being sees that there is absolute freedom, though it need not be fully realisable in life. I took Soviet language as the most functional at that time, the most obvious and accessible, which was the representative of ideology and presented itself as the absolute truth, sent down from Heaven. The human being was oppressed by this language not from outside, but from within himself. Any ideology lays claim to you entirely, any language has totalitarian ambitions to seize the whole world, cover it with its terms and show that it is the absolute truth. I wanted to show that there is freedom. Language is only language, and not the absolute truth and, having understood that, we shall win freedom.
>
> (Gandlevskii and Prigov 1993: 5)

Sorokin's writing may be understood as an attempt to restore to literature Roland Barthes's notion of *jouissance*, almost by directly imitating Barthes's description of de Sade, with whom Sorokin has been compared (see, for example, Vladiv-Glover (ed.) 1999: 273). In *The Pleasure of the Text*, Barthes argues that the pleasure of reading de Sade 'proceeds from certain breaks (or certain collisions)' (Barthes 1976: 6) resulting from the redistribution of language. Barthes continues:

> such redistribution is always achieved by cutting. Two edges are created: an obedient, conformist, plagiarizing edge (the language is to be copied in its canonical state, as it has been established by schooling, good usage, literature, culture), and *another edge*, mobile, blank (ready to assume any contours), which is never anything but the site of its effect: the place where the death of language is glimpsed. [...] Neither culture nor its destruction is erotic; it is the seam between them, the fault, the flaw, which becomes so.
>
> (Ibid.)

Whereas satiation is comforting, *jouissance* constitutes a sudden experience of loss or emptiness which Sorokin frequently symbolizes in his 'frame-breaks' through images of physical voiding, orgasm or violent death. As Sorokin demonstrates through his repetitive use of the 'frame-break' device in 'Pervyi subbotnik', however, the reader quickly becomes comfortable with the formula, and the moment of *jouissance* turns into a ritual of satiation, the self-confidence of knowing that forms the basis of conviction and action. Unlike Ajvaz, Sorokin, in his resistance to the formulaic, to petrification in the manner of Denisov's monument in 'Somnambula v tumane', is prepared to subvert his own method. Like Hodrová, Sorokin asserts the openness, multiplicity and uncertainty of linguistic meaning, for example in the anagrammatic titles of *Norma* and *Roman*, in which characters at one point listen to arias from Bellini's opera *Norma*. The title of his controversial novel *Goluboe salo* (1998) translates literally as 'blue fat', but also combines an allusion to *Salo*, Pasolini's cinematic encyclopaedia of sexual perversion, with the most common pejorative adjective for 'homosexual'. This novel, which contains passages written in a futuristic 'new Russian' exploiting such multi-lingual puns, is prefixed with a quotation from Rabelais in which Pantagruel rescues from the sea frozen words which melt into a barbarian language (see Sorokin 1998: 5).

For Lipovetskii, Sorokin's simulation of styles exemplifies Fredric Jameson's understanding of the notion of 'pastiche', which he describes as the

> imitation of a peculiar or unique style, the wearing of a stylistic mask, speech in a dead language [...] without parody's ulterior motive, without the satirical impulse, without laughter, without that still latent feeling that there exists something *normal* compared to which what is being imitated is rather comic.
>
> (Quoted in Rose 1993: 222)

However, in Sorokin's writing, through the 'frame-break', it is precisely the 'normal' which is shown to be comic. Henri Bergson writes:

> We begin to become imitable only when we cease to be ourselves [...]. Our gestures can only be imitated in their mechanical uniformity and therefore exactly in what is alien to our living personality. To imitate anyone is to bring out the element of automatism.
>
> (Bergson 1911: 33)

Sorokin's 'frame-breaks' correct the 'rigidity' of the formulaic text, momentarily restoring life before themselves lapsing into formula. For example, in 'Vozvrashchenie' (The return), a parody of a typically chaste Soviet love story in which a young man takes his sweetheart home for the first time, Sorokin repeatedly interrupts the characters' timid gestures and expressions of affection with sudden, incongruous vulgarisms that intrude on the reader's experience but not that of the characters. For example, near the end of the story the reader is told:

> They crossed the deserted square with two bright blue lamps and turned into Veronika's street. 'You have such a lovely mum,' said Veronika, straightening her hair. 'I reckon all mums are lovely,' laughed Vladimir. 'And

> your brother's sweet. It must be good to fuck with him till you get heartburn…'. Vladimir nodded silently. They went into the garden, and the young linden trees closed over their heads.
>
> (Sorokin 1998: 472–3)

The vulgarity, by raising awareness of the banality it replaces, causes the reader to hesitate, perhaps even to recoil. Sorokin's texts seek to teach this hesitation, a sudden awareness of helplessness, an extreme version of what Venichka in *Moskva–Petushki* calls 'universal faint-heartedness'. In effect, Sorokin suggests that by sustaining change in the text, the writer resists both the 'will to power' of the text and the concomitant momentum for change in life.

As Prigov indicates in the passage quoted above, the Conceptualists perceive the notion of language as a surface over reality, arising initially from their play with the 'disembodied' signs of Socialist Realism, as a liberation. Speaking in 1987 about the appeal of the Conceptualists, Sorokin comments:

> In principle the conceptual artist doesn't have his own language – he uses only the language of others.[…] This idea seemed to me very natural; it had an obvious relevance to our situation here, to our attitude towards the language of our state, its literary language. I feel acutely that I can't be *inside* this language, because to be inside it, to use it as mine, means that I'm inside this state – and that's something that I've always feared. […] [F]or me, the only kind of freedom there is is the freedom to choose different languages, make use of them, and remain an outsider in the process.
>
> (Laird 1999: 149)

This freedom is typified by the implied authorial 'role-playing' in Prigov's poetry. Mary A. Nicholas writes:

> In the place of a single lyric persona, Prigov relies instead on a variety of literary types, which he calls 'images' (*imidzhi*). These images vary from the best known of his personages – the policeman or '*militsioner*' – to the civic poet, the writer of 'women's verses', the journalist, the unofficial artist, the simple worker and so on.
>
> (Nicholas 1996: 21)

What Prigov and Sorokin, however, regard as freedom is presented in Kolenič's first books of fiction and Litvák's collection of prose pieces *Samoreč* as imprisonment in relativity. The narrators in *Samoreč* repeatedly assert 'Everything is the same' (Litvák 1992: 16). In the piece entitled 'Zlosť' (Anger), the narrator says to the reader, or perhaps just to himself: 'From where to where don't you want to understand the incomprehensible, when everything merely imitates itself?' (ibid.).

In common with other writers discussed in this study, Litvák seeks to strip literature and human beings of their pretensions. Štefan Moravčík describes the work as a 'report on the catastrophe of youth and humanity, and on the catastrophe of literature which cannot, does not want and does not know how to go on in the old way' (Moravčík 1992: 36). In 'Chorobne ľubím písať' (I morbidly love to write), the narrator defines what he is writing as 'the purgatory of Slovak fiction', ridding Slovak literature of its sinful delusion of potency as it rids signifiers of any relationship to their signifieds. Like Mitana in *Hľadanie strateného autora*, though more savagely, Litvák rejects the notion of story and story-telling because they sustain the illusion not only that words can give shape and order to the world, but also that the accumulation of words, as memories or experiences, may give rise to the notion of a self: 'I hate stories. They are distorted memories and nothing is more monstrous than the epic. It is something as terrible and useless as my experience' (Litvák 1992: 21).

In effect, Litvák replaces literature with 'autospeak', not language which gives shape to the self, but the incessant production of sounds, the futile accompaniment to futile existence. Whereas Hodrová and Ajvaz characterize the activity of writing as a constant movement to-and-fro, through which meaning is endlessly revealed and reconstituted, in the first piece from *Samoreč*, 'Zvyšný' (Superfluous), Litvák's narrator indicates that his revolt against meaning merely renders him as helpless as a tight-rope walker, stationary on his rope: 'from his debilitating bird's-eye view he can only smile, whisper his sorrows to the emptiness beneath the sky, suffer from dizziness, stand on tiptoe and enjoy the balancing' (ibid.: 10).

The impact of *Samoreč* was, however, eclipsed by that of Kolenič's first novel, *Mlčať*, in the context of which *Samoreč* appears as little more than preparatory sketches. A decade younger than Sorokin, Kolenič established his reputation as the *enfant terrible* of contemporary Slovak literature at almost exactly the same time as Sorokin did the same for himself in Russia. In 1986, just as the publication abroad of *Ochered'* was causing a scandal in official Soviet circles, Kolenič's first collection of poetry, *Prinesené búrkou* (Brought by the storm) was published in Slovakia, provoking much critical discussion (see *Romboid* 1988: 114–22). Pynsent argues, however, that the appearance of *Mlčať*, coincidentally in the same year as Sorokin's first book publication in Russia, 'did more [than his verse] to prepare the way for [the] new writing' of post-Communist Slovakia (Pynsent 1999: 17). Whereas Sorokin and Prigov sought to evade absorption into the language of the Soviet state, *Mlčať* constitutes an attempt to escape from the relativity of language, which, as Kolenič scathingly contends in 'Diletant 1', renders the writer nothing more than a 'dilettante', as superficial and superfluous as the language with which he is condemned to work. Pavel Minár writes of *Mlčať*:

> at the centre of the thematic action of Kolenič's text are the human being as an instrument of language, and the trauma arising from the impossibility of

> escape, of eluding the clutches of "ever-present" language; that is to say, the fundamental non-existence of any condition outside language.
>
> (Minár 1992: 20)

Writers like Tolstaia, Hodrová or Topol present language as a gift; in Kolenič's fiction it is a curse, since it constitutes the only means of expressing knowledge of reality, but proves inadequate to the task.

The title of *Mlčať* may be understood simultaneously as an imperative and an aspiration, denoting a piece of writing which paradoxically advocates an end to writing. It recalls Tiutchev's poem 'Silentium!' (1832), where the first word is 'Molchi' (Be silent). In the poem, Tiutchev rejects externally directed language in favour of an inner language of thoughts, dreams and emotions. For Tiutchev, this inner language cannot be conveyed through externally directed language – 'The thought uttered is a lie' – and therefore he exhorts the reader to fall silent and live inside himself: 'There is a whole world in your soul / Of secret magical thoughts' (Tiutchev 1984: 61). In 'Diletant 1', the narrator virtually paraphrases Tiutchev's poem when he comments: 'In fact there's only one problem: to end one's inclination towards the manifest world with its lures and confusing feelings. And to plunge into the endless depths of one's own interior, into spaceless and timeless peace' (Kolenič 1993: 77). This aspiration recalls that of Mameev in Ivanchenko's *Avtoportret s dogom*.

Like Tiutchev, the narrator of *Mlčať* suggests at the beginning of the work that he has a choice between speaking and remaining silent. He mocks the high value traditionally placed on speech, describing it as 'too primitive and limited' to convey meaning, and concludes that it makes no difference whether one speaks or not, since speaking and being silent merely represent alternative ways of saying nothing: 'speech is organized silence' (Kolenič 1992: 5). However, even as he writes this, he is aware of his dependence upon the presence of words for knowledge of his existence. His first words – 'I don't have to say anything' (ibid.) – are consciously ironic because he knows it is this utterance which brings him into being for the reader, while it is the sound of his thoughts which makes him aware of his own existence. The apparent distinction in Tiutchev's poem between externally and internally directed language is therefore obscured in *Mlčať*, since as the narrator puts it, 'thinking too is controlled by words and sentences' (ibid.: 89). Kolenič employs both the 'stream of consciousness' technique, reminiscent particularly of Samuel Beckett's trilogy, and the diary form as types of communication that are directed neither entirely inwards nor entirely outwards, but constitute an incessant flow of language – 'autospeak' – upon which the narrator's existence both for himself and for others is conditional. The initial question of whether to speak or be silent is thus shown to be, in effect, a recasting of the opening of Hamlet's soliloquy (Act III, Sc. 1, l.56f.). Being equates with narration, and therefore silence represents an impossible aspiration during life.

The problem for the narrator of *Mlčať* is that he experiences an intolerable discrepancy between himself and the words that give him being, which appears to him to emanate from an alien source: 'I cannot silence within me that voice which wants to show itself' (ibid.: 28). This same Beckettian alienation is also expressed by Litvák's narrator in 'Zvyšný', who demands: 'How could I blindly fall for speech which treacherously emits groans and suspiciously imitates with them the voice of a human being (about whom I am not entirely sure if he considers me as himself)?' (Litvák 1992: 6). Beasley-Murray links the estrangement of Kolenič's narrator to Jacques Lacan's notion of the Symbolic Order, within which the signifier has meaning only in so far as it differs from other signifiers, and therefore its relationship to the signified appears arbitrary. As a result, thinking and being can never be simultaneous; hence Lacan's reworking of Descartes: 'I think where I am not, and therefore I am where I am not thinking' (quoted in Beasley-Murray 1999: 38). The result for the narrator is a constant, inescapable sense of inauthenticity.

Kolenič's narrator conveys his sense of alienation from the words which create him by giving himself a name which he says is made up. The name, Jaroslav Varga, appeals to him because he claims that the repeated 'v' renders it impossible to pronounce properly, thus exposing the inadequacy of language. For the narrator, the invented name serves as a model for all words, which in his view do not represent, but rather replace what they signify. Through the narrator's creation of Varga, Kolenič actualizes the sense of estrangement which the writer experiences on looking back at words which he has just 'uttered'. At the same time, Kolenič uses the narrator's acknowledged untruth to demonstrate what he perceives as the futility and dishonesty of writers' endeavours to tell the truth.

The relationship between Varga and the narrator of *Mlčať* cannot be understood simply as the relationship between a fictional and a 'real' narrator; Varga constitutes a 'narrator-within-a-narrator', neither identical to the narrator, nor entirely separate from him. Through the invention of Varga, Kolenič foregrounds what Waugh terms the 'creation/description paradox' in fiction, which arises because 'all literary fiction has to construct a "context" at the same time that it constructs a "text", through entirely *verbal* processes. *Descriptions* of objects in fiction are simultaneously *creations* of that object' (Waugh 1984: 88). As she argues, the foregrounding of this paradox has implications not only for worlds in fiction, but also for the world outside it, which, if it can only be known through words, is similarly created as it is described. Through the 'narrator-within-a-narrator' device, Kolenič shows the self, in fiction and in life, to be a creation of words, and therefore suggests that each new utterance, though apparently emanating from a single physical source, may constitute a new self: 'So who is speaking? Me, or an invented name. We're speaking together, Mr Varga, each of us will say what he has to say. His own silence' (Kolenič 1992: 30).

The self in *Mlčať* is a story (*príbeh*), one of a notionally infinite number which the teller may tell without ever being able to convey his 'real self', the self which would establish a hierarchy of true and false. Whereas Prigov celebrates the freedom of 'role-play', near the end of *Mlčať*, Kolenič's narrator furiously asserts the absurdity of the situation brought about by language by listing dozens of possibilities from an implicitly infinite list of what 'Varga' could be. As in *Dusha patriota*, writing is thus shown to be a process not of self-discovery, but of self-creation. However, while Popov's narrator feigns indifference to the consequent 'emptiness' of writing, Kolenič's narrator is stricken with writer's block: 'If I could just get out a story, any invented story at all. My story' (ibid.: 29). He does not perceive his inability to write as a consequence of his own inadequacy, but of the inadequacy of language. His desire for a story with which to write himself out of his block therefore also becomes a desire to take revenge on language: 'I must drive words to a place where they will not be able to manifest their dim-witted supremacy' (ibid.).

In the novel's central episode – which the narrator subsequently calls his 'story' – the narrator describes how he rapes his mother, driving her insane, and murders her lover who disturbs them. The mother's madness manifests itself in her inability to use words, which are replaced by meaningless sounds. Beasley-Murray equates this situation with Lacan's Imaginary, the infantile state in which sign and referent reflect each other, for which the narrator longs but which he is unable to attain (see Beasley-Murray 1999: 41). The narrator's assault on his mother may be understood as a metaphor for his attack on language in the novel, since, as the narrator demonstrates in the opening pages, it is language that gives him being. However, more immediately, like the various forms of violence in Sorokin's writing, the assault constitutes an attack on the implied reader, whom Kolenič's narrator considers complicit in the social codes and systems of organization which perpetuate the hegemony of words.[13] From the very beginning of the novel, the narrator rejects all notions of the importance of the individual and the community, since he regards them, and the principles on which they are based, including the notion of the value of communication itself, to be mere linguistic inventions with no basis in reality:

> We're not going to make anything up; we're as indifferent to each other as the paper with which someone has wiped their arse and shit waiting for the flush. Why deceive oneself with talk about some kind of sincere human understanding?
>
> (Kolenič 1992: 10)

As in Pišťanek's assault on the apparently liberal intellectual in his fiction, the reader in *Mlčať* is implicated in the unthinking perpetuation of such notions to the extent to which he or she is offended by the narrator's attitude to them.

As the narration progresses, the narrator increasingly attempts to rid words of their capacity to create hierarchies, in effect, to sanctify. His inability to empathize with other human beings in the novel gradually worsens, as though he has broken through the psychological attachment to others of his own kind and seen it as nothing more than a verbal formulation: 'suddenly I saw people as things, in their insurmountable solitude, as they tottered towards each other in the rain: a chaos of steps, a labyrinth of movements, a silent mechanism which someone had activated' (ibid.: 53). As Mária Bátorová points out, 'ordinary words and names, for example the word mother, have lost their sense for him, have been emptied and mean nothing' (Bátorová 1993: 58).[14] In the pages leading up to the rape, he mentally strips his mother of the social and emotional significance that turns the word into a cultural concept, and is surprised how easily he can rid her of her taboo status and persuade himself of her sexual attractiveness:

> I don't know why I pushed her being to the periphery of all that is untouchable for so long.[…] Words merely tediously and bitterly name; they name only what they name. It has always been thus. Why did I think I was missing some meaning, some sense? Some secret symbol?
>
> (Kolenič 1992: 56)

In what follows, the narrator seeks to expose to the reader what he perceives as the exclusively linguistic basis of notions of human morality and decency, the dignity of death and the beauty of the erotic. After the rape and murder, the narrator describes how he chops up the corpse, stuffs it in a trunk and dumps it in a cellar. He then brings a girl to the flat and has violent sexual intercourse with her beside his stupefied mother. In these scenes, the reader is encouraged to 'suspend disbelief', as when reading conventional realism. Kolenič is thus able to 'break the frame' when the narrator suddenly declares that he has made everything up.

As, for example, in Sorokin's short stories, the aim of the 'frame-break' is to reveal the reader's helplessness, exposing both his willingness to accept the products of language as reality and the impossibility of doing otherwise. However, whereas in Sorokin's writing the 'frame-break' confirms the position of the author outside the 'frame', in *Mlčať* on the contrary it reveals the failure of the narrator's attempt to defeat language, his own imprisonment in the relativity of language, represented by the potential infinity of frames. At the end of *Mlčať*, the narrator reiterates in terms reminiscent of Dostoevsky's Underground Man what he knew at the beginning, that being is dependent on words whose content is irrelevant: 'After all, what else is speaking, if not raw being against emptiness?' (Kolenič 1992: 115).[15]

Whereas writers like Tolstaia, Popov and Kratochvil seek to free literature from expectations of its capacity to affect 'reality', and others, like Venedikt Erofeev or Sorokin, at least attempt to neuter its potential to do harm, in *Mlčať* Kolenič strives in vain to restore the potency of literature by resorting to shock tactics, which only intensify the awareness of impotence.[16] This approach is made explicit by the narrator of 'Diletant 1', who suggests: 'I could start writing a new book. The beginning would go like this: "Just disappear up a cunt once and for all! Who the hell wants to listen to that bollocks of yours?" That would shock people' (Kolenič 1993: 72). *Porušenie raja*, which includes half-hearted pastiches of 'video-nasties', erotic and pornographic fiction, lacks any of the inspiration or conviction of *Mlčať*, suggesting that the defeat of the narrator in that novel is also the defeat of the author. The narrator of 'Diletant 1' is suffering from writer's block, a reflection of the unceasing desire to use words, combined with the debilitating awareness of its pointlessness. His artistic redundancy is matched by the physical redundancy of sexual impotence.[16]

Whereas in the fiction by Sorokin discussed in this chapter, the adoption of 'literary masks', always exposed by 'frame-breaks', reflects a fear of the consequences of unself-conscious creative activity, in Kolenič's case, the process of writing, understood as the arbitrary manipulation of meaningless symbols, serves as a metaphor for the futility of existence. Both writers, however, assert the impossibility of stilling the compulsion to write, Kolenič explicitly in his texts, Sorokin through his high productivity. In the latter half of the 1990s, both sought to change direction, in both cases away from parody or simulation and towards more conventional story-telling. *Goluboe salo*, Sorokin's first novel since *Serdtsa chetyrekh* (Hearts of four, 1998, dated as written 1991), was described by Lipovetskii as his most 'neo-Baroque' work, a comment which might also apply to Kolenič's Surrealist-influenced *Ako z cigariet dym* (Like smoke from cigarettes, 1996), in which the implied author is virtually unrecognizable. Their shift towards a writing less hampered by its own self-consciousness is reflected in the work of many of the writers of the Changes as the 1990s wore on, and in the work of writers like Pelevin, Balla and Kahuda, who emerged in their wake and form the subject of the final chapter.

7 Learning to live with emptiness

Viktor Pelevin, Václav Kahuda, Vlado Balla

Irina Rodnianskaia begins her review of Pelevin's third novel, *Chapaev i Pustota*, with a quotation from Blaise Pascal:

> What then does this avidity and powerlessness cry to us, if not that there was once a true happiness in the human being, of which there remains now for him only an empty sign and trace, and which he tries needlessly to fill with all that surrounds him, seeking in absent things the succour that he cannot gain from present things. These things, however, cannot help, since this infinite abyss can only be filled by an infinite and immutable object, that is to say by God himself.
>
> (Pascal 1991: 226)

In the fiction of the Changes, this perception of human activity as a futile attempt to fill emptiness – in effect, to restore Eden – finds its metaphor in the acts of filling silence with speech or putting pen to paper. All the writers discussed here reject the use of writing apparently to assert a fixed, substantial world designed to replace or deny the emptiness of existence. Some, particularly Czech writers like Hodrová or Topol, present the activity of writing as a metaphor for the unceasing dynamic struggle of being against emptiness, comic but not ignoble resistance to the end which will none the less come.[1] Others, like Sorokin and Kolenič, use the seemingly compulsive need for human beings to assert their presence through words as a metaphor for the futility or inevitable noxiousness of human existence. Their work reflects a paradoxical yearning to give way to silence and emptiness once and for all. This final chapter focuses on works by Pelevin, Balla and Kahuda which represent simultaneously the culmination and the subversion of the strategies and techniques used by their immediate predecessors. In effect, Pelevin and Balla move towards the perspective of the Czechs, seeking to restore faith in the activity of creation, while Kahuda, by rejecting the sentimentalization of writing, moves towards the Russian and Slovak perspective. In the process, however, each writer finds a way of living with emptiness.

Kahuda's third novel, *Houština* (Thicket, 1999) begins with a description of how the narrator, as a toddler standing on a river bank, is born into consciousness of himself from the 'nameless timelessness' of eternity, represented by the blue of the sky which 'motionlessly floats away' (Kahuda 1999: 9). The narrator first describes how a town, a canoeists' hut, a sugar refinery and his shoes emerge from the landscape, then comments: 'I also sketch myself out, I separate myself from the glycerine, multi-coloured emptiness. Thanks to my sharp eyesight, thanks to my young eyes' (ibid.). This coming to self-consciousness is not, however, presented as an instant of self-discovery, in which the child begins to become aware of the physical world and of itself as an object within that world, but as an act of self-creation, a fascinated realization of the power of imagination. Kahuda here implicitly contrasts the reader's 'adult' interpretation, based on a confident belief in the reality of the physical world, with that of the child, who requires no firm, lasting definition of reality, but perceives himself as the unceasing creator and dissolver of his world. This perception of the child recalls Wordsworth's Romantic description of the infant in *The Prelude* as

> an inmate of this active universe.
> For feeling has to him imparted power
> That through the growing faculties of sense
> Doth like an agent of the one great Mind
> Create, creator and receiver both,
> Working but in alliance with the works
> Which it beholds.
>
> (Wordsworth 1994: 331)

Pelevin makes a similar contrast in *Chapaev i Pustota*, through the narrator, Pet'ka, who, as the post-Revolution Civil War rages, notices some children skating and remarks:

> while all the idiot adults are busy reconstructing the world they have invented, children continue to live in reality – amid the snowy hills and sunlight, on the black mirrors of frozen reservoirs and in the mystical silence of nocturnal, snow-covered yards. And although these children were also infected with the germ of madness which had attacked Russia [...] all the same the memory of something I had long forgotten still shone in their clear eyes; perhaps it was the unconscious recollection of the great source of all that exists, from which they, while going deeper into the shameful desert of life, had not yet had time to become too distanced.
>
> (Pelevin 1996: 88)

Whereas the children have no fear of emptiness, indicated by the images of blankness – snow, black mirrors and darkness – which surround them and are equated with reality, adults are no longer able to accept the reality of emptiness, but seek repeatedly to fill it by asserting the reality of their own inventions. In *Houština*, the narrator presents this behaviour as the artificial limitation of the activity of the imagination through the random designation of certain of its products as 'real': 'The world of ideas is a living hand. A hand which has drawn over its limpid, transparent fingers the rubber gloves of reality' (Kahuda 1999: 241). In common with writers like Hodrová, Ivanchenko and Tolstaia, both Kahuda and Pelevin aspire in their fiction to return to the child's way of seeing, not only as a preferred artistic position, but also as a stage towards liberating the mind from its attachment to a substantial reality. Kahuda's second novel, *Veselá bída* (Merry misery, 1997) ends with the lines:

> Through a child you will guess the secret of the world. And you will look it over from horizon to horizon. You will come to know the remote spaces at the end of the universe. And when you crash through the last black star, which is twinkling with horror, you will find yourself at the bottom, in the deepest crevice of your soul. And you will rise towards the surface, towards an eternal present, which is as simple as a forget-me-not on the bank of a stream, as simple as creation.
>
> (Kahuda 1997: 134)

In 'Ontologiia detstva' (The ontology of childhood), from his first publication, the collection of short stories, *Sinii fonar'* (The blue lantern, 1991), which was awarded the Little Booker Prize in 1994, Pelevin suggests that the moment of perceiving oneself as a physical object among physical objects, like that described by Kahuda in *Houština*, marks the beginning of the end of the happy creative innocence of childhood, and the gradual absorption of the child's mind into the adults' world of everyday terrestrial existence:

> it turns out that just by seeing this world one becomes sullied and participates in all its abominations – and in the evenings in the dead-ends of corridors and dark corners of cells there are many terrifying things. And just like that – like a magic trick – from the shifting mists of a childhood which is being forgotten emerges the comprehension that you were born and grew up in prison, in the filthiest, most stinking corner of the world. And when you finally grasp this, the rules of your prison begin to absorb you totally.
>
> (Pelevin 1991: 212–13)

In his second novel, *Zhizn' nasekomykh* (The life of insects, 1993), the title of which is taken from the play *Ze života hmyzu* (From the life of insects, 1921) by Josef Čapek (1887–1945) and Karel Čapek (1890–1938), Pelevin with an uncharacteristic lack of originality compares this existence to that of insects. In the chapter entitled 'Initsiatsiia' (Initiation), a young dung-beetle's curiosity and imagination is steadily eradicated by his 'slightly threatening' father, who teaches him that the meaning of life is to push his gradually expanding ball of dung – his

'Ia' (*Ich*) – along in front of him. 'Ia' is written 'Йa' rather than 'Я', a defamiliarization that satirizes its mystical, quasi-religious significance to the dung-beetles and therefore, implicitly, to contemporary society. Whereas in the Čapek brothers' play, the dung-beetle represents those human beings who devote their lives to material accumulation, in his chapter Pelevin turns that material accumulation into a metaphor for the notion of 'self-realization', equating the resultant 'self' with a ball of dung. Rodnianskaia describes what happens to the dung-beetle as the 'socialization of the personality' (Rodnianskaia 1993: 226), whereby the young dung-beetle learns to identify his self with a discrete physical object which, in accordance with the laws of physics, must follow a single specific path, thus permitting the continued smooth running of society. By the time the father has been trodden on, an indication from the implied authorial perspective of the actual ephemerality and expendability of the physically conceived self, the young dung-beetle's training is complete, as his utterly clichéd eulogy over his father's corpse demonstrates:

> I'll grow up big, I'll get married, I'll have children, and I'll teach them everything my dad taught me. And I'll be as kind to them as he was to me, and when I get old, they will take care of me and we'll all live a long and happy life.
>
> (Pelevin 1997: 184)

The dung-beetle's accumulation of self may be compared with Kahuda's implicit perception of the conventional nature of autobiography-writing in *Houština*. *Houština* itself is implicitly autobiographical, describing the narrator's life from early childhood in the late 1960s until the mid-1990s, but constitutes a reaction to the dominance of autobiography and overtly autobiographical fiction appearing in Czech literature in the 1990s. The sheer length of *Houština* – five hundred pages – mocks the 'physicality' of autobiographical writing, in which the experiences related steadily amount to a self, represented by the volume itself. In the novel, Kahuda uses autobiographical writing not to show the self that he has become, but to rid the mind of the very notion of the self. Vladimír Novotný describes the novel as an 'anti-*Erziehungsroman*, an anti-novel of coming of age' (Novotný 2000: 5). Like Pelevin, Kahuda perceives the imposition of the notion of the individual self by adults on children as an attempt to assert the civilizability of the human being; this merely serves to intensify homogeneity and encourage herd behaviour. In *Houština*, the narrator comments of adults:

> themselves unbalanced, unexpectedly giving way to fluctuations in feelings, they burden the weak, inexperienced child so that it will live and fulfil this dependency of its parents on its person. So that it can bear the burden of their terrified instincts, well knowing that its guardians see it not as it really is, but love that picture, that image in which the deformed picture of their world is mirrored, of the one that they love, their image of themselves. Woe betide the

> offspring which refuses to play the nurseling, the little fellow and ultimately the young man.
>
> (Kahuda 1999: 400)

The narrator of *Houština*, rejects the assertion, implicit in the notion of the individual self, that the physical individuation of the human being is matched by psychological individuation, declaring:

> What do I have in common with this flesh? And what about these thoughts? How on earth can this fleeting consciousness which will be blown away into oblivion in a second, how on earth can it calls itself 'I'? This pile of memories of a body [...] Where did this enormous arrogance and blindness that it can call itself 'I' come from?
>
> (Ibid.: 233)

Kahuda here echoes David Hume, who writes:

> I may venture to affirm to the rest of mankind that they are nothing but a bundle or collection of different perceptions, which succeed each other with an inconceivable rapidity, and are in a perpetual flux and movement.[...] What then gives us so great a propension to ascribe an identity to these successive perceptions, and to suppose ourselves possest of an invariable and uninterrupted existence thro' the whole course of our lives?
>
> (Hume 1978: 252–3)

Throughout his fiction, in an altogether more aggressive way than Pelevin's insect metaphors, Kahuda contrasts the activity of the mind with that of the body, which is shown to behave like a herd animal, in the thrall of biological functions and instincts; that is reflected in his anatomical depictions of urination, defecation, masturbation, vaginal and anal penetration and ejaculation. In his first published work, the very short novel, *Příběh o baziliškovi* (A story about a basilisk, 1992, dated as written 1988), Kahuda implicitly associates the veneration of the physical, equated in the story with filth and stench, with Marxism-Leninism, which engenders a homogeneous collective of deformed, sexually perverted physical selves. This is comparable with Sorokin's depiction of Soviet human beings eating faeces and committing ritualistic acts of violence in works like *Norma* and 'Pervyi subbotnik'.[2] Kahuda's story describes the life of Slezák, a retired guard from the Communist prison camp in Jáchymov who keeps a basilisk, repeatedly associated with the Devil, as a pet. Slezák is utterly beholden to the intense and exclusively physical experience of existence enjoyed by the basilisk, ultimately participating in sado-masochistic sexual intercourse with an apparently consenting youth. The first of several Kahuda characters to derive sexual pleasure from observing women defecate, Slezák is permitted to watch a certain Dr Eva defecate in return for fresh faeces, which Dr Eva hungrily devours. Dr Eva, perhaps the victim of a stroke, can only smile with one side of her face, an indication of the distorted and reduced nature of her existence.[3]

In *Příběh o baziliškovi*, Kahuda attempts to arouse the implied reader's disgust for the ordinary, rank-and-file collaborator, whose perversion reflects the nature and effects of the autocratic regime in which he has become embedded. In the later novels *Veselá bída* and *Houština*, however, he departs from the conventional demonizing of Marxism-Leninism in post-1989 Czech fiction, including that written by fellow members of the 1980s underground generation like Placák and Topol, implicitly presenting it as merely a stage in a process which began with the Czech national idea and continued with Masaryk's liberal individualism, for which Kahuda reserves his strongest invective. In the final chapter, the narrator refers to Masaryk as 'Tuchcáč Žarig Masorád', equating him with a forever pissing, meat-loving dog, and describes him as a 'totem of banality' and, in another insect metaphor, a 'beetle of hopes' (Kahuda 1999: 412, 419). For Kahuda, the latest manifestation of this assertion of the individual self is political correctness. The narrator comments:

> The level of humanity and the need to be caring towards fellow-citizens has reached such a degree that when an accident, a car accident or some other tragedy happens, the ethics service are the first on the scene. They surround the site of the accident with an opaque barrier.
>
> (Ibid.: 409)

Whereas in works like Topol's *Sestra*, Brabcová's *Zlodějina*, Hrabal's 'Listopadový uragán' (The November hurricane, 1990) and *Kobova garáž* (Koba's garage, 1992) by Zdeněk Zapletal (b.1951), the events of November 1989 in Czechoslovakia are presented as a sudden, disorientating, liberating change, in *Houština*, they apparently have no impact on the narrator and thus are not mentioned at all. In *Zhizn' nasekomykh*, Pelevin similarly mocks the hypocrisy of the 'importation' of Western liberal values, when the blood-sucking American mosquito-businessman, on hearing from the young Russian ant-prostitute with whom he has just slept about the horrors of crop-spraying, points out that at least she has 'insect rights' now (see Pelevin 1997: 290).

The rapturous reception which Russian critics accorded Pelevin's early works, especially his first novel, *Omon Ra* (1992), was above all motivated by a perceived change in the treatment of the Soviet experience from that found in Conceptualism, which for many indicated decisively the transition to a genuinely post-Soviet period. In a review of new fiction in 1992 expressing the widespread critical weariness with the Conceptualists, Sergei Kostyrko argues: 'Sots-art and postmodernism will appear to be independent, original trends until an artist is found who is capable of exploiting the material opened up by them precisely as material' (Kostyrko 1992: 256), before suggesting that Pelevin was just that artist. In Kostyrko's view, which echoes Boris Groys's decision to include the Conceptualists within his analysis of the 'total art of Stalinism', Conceptualist art could not be separated from the Soviet art and ideology it sought to deconstruct. In contrast, Pelevin, though working with the same cultural context, had moved away from pure opposition to explore 'metaphysical, eternal' problems. Writing in 1995, following the publication of *Zhizn' nasekomykh*, Genis concurred: 'Pelevin does not destroy; he builds. Using the same fragments of the Soviet myth as Sorokin, he constructs both subject-matter and concepts' (Genis 1999: 214).

In contrast to Sorokin's first novels and short stories, written in the early 1980s, in *Omon Ra* the Soviet system has lost its potency and becomes, like the deposed king in Bakhtin's account of the medieval carnival, a figure of fun. Whereas writers like Hodrová and Kratochvil explicitly borrow Bakhtin's notion of carnivalization as a literary technique, Pelevin's work resonates with the popular mood of liberation that infused intellectuals at the time of writing. In *Rabelais and His World*, Bakhtin writes that carnival feasts were 'linked to moments of crisis, of breaking points in the cycle of nature or in the life of society and man. Moments of death and revival, of change and renewal always led to a festive perception of the world' (Bakhtin 1984b: 9). Writers like Sorokin and Prigov correspond, in effect, to Bakhtin's description of the 'satirist whose laughter is negative', who 'places himself above the object of his mockery; he is opposed to it. The wholeness of the world's comic aspect is destroyed, and what appears comic becomes a private reaction' (ibid.: 12). By contrast, according to Sergei Chuprinin, Pelevin's burlesquing of Soviet and post-Soviet reality 'left no one feeling offended' (Chuprinin 1993: 182), thus in effect reflecting Bakhtin's assertion that

> carnival laughter is the laughter of all the people [...] it is universal in scope; it is directed at all and everyone, including the carnival's participants. The entire world is seen in its droll aspect [...] this laughter is ambivalent; it is gay, triumphant, and at the same time mocking, deriding. It asserts and denies, it buries and revives.
>
> (Bakhtin 1984b: 11)

The universality of Pelevin's laughter was reflected in his instant commercial success, which for many critics represented a final break with Soviet literary culture. Writing in 1993 on the problems facing literature with the introduction of market forces, Sergei Chuprinin identified Pelevin as the type of writer likely to survive in these new circumstances because of his ability to overcome the distinction between élite and popular culture, to win commercial success at the same time as critical acclaim and therefore, in Fiedler's terms, 'cross the border, close the gap'. In Chuprinin's view, while the 'postmodernists, Conceptualists and other "-ists"' had followed a path to academic élitism, through Pelevin 'the zone of artistic risk and of shocking innovation has moved closer to the line which divides (connects?) high art and the mass-market books which our critics loathe' (Chuprinin 1993:182).

Nowhere was this shift more apparent than in the success of *Chapaev i Pustota*, which briefly returned the sales of the journal *Znamia* to *glasnost'*-period levels when it was published there in successive issues in 1996. Viacheslav Kuritsyn describes 1996 as the 'year of the birth of the new Russia', when, after several false starts, Russia voted decisively against Communism and proved it could survive while the President was seriously ill (Kuritsyn 1997: 12). This mood of optimism appeared to be reflected not only in the enthusiastic reception of Pelevin's novel, but also in the extravagantly self-confident length and breadth of the novel itself. Kuritsyn identifies Pelevin's readers as 'those whom we don't have, but whom we need, the middle-class, rumours of whose existence are gradually beginning to be proven true, the layer which affords a society stability' (ibid.: 8). Nikolai Aleksandrov, who himself found the work flawed, nevertheless described the novel as the 'undoubted literary event of the year' (Aleksandrov 1997: 27), and lent his voice to the widespread criticism of the 1997 Russian Booker Prize jury, whose failure to short-list the novel demonstrated the enduring resistance of Russia's mainstream literary intelligentsia to any hints of commercialism. In effect, rather like Pišťanek in Slovakia, who 'crossed the border and closed the gap' in post-Changes literature there slightly earlier, Pelevin's work became synonymous with the explosion of the market economy in 1990s Russia, and enormously popular with its actual and potential beneficiaries – the so-called 'new Russians' and the young – despite the fact that, particularly after *Omon Ra*, the central target of his satire, like Pišťanek's, is precisely the amoral barbarism of the new consumer society.

In *Omon Ra*, Pelevin, rather like Kahuda, presents the Soviet system as a symptom rather than the cause of the belief in the identity of the self with the body. In the model of self-realization that flows from this belief, the mind, in imitation of the body, must find and submit to a single direction forward, which at one point, for a great many people, proved to be the Soviet direction. Early in *Omon Ra*, the narrator and central character, Omon, articulates this understanding of the purpose of life when he comments: 'In early childhood (as, perhaps, also after death), a human being moves in all directions at once, therefore one may consider that he does not yet exist; the personality emerges later, when an attachment to one single direction appears' (Pelevin 1997: 25). This prescriptive notion of the development of the self is first encapsulated in Omon's name, in which 'om', the 'basic sound of the universe' (Harvey 1990: 136) in the Vedas, becomes 'on' ('he'), the concrete, individuated self, and, second, exemplified by the Socialist Realist *Bildungsroman* structure which Pelevin parodies in the work.[4]

Omon devotes his life to becoming a Soviet cosmonaut, training for a mission to plant a radio beacon on the Moon, after which he is supposed to shoot himself, because the Soviet Union cannot spare the fuel for his return journey. His discovery of his 'single direction' is indicated by the red line drawn on the map of the Moon to show the route of his moon-mobile. During a demonstration, however, a model of the moon-mobile rolls along the line, off the table and on to the floor, recalling the objections made when Columbus suggested the world was round. Pelevin here inverts the situation, poking fun at those who believe in the *Bildungsroman* model of existence by implicitly equating them with those who claimed the world was flat. Like the journey of the model moon-mobile, Omon's path to glorious self-realization ends bathetically when his revolver malfunctions, a metaphor for the collapsing Soviet military-industrial complex. At this point he is torn out of the Socialist Realist fairy-tale and plunged, with the reader, into a Western science-fiction thriller, a structure which serves as a metaphor for the sudden and chaotic westernization of the late Soviet period, comparable to the 'explosion of time' that motivates the disorientating narrative in Topol's *Sestra*. Utterly confused, Omon is pursued across the Moon by people trying to kill him, before finally escaping into what turns out to be the Lenin Library Metro station. Even then, however, Omon does not fully realize that the Soviet space programme appears to have taken place entirely in a disused Metro tunnel. In the final lines of the novel, he continues to think of himself in terms of a physical object. Standing in the Metro train, he comments: 'I raised my eyes to the route-plan hanging on the wall beside the emergency-brake button, and began trying to see where exactly on the red line I was' (Pelevin 1997: 152).

In parodic imitation of Socialist Realist fiction, Pelevin dedicates the novel to the 'Heroes of the Soviet Cosmos'. In the context of the conclusion, the dedication appears to refer not to the cosmonauts, who may not even have existed, but to all those who submitted their lives in the Soviet-ordered world, particularly those, like Omon, the implied author and reader, who by luck rather than by design managed to survive. Writing on the mass heroization of the Soviet people under Lenin and especially Stalin, Rosalind Sartorti comments: 'heroic behaviour had become a "civic duty", not only for the few but for everybody. It was transformed into an "innate" characteristic of Soviets, as pronounced by official Soviet discourse' (Sartorti 1995: 178). The hero's rite of passage in the Socialist Realist novel conventionally stood for the progress of the nation towards the Marxist-Leninist ideal, as Katerina Clark points out:

> In Socialist Realist fiction, the Soviet "divine plan of salvation," or Marxist-Leninist account of History, is condensed by means of highly codified conventions and told as a tale. This tale is of a questing hero who sets out in search of "consciousness". [...] On the one hand, he has before him a task from the public sphere. [...] But his second, and more important, goal is to resolve within himself the tension between "spontaneity" and "consciousness". Since the public and private goals are fused, the hero's personal resolution becomes a historical allegory.
>
> (Clark 1981: 162)

Pelevin parodies this allegorical function in *Omon Ra*, using Omon as a metaphor for the Soviet people, presented not as helpless victims of tyranny, but, as in Sorokin's fiction, as participants in an act of collective self-delusion from which they have had a lucky escape. Omon reveals little of the 'spontaneity' supposed to mark out the Socialist Realist hero. On the contrary, unlike his clever, inquisitive and sceptical friend Mitek, who 'disappears' following a 'reincarnation examination' which suggests that he had been a subversive element in each of his many former lives, Omon resembles Voltaire's Candide, dogged, obedient, passive and incorrigibly naive. Early in the novel, an old man tells how he and his sado-masochistically named son, Marat, used to impersonate bears when leading Soviet and foreign dignitaries went hunting, until one day Kissinger stabbed Marat, who bled to death because his father, to sustain the pretence, could not go to his aid. Pelevin suggests that Kissinger knew the bear was not real, and by stabbing it, indicated that he had seen through the Soviet illusion. This detail also reflects a recurrent anti-Western attitude in the 'fiction of the Changes', which distinguishes it from other implicitly or explicitly anti-regime fiction in the late Communist and early post-Communist period. When Omon later prepares himself for suicide, he is frustrated that all he can think of is Marat, unable to grasp that their fates, as men willing to sacrifice their lives to the deception of Soviet reality, are identical:

> I [...] tried to remember the most important thing in my short existence, but nothing came into my head except the story of Marat [...] it seemed awkward and offensive that I should die with this thought, which had nothing whatsoever to do with me.
>
> (Pelevin 1997: 139)

Omon's reaction recalls that of Makar Devushkin in Dostoevsky's first novel, *Poor Folk* (1846), who criticizes the lack of verisimilitude in Gogol's short story 'The overcoat' (1842), unable or unwilling to recognize himself in the central character.

This episode exemplifies how Pelevin, in contrast to Sorokin, tempers his criticism with a certain implied authorial sympathy, and indeed empathy with 'those who were deceived and deceived themselves' (Rodnianskaia 1996: 215). The shared sense of relief permits the grim absurdity of the Soviet period to become comic in Pelevin's work. The implied author's sympathy even extends to those knowingly engaged in perpetuating the illusion, like Omon's military instructors Urchagin and Burchagin, who, instead of guiding Omon to 'consciousness' of the truth of Marxism-Leninism, repeatedly expose its disintegration.[5] Sergei Kostyrko writes: 'We may speak here of the tragedy of people convinced of the impossibility of embodying their idea in reality and presenting society not with life, but with its TV version, a theatre of shadows' (Kostyrko 1992: 257). This empathy with the reader disappears only in Pelevin's fourth and critically least successful novel, *Generation P* (1999), in which he becomes more of a 'satirist whose laughter is negative'. The work expresses disillusion and despair, thus perhaps once again reflecting the popular mood, but is permeated by implied authorial frustration at the unthinking adoption of

Western capitalism and media manipulation in Russia and perhaps particularly the failure of readers to learn the lessons of his earlier fiction, in which he points out the dangers of becoming imprisoned in a manufactured reality.

Throughout *Omon Ra*, Pelevin characterizes the effects of committing oneself to the 'Soviet Cosmos' as the replacement of the natural with the artificial. As Norman Shneidman points out, the key intertextual reference in the novel is the best-selling hagiographic account of the Second World War pilot, Aleksei Mares'ev, *Povest' o nastoiashchem cheloveke* (The story of a real man, 1946) by Boris Polevoi (1908–81), which was made into a hugely popular film in 1948 (see Shneidman 1995: 167). Sartorti describes how Mares'ev, a Soviet counterpart to Douglas Bader, survived being shot down by the Germans and crawled back to Soviet territory, where he was given artifical limbs which enabled him to take to the skies again (Sartorti 1995: 180). In *Omon Ra*, at the flying school named after Mares'ev, the new recruits are made into 'real men' by having their legs cut off and replaced with artificial limbs.

This physical violence is equated with the attempts of ordinary people to adapt their children to the 'new world' by inventing names from Soviet phenomena, typified by the unfortunate Squadron Leader Pkhadzer Vladilenovich Pidorenko. His parents could apparently do nothing about his surname, which suggests 'pederast', but produced his first name from the acronym of 'Party Economic Activists of the Dzerzhinskii District', while his father's name, genuinely used in the Soviet period, is a contraction of Vladimir I. Lenin. Moreover, the reader is told, taken together Pkhadzer and Vladilen have fifteen letters in Russian, corresponding to the number of Soviet republics. Omon himself was given his name because his father wanted him to have a successful career in the police (OMON is the acronym for the Soviet and post-Soviet Special Branch). This desire to ordain Omon's destiny founders, however, in the face of the multiple interpretations of the name. Omon later adds the epithet Ra to evoke Amun-Ra, the Egyptian god with the falcon's head, in an attempt to associate himself with the polar airmen, who were known as 'Stalin's Falcons'. (For a discussion of their feats, their leading role in the creation of Stalinist culture and the popular reaction to them, see McCannon 1997: 346–65.) The words of their anthem, 'Vse vyshe' (Ever Higher) – 'Reason gave us steel wings for arms / And in the place of a heart they gave us a fiery motor' (quoted in Clark 1981: 138) – typify the confusion of the symbolic and the material in Stalinism, satirically imitated by Pelevin in the novel. By noting the condescending assertion in Omon's Soviet dictionary that the ancient Egyptians created the 'poetic myth' of Amun-Ra because they did not have the scientific knowledge to determine that the Earth orbits the Sun, Pelevin implicitly draws attention to the 'poetic myth' of Marxism-Leninism. At the same time, through Omon, he suggests a subconscious yearning for other 'ways of seeing', effaced by the 'Soviet cosmos'.

Pelevin's presentation of the Soviet experiment as an attempt to reincarnate the physical through words recalls the vain attempts by Tolstaia's characters in her 1980s stories to escape the bleak mundanity of daily life by imposing a brighter, invented alternative, an activity which implicitly refers to the aspirations of Soviet myth-making. The outcome, however, is the artificial ugliness of Denisov's monument or Pkhadzer's name. At the beginning of *Omon Ra*, Omon indicates that his desire to go into space is motivated by a desire to escape the oppressive homogeneity of terrestrial existence:

> I understood once and for all that only weightlessness could give a human being genuine freedom – that's why, incidentally, throughout my life Western radio voices and the works of various Solzhenitsyns aroused such boredom in me. In my soul I, of course, felt loathing for a state whose threatening demands forced any group, even if it only formed for a few seconds, to imitate assiduously the most obscene of its members, but realizing that peace and freedom could not be achieved on Earth, I aspired in spirit to the heavens.
>
> (Pelevin 1997: 27)

In Pelevin's subsequent works, this yearning upwards marks out those destined for enlightenment, like Dima, the moth seeking the light in *Zhizn' nasekomykh*, and Pet'ka, the Symbolist poet in *Chapaev i Pustota*. Omon's error is to believe that the physical can be reincarnated, that the ideal can be realized in the physical world. At the end of the novel, he finds himself sitting next to an old woman with her shopping, which Kostyrko describes as a 'symbol of the fatal immobility and unchanging nature of the *byt* of Soviet human beings' (Kostyrko 1992: 257).[6] The transformation of Omon's linear journey into a circle recalls Erofeev's *Moskva–Petushki*, the work with which this study began, except that where Venichka's journey is implicitly that of the Russian intellectual through history, Omon's is that of the masses. The fact that Omon's journey, unlike Venichka's, does not end in death, however, suggests a more optimistic mood in 1992 than in 1969. For Pelevin, as the cautionary nature of Omon Ra indicates, the disintegration of the 'Soviet cosmos' offers the post-Soviet everyman the chance not to enthrone a new cosmos, but to free himself from his absorption in the physical once and for all.

Pelevin's subsequent fiction, set in the early post-Soviet period, suggests, however, that those who have survived the 'Soviet cosmos', while no longer having any ambitions to reincarnate the flesh, have instead embedded themselves in a way of life utterly subordinate to the limits and needs of the body. In her discussion of early post-Soviet literary conditions, Ivanova argues that Pelevin's writing typically reflects the 'triumph of the ideology of consumption, which corresponds to the biological nature of the human being (unlike all other ideologies)' (Ivanova 1993: 192). Rather as Kahuda places Marxism-Leninism on a continuum of 'official morality', in *Chapaev i Pustota*, one of the patients undergoing psychiatric treatment with Pet'ka blames both Marxism-Leninism and market economics on Aristotle, whom he perceives as the father of materialism. Pelevin indicates his own scepticism regarding Aristotle's theory of substance when, in the ensuing quarrel, Pet'ka is struck on the head by the bust of Aristotle which they have been painting. The bust turns out to be hollow, and Pet'ka reflects how much worse it would have been if the bust had been of Plato.

Whereas in *Omon Ra*, like Tolstaia in her 1980s fiction, Pelevin satirizes people's attempts to impose grandiose inventions on bleak reality, in his later fiction, like Pišťanek, he mocks their lack of imagination. In 'Zheltaia strela' (The yellow arrow, 1992), Pelevin depicts post-Soviet Russia as a train hurtling inexorably towards a ruined bridge, a more disillusioned interpretation of Gogol's image in *Dead Souls* (1842) of Russia as a troika rushing forward, not fully certain of its direction but nevertheless charged with a mission. As Gerald McCausland points out, Pelevin only gradually makes the reader aware that the action of the work is taking place on a train, thus indicating that the people on board have become so embedded in this existence that they appear no longer aware that they are on a train, and equate leaving the train with death (see McCausland 2000: 226).

In this work, Pelevin explicitly distances himself from the Conceptualists through the character of the postmodernist painter, Anton. According to the central character, Andrei, Anton's work has become repetitious and therefore descended into kitsch. Anton, however, responds: 'There's life and on the other hand there's art, creation. Sots-art, Conceptualism, the modern, the postmodern. I stopped confusing them with life a long time ago. I've got a wife, a child on the way; that's what's serious, Andrei' (Pelevin 1998: 46). Having exposed the complicity of art in Soviet oppression, Pelevin suggests, the Conceptualists appear happy now to co-opt art into consumerism, the new form of oppression, in order to make a living. Rather as Pišťanek mocks the young Slovak would-be avant-garde, in *Zhizn' nasekomykh* Pelevin further asserts the inconsequentiality of postmodernist artists by portraying them as drug-addled hemp bugs who combust in an American's spliff. In their hands, art has lost its capacity to express the spiritual dimension of existence; Pelevin asserts his intention to restore this through his account of Andrei's passage from the train into Nirvana at the end of the work.

In her review of *Zhizn' nasekomykh*, Rodnianskaia suggests that the secondary characters embody various ways of life adopted in the post-Soviet period to give life meaning, including business, home-building, prostitution and recreational drug use (see Rodnianskaia 1993: 217). All reflect the chaos of the Changes and represent individual attempts to find a refuge from that chaos. This creation of an illusion of ordered existence in an attempt to block out chaos is also satirized by Balla in his first collection of short stories, *Leptokária* (1996). Balla, however, refers here not to the socio-political chaos prompted by the sudden absence of an officially-approved way of life, as in Pelevin, but the ever-present chaos of desire. Whereas in *Houština*, Kahuda associates attempts to deny or eradicate this desire with the imposition of an officially ordained notion of reality, Balla portrays such attempts as a private activity, in essence an act of self-denial. For example, in 'Úzkosť' (Anxiety), the central character's life possesses a comforting rhythm through his regular seduction and abandonment of women, until one day he suddenly falls in love and is himself rejected. While wandering drunk in the countryside, he discovers a shed containing a mass of bleeding human limbs and penises, intertwined as though in the form of a hideous creature, the embodiment of the turmoil which has suddenly been exposed within him. The creature recalls Ovid's description of Chaos at the beginning of *The Metamorphoses*: 'a shapeless, uncoordinated mass, nothing but a weight of lifeless matter, whose ill-assorted elements were indiscriminately heaped together in one place' (Ovid 1955: 29). Apparently unable to bear this vision, the drunken protagonist sobers up and reverts to his former life-style. At the end of the story, having once again erased desire from his life, he cannot comprehend the jealousy of the husband of one of his conquests, who sticks a pitch-fork in his unfaithful wife's back.

The pain of desire described by Balla may be compared with Hodrová's notion of *trýzeň* in her trilogy, an unceasing longing to escape intermediacy which is inseparable from human existence. In *Kukly*, Mr Turek comments that only some people experience life as metamorphosis. Mr Turek does not wish to say whether this is good or bad for them, but remarks: 'It is certain that the instant of metamorphosis causes them agony, a pain bordering on pleasure, which those others do not know' (Hodrová 1999: 267). Those who manage to shield themselves from this experience appear in *Kukly*, as in *Podobojí*, to be those most firmly embedded in day-to-day material existence, like the caretaker of the block of flats or the shopkeeper. In 'Jaskyňa' (The cave), Balla suggests that to try to blunt the pain of desire is to seek to reduce the experience of living. The story describes how a group of students travelling in the countryside hear of a secret cave which the locals believe has the power to ease the pain of living. One villager comments: 'I know that the cave in fact just dulls the pain. Except…except even for that kind of relief we're grateful! The diseases have remained, true enough, for the diseases are somewhere very deep, but they don't hurt any more' (Balla 1996: 122).

Those who visit the cave return with one finger missing, a reference to Tolstoy's short story 'Father Sergii' (1911), in which a hermit priest cuts off his finger to force himself to forget his desire for a woman. Unlike Tolstoy, however, Balla, who appears as an actant in the tale, finds nothing admirable in this self-mutilation, and alone of his companions refuses to visit the cave. His refusal to relinquish desire may be seen to do him no good, because the object of his desire, Andrea, does visit the cave, and on her return, one finger short, she rejects his clumsy advances, apparently because she regards him as evil. However, he may have attempted to seduce her only because he knew she would refuse. The narrator of the title story asserts the need for the story not to preserve but to disrupt the existing order, commenting: 'A story which is not impossible is trivial' (Balla 1996: 146). In the same way, Balla is interested only in desire which is impossible, which cannot be realized, because such desire constitutes the source of creativity.

This contrast between the pursuit and the denial of satisfaction is expressed in 'Odpočinok' (A rest), in which the narrator scornfully observes how a young couple in a pub attempt to enclose themselves in a self-perpetuating shell of domesticity:

> That young man is the demiurge of his world, into which he will take Jana. Jana is also just a word. They will make a cycle for themselves. First of all they were children; soon they'll have their own children. If those two are healthy, they'll make a cycle for themselves. Nothing will touch them from outside, for the young man's world isn't outside.
>
> (Ibid.: 89)

The establishment of a 'normal' family life is shown to be an act of fictionalizing by the comment that 'Jana is also just a word'. The young man may ordain whatever self he chooses for 'Jana', but that has no basis in reality. In contrast to the young man, the narrator seduces married women, taking them to the point of penetration before feigning impotence. He says: 'My concern is the implantation of evil, of decay, and above all of uncertainty and mistrust. Let the essence of evil at least be freedom' (ibid.: 93). The substitution of contentment for desire constitutes for Balla an act of imprisonment, whereas unfulfilled desire represents absolute freedom, in which all possibilities remain.

Before *Leptokária*, however, those writers like Tomáš Horváth, Marek Vadas and Tom von Kamin, labelled the Genitalists, wrote pointedly lightweight texts which sustained the assertion of the futility of writing expressed in Koleníč and the self-styled Barbarians, albeit more playfully. For example, Horváth's doggedly intertextual collection of parody stories and essays, *Akozmia* (1992), regularly refers to Existentialist, post-Structuralist and Phenomenological texts, above all to demonstrate how the post-Structuralist attempt to liberate the text from dogma becomes itself a dogma which disarms the text. As a result, however, his writing suffers from the same dependency on its sources as Russian critics observed in the work of the Conceptualists. This dependency is reflected in the title, which is a pun on 'acosmia' and the Slovak for 'like a viper', a reference to venomous-tongued woman, or 'like a snake', a reference to the image of the Uroboros, understood here as a metaphor not for time, but for the text which turns in on itself, seeking to leave its reader speechless and helpless.

Balla's intention to break with this dependency is reflected in his use of the metaphor of sexual impotence in 'Odpočinok' and other stories in *Leptokária*. As discussed in the last chapter, Koleníč repeatedly uses sexual impotence as a metaphor for the impotence of the writer, for example in *Mlčať* the narrator compares communication to the slithering of a limp penis on the labia of a vagina. The Genitalists link this rejection of the traditional notion in Slovak literature of the 'potent', world-shaping writer with a general satirization of the Slovak male stereotype, most obviously in von Kamin's *I. alebo Žltý penis* (Volume One, or The yellow penis, 1996), in which writing is presented as a substitute for 'real life'. Haunted by a yellow penis which appears at his window to mock him, the narrator, in playful imitation of Sheherezade (a favourite of post-Structuralist and feminist theorists), feverishly writes the parody picaresque text of the novel to delay the moment when he has to go into the bedroom next-door and satisfy – or fail to satisfy – the woman who is eagerly anticipating him there.

In *Leptokária*, Balla very much continues the social satirization of masculinity, but at the same time transforms sexual impotence from a condition of weakness into an ideal state for the writer, the endless promise of creation that is never finally realized. In the context of Balla's writing, the outright assertion of potency or impotence constitutes a position of comfort or self-satisfaction, whereas the feigned impotence – or feigned potency – in 'Odpočinok' represents a position between potency and impotence from which, in Lipovetskii's phrase, a 'dialogue with chaos' may be interminably conducted. The nature of this location is expressed in the story 'Pustovník' (The hermit), in which the narrator's friend refuses to sleep with the woman the narrator has made from sand, because, the narrator suggests, he was hoping for a threesome. The narrator comments:

> of course, under no circumstances would there have been any sort of threesome that evening, because I wouldn't have taken part in the act, but both he and she could have got what they wanted. I would have had a drink and observed the pair and I would have deliberately moved as close as I could and leaned over them and watched their bodies, their movements and scents, to become most clearly aware of how alien it all was to me, this sincere joy, this surrender to a partner, a surrender without pretence.
>
> (Balla 1996: 52)

For Balla, writing constitutes the implicitly endless negotiation of this voyeuristic position, at once most intensely involved in the fulfilment of desire and most completely detached from it. This perception of writing compares, in the context of this study, not only to Ajvaz's notion of the writer moving endlessly between Chaos and Cosmos, but also to Hodrová's notion of the threshold in her trilogy and to Kratochvil's 'lamb in bear's clothing', although in contrast to Kratochvil Balla is concerned more about texts which lack rather than wield power.[7]

Balla's rejection of the helplessness of the writer in *Leptokária* brings him close to the perspective of the leading Slovak feminist prose writer of the 1990s, Jana Juráňová. Her novel *Utrpenie starého kocúra* (The sufferings of an old tom-cat, 2001) is, in its own way, a version of the in-joke-filled 'gossip-novel', set in the small world of the Bratislava intelligentsia, employed by several of the Genitalists. At the same time, however, it constitutes a feminist response to Vilikovský's attempt in the story 'Eskalácia citu 1' (The escalation of emotion 1, 1989) to describe the experience of rape from the perspective of its victim, a wheelchair-bound woman. Vilikovský's story, written in the 1970s, makes a sincere attempt to relativize or at least problematize the question of authorial gender. Juráňová, however, presents it as symptomatic of an attempt by the male Slovak author to absorb all perspectives within his own.

The first part of *Utrpenie starého kocúra* describes how a conformist female intellectual is rendered helpless by the disappearance of her lover, a leading writer, who is immediately declared dead and nationally mourned. In effect, she allows herself to be imprisoned by the announcement of the 'death of the author'. In the second part of the novel, it transpires, however, that the writer has merely been kidnapped by Zuzana, the wheelchair-bound woman whose rape, reported in the press, had inspired his story, in revenge for his claiming to know how she felt. Throughout the novel, Juráňová satirizes the male writer's preoccupation with the theme of identity as nothing more than pointless self-absorption, and rather mocks his vague notions of empathy and understanding as means of sustaining his extra-marital affairs. His ineffectuality contrasts with Zuzana's strength, which her appearance of vulnerability and powerlessness belies. In essence, Juráňová's fiction, like that of the more commercially successful Michal Hvorecký (b.1976), whose first collection, *Silný pocit čistoty* (A strong feeling of purity) was published in 1998, seeks to break with the Existentialist-influenced themes of writers like Johanides and Vilikovský that have effectively dominated Slovak 'urban' fiction since the 1960s. The male author, the 'old tom-cat' may assert his weakness, suggests Juráňová, but the female is not obliged to feel the same.

Whereas Juráňová's fiction tends towards a moralizing essentially at odds with the inclinations of the 'fiction of the Changes', Balla seeks simply to suggest that a literature that reflects on its own exhaustion need not be exhausted. Instead of a single swing from an extreme of integrated meaning, understood as the co-operation or complicity of author and reader in the manufacture of a shared world in realist writing, to an extreme of disintegrated meaning, Balla advocates a constant, unsettling oscillation between the two extremes, dramatized in the very title of the story 'Večerná úzkosť. Pieseň plavecká' (Evening anxiety. A swimmer's song), a disordering of the more conventional 'Evening song. A swimmer's anxiety'. In this story, Balla depicts the writer as a poor swimmer, struggling between the surface, the veneer of order obscuring what lies beneath, and the depths, the chaos of the unconscious, in which contradictions co-exist and everything is possible. One of the narrators declares:

> let the talk be of the surface, for beneath it is the world: its energy, movement, events, multicoloured, blinding light… The calmer and darker the surface, the more mysterious the depths it hides: or rather, it does not hide: the depths are simply covered by the surface: the surface does not know about anything. Beneath the surface is everything – both the Bible and the impossibility of a god.
>
> (Balla 1996: 37)

As elsewhere in the collection, the story oscillates between the metaphor and its actualization, creating an experience of uncertainty for the reader. The third-person narration in the piece describes a young writer who, rather as Ajvaz's sculptor constantly exposes himself to the dangers of the underground lake, cannot resist repeatedly returning to a lake to swim, despite nearly drowning each time. The writer shows no signs of wanting to become a better swimmer, since knowing how to swim would keep him on the surface, making him a collectivizing writer, a perpetuator of surfaces. On the contrary, in fact, the young man is drawn to the lake by the lure of the depths. At one point, in an implicit reference to the Slovak writer's enduring duty to sustain the Slovak language as a guarantor of Slovak nationhood, he declares that he longs to be part of a nation of people who cannot make themselves understood to each other. The realization of this longing, however, is equated with the drowning of the writer at the end of the story; Balla posits here an alternative 'death of the author', in which the author disappears in his exploration of the depths of his self and becomes lost to the reader. The writer cannot completely lose contact with the surface, but must seek constantly to penetrate and subvert it to avoid becoming a denier of desire, and therefore of life.

This position between the surface and the depths is reflected in the co-existence of the notion of the single individual self matching the body and its rejection in the narrative structure of the story. In the story, the third-person narration describing the young writer is interspersed with the first-person narration of a writer, and also with the commentary of an unmarked third narrative voice. The fluctuation between narrative voices does not simply represent an alternation of external and internal perspectives on the same character. Rather, the young writer is apparently the subject of the text the first-person narrator is writing, while the first-person narrator may be the subject of the third narrative voice, and each represents a fictional self-characterization of his narrator. The reader may therefore choose either to reduce these voices to identification with a single authorial self, or to accept them as a representation of the chaos inherent in selfhood. Balla essentially parodies here the altogether more earnest anxiety about the nature of the self expressed, for example, in Kolenič's *Mlčať* or Litvák's *Samoreč*. At one point, one of the narrators comments: 'Someone caught me by the shoulders. 'Do you recognize yourself? Is it still you? Your body?' 'Yes, it's me… My body.' I'm holding myself by the shoulders' (ibid.: 42). Like Pelevin and Kahuda, Balla is untroubled by questions of self-preservation or self-discovery, presenting the notion of the individual self as part of the language of the surface, an invention designed to make life easier, and populating his collection with a series of alter-egos, sometimes unnamed, or sometimes called Balla, Martin Ajn, or just Ajn (the German *Ein*), which playfully suggests the existence of a prototype from which the other alter-egos develop. In his rather disappointing novel, *Outsideria*, Balla uses all the personal pronouns singular and plural in turn in an attempt to assert their arbitrariness.

Balla's response to the techniques of his contemporaries closely resembles that of Pelevin to Conceptualism. Perceiving in the work of their predecessors an apparent effacement of the imagination, both seek out a threshold position from which writing may be seen again as a productive process, expressing the unceasing creative activity of the imagination. Citing a passage from 'Ontologiia detstva' in which Pelevin describes the child's view from a window, Genis writes:

> In Pelevin's stories everything takes place on the 'windowsill', the border between different worlds. Every border both underlines and creates difference. But a border not only divides, it also unites. The more numerous the borders, the more border zones proliferate. […] The author of the new post-Soviet literature is a poet, a philosopher, and a physiologist of these border areas. He dwells in the zone where realities collide. The site of this contact generates expressive artistic effects: one picture of the world succeeds another, creating a third that is distinct from the first two.
>
> (Genis 1999: 217)

This effect is epitomized by characters who are both human beings and insects in *Zhizn' nasekomykh*; similarly, in the story 'Živočích' (Animal) in *Leptokária*, the narrator keeps a pet which appears simultaneously to be a mouse and a spider. Developing Genis's argument, Gerald McCausland suggests that Pelevin, in effect, returns in his writing to the beginnings of Sots-Art in visual art. For McCausland, the 'false perception set up in many of [Pelevin's] stories derives not from language games, but from sensory, above all, visual tricks' (McCausland 2000: 228–9). By contrast, Sorokin's aggressive 'frame-breaks' may be seen as an attempt to prevent words from becoming an image in the reader's mind by providing a counter-image which exposes both images as nothing but letters on a page. This fear of the consequences of any creative act, directly associated with the imposition of a single invented notion of reality in the Soviet period, is no longer present in Pelevin's writing. Pelevin's response to the attempt to impose a single meaning upon words is rather, somewhat like Hodrová, to assert the multiplicity of co-existing meanings which arises from this attempt.

This approach is typified in Pelevin's work by his exploitation of the figure of Chapaev in *Chapaev i Pustota*. Historically a local Red Army leader during the Civil War, in the 1920s Chapaev became the subject of a Socialist Realist reportage by Dmitrii Furmanov (1891–1926), and then, in the 1930s, of a hugely popular film, in which Pet'ka was a clumsy but earnest peasant soldier. Following the film, Chapaev and Pet'ka became stock characters in Russian jokes. In *Chapaev i Pustota*, the writer of the parody foreword claims that Chapaev was 'in fact' a Buddhist teacher, and Pet'ka his disciple.[8] However, as Nikolai Aleksandrov points out, noting Pelevin's frequent use of 'na samom dele' (in fact), in Pelevin's writing there is, in fact, no 'in fact' (Aleksandrov 1997: 27); Chapaev exists equally and simultaneously in all these versions. In the novel, Pelevin implicitly extrapolates this situation to assert the absurdity of the human being's efforts to identify his self with a single space, time and direction, as Omon continues to do at the end of *Omon Ra*. In *Chapaev i Pustota*, Pelevin seeks to teach the reader not to look for himself on the plan of the Metro, but to see himself represented by that plan, as the first stage in the reversal of the journey from 'om' to 'on'. The Metro-plan image recalls Hodrová's conception of the self in *Kukly* as a labyrinth or spider's web, a 'place in which past and future events run together like the radii of a circle'.

Chapaev i Pustota may be seen as sequel to *Omon Ra*, beginning at the point where that novel ends, with Russia still trying to establish exactly what it is. The same desire to abandon the notion of the individual self appears in Czech fiction of the 1990s only with the work of Kahuda, in particular *Houština*. This identity crisis is represented by the schizophrenic central character, Pet'ka, like Omon a metaphor for Russia. In the novel, Pet'ka believes he is a Symbolist poet in 1919, suffering a delusion that he is a patient in a Moscow psychiatric hospital in the early 1990s, while in the hospital the staff believe the reverse. Rodnianskaia notes that the periods 'rhyme' as times of turmoil in which Russia seeks a new direction. Like Hodrová, Pelevin attempts to remove any sense of the uniqueness of a particular historical situation by presenting history as a kaleidoscopic repetitive cycle. While Hodrová, however, suggests that this cycle is inescapable, Pelevin blames it on a persistent belief that such periods of 'crisis' must be 'resolved' through the adoption of a single direction forward.

In *Chapaev i Pustota*, that single direction is advocated by Pet'ka's psychiatrist, Timur Timurovich. His name alludes to Egor Timurovich Gaidar, the architect of the 'shock therapy' economic reforms of the early 1990s through which Russia was to be transformed into a market economy, not only through the shared patronymic, but also because Timur was the hero of a novel by the children's author Arkadii Gaidar (1904–41), the economist's grandfather, set during the Russian civil war. According to Timur, Pet'ka has created a highly developed false personality because he is unable to accept the new situation in which he and Russia find themselves. Seen from Timur's perspective, Pet'ka's condition corresponds closely to R.D. Laing's description of schizophrenia in *The Divided Self*. Laing suggests that while most people identify themselves with their bodies, the schizophrenic experiences himself as 'unembodied' (Laing 1969: 66). This denial of one's physical existence in linear time and three-dimensional space corresponds to the persistent attempt to escape *byt*, typified by Omon's flight into space, and also documented in Tolstaia's stories. This denial results in a vacuum, indicated in Pelevin's novel by Pet'ka's surname, Pustota, meaning 'emptiness', which the 'unembodied' mind is unable to tolerate. It consequently creates a 'false-self system', made up of a 'number of partially elaborated fragments of what might constitute a personality if any single one had full sway' (ibid.: 73).

These fragments are depicted in the novel by the four patients in the hospital who, in Rodnianskaia's description, represent various potential 'ways out' of post-Soviet circumstances (Rodnianskaia 1996: 214), all tried by some, but none adopted to the exclusion of all others. The representative of the masses, confused about his gender and described by Timur as a collision of 'Mexican soap opera, Hollywood blockbuster and unstable Russian democracy' (Pelevin 1996: 54), stands for grotesque westernization, the down-and-out dreamer for the impossible marriage of the Russian and Japanese, the 'new Russian' for consumerist hedonism, and the intellectual, Pet'ka, for the restoration of the Silver Age. As Rodnianskaia points out, however, the dominance of Pet'ka's perspective means that the two periods are not weighted equivalently; rather, the 1990s are presented as a hideous, trashy parody of the earlier period. In his 1919 existence, Pet'ka opposes the political direction taken by Mayakovsky and is nostalgic for the monarchy. The co-opting of the Avant-garde into the revolutionary movement may be implicitly compared to the Conceptualists' descent into consumerist kitsch depicted in 'Zheltaia strela'. Pelevin evokes here the ancient Chinese perception of time as an inevitable decline from an initial 'golden age', playfully linked to the conventional account of the development of Russian literature from the 'Golden Age' of Pushkin to the 'Silver Age' to the contemporary period.

Timur's aim is to persuade the patients once again to accept their 'embodied' selves, to become re-absorbed in *byt*, like the passengers on the train in *'*Zheltaia strela*'*, by using a form of group therapy in which each patient, by hearing for a time the 'false personalities' of other patients, gradually comes to a realization of the fictional nature of his own delusion. Timur's counterpart in the Civil War period is Chapaev, who considers the cause of Pet'ka's illness to lie not in the fact that he appears to exist in two time planes at once, but in his desire to find out where he 'really' is, to return to an 'embodied' notion of the self. Whereas Timur equates this outcome with healing, for Chapaev and the implied author it simply represents the adoption of another 'false self'. In *Houština*, the narrator scathingly describes his mother's mental illness, presenting it essentially as weakness brought on by dependence on the notion of a single, integrated self. Kahuda's outright rejection of this notion means that he does not experience its disintegration in the novel with any anxiety, in contrast, for example, to the treatment of the personality crisis in Brabcová's *Daleko od stromu* or *Zlodějina*, where characters seek ways to restore a sense of wholeness.

In place of this notion of the single self, obedient to the laws of physics, Pelevin proposes a conception corresponding to the image of time as a labyrinth apparently conceived by one Ts'ui Pen, a Chinese provincial governor, in Borges's short story 'The Garden of Forking Paths' (1956). In the parody introduction to the novel, Pelevin suggests that it might have been called 'The Garden of Forking Pet'kas' (Pelevin 1996: 9). In Borges's story, a scholar of Ts'ui Pen's work comments:

> 'In all fictional works, each time a man is confronted with several alternatives, he chooses one and eliminates the others; in the fiction of Ts'ui Pen, he chooses – simultaneously – all of them. *He creates*, in this way, diverse futures, diverse times which themselves also proliferate and fork.'
>
> (Borges 1970: 51)

According to the scholar:

> [Ts'ui Pen] believed in an infinite series of times, in a growing, dizzying net of divergent, convergent and parallel times. This network of times which approached one another, forked, broke off, or were unaware of one another for centuries, embraces *all* possibilities of time. We do not exist in the majority of these times; in some you exist, and not I; in others I, and not you; in others, both of us.
>
> (Ibid.: 53)

At one point in *Chapaev i Pustota*, Pet'ka confides in Chapaev that he dislikes the political commissar, Furmanov, suggesting that he might not work well together with him in the future. Chapaev, however, rejects this line of thinking, arguing:

> 'One still has to contrive to get to the future of which you speak. Perhaps you will get to a future where there won't be any Furmanov. And perhaps you will get to a future where there won't any "you"'.
>
> (Pelevin 1996: 99)

Furmanov, as the author of *Chapaev*, is responsible for one of Chapaev's 'futures'.

As the history of Chapaev's 'self' indicates, these 'futures' or 'times' represent infinite selves, understood, as in Balla, as nothing more than verbal constructs of the mind. The belief in one particular construct does not eradicate the other constructs, but merely succeeds for a time in concealing them from the believer. Through his depiction of Pet'ka's ability in the novel not only to pass freely between different time-planes, but also to enter the minds of other characters and experience their experiences as though they were his own, Pelevin seeks to expose the borders erected to delineate the individual mind as illusory. He asserts instead a universal consciousness, like the child as portrayed in Pelevin's work, endlessly dreaming up and dissolving the world.

The novel may thus be seen as the most expansive, celebratory expression in Russian fiction of the Changes of the 'death of the author' as a liberation to wander amid the products of this consciousness; this activity contradicts the adoption of a 'single direction' and, like the 'wandering' in Hodrová's fiction or the narrator's rambling in Popov's *Dusha patriota*, purports to represent the 'true' nature of terrestrial existence. In this respect, according to Sergei Kornev, *Chapaev i Pustota* constitutes the first example in Russian literature of what is regarded in Western criticism as 'classical postmodernism' (Kornev 1997: 244), a view shared by Sally Dalton-Brown, who argues that, until Pelevin, Russian prose had 'not learnt to play the postmodernist game nonchalantly' (Dalton-Brown 1997: 218).

Kornev writes: 'The ideal of postmodernism is the schizoid consciousness, a consciousness entirely splintered ideologically, the fragments of which peacefully co-exist among themselves' (Kornev 1997: 248). Kornev alludes here to *Anti-Oedipus* (1972) by Gilles Deleuze and Félix Guattari, a key work of post-Structuralism whose influence is evident in the writing of not only Pelevin, but also Kahuda and Balla. In *Anti-Oedipus*, Deleuze and Guattari contend that psychoanalysis, by seeking to make human psychology conform to the Oedipal model, participates in the 'work of bourgeois repression', the circumscription of unconscious desire and the socialization of the human being which begins, as Pelevin and Kahuda depict them, with the parent–child relationship. In place of psychoanalysis, they call for 'schizoanalysis', analysis of what psychoanalysts consider the pre-Oedipal phase, but which, according to Deleuze and Guattari, manifests itself in the schizophrenic as a form of progress or liberation from the 'oedipalized' state: 'Wouldn't it be better to schizophrenize – to schizophrenize the domain of the unconscious as well as the sociohistorical domain, so as to shatter the iron collar of Oedipus and rediscover everywhere the force of desiring-production [...]?' (Deleuze and Guattari 1984: 53). Deleuze and Guattari's descriptions of the schizophrenic mind, drawing particularly on Beckett's *The Unnameable*, find their echo in the explicit rejection of 'I' in Kolenič, Kahuda and Balla (see, for example, Deleuze and Guattari 1984: 23). As Kornev points out, this position is necessarily amoral, since no one fragment may be advocated or rejected over any other. In keeping with the assertion of the impotence of literature, the irony in 'classical postmodernism' is not, arguably unlike in Sorokin's writing, corrective, but may even serve as an alibi for continued immoral or amoral activity, hence Pelevin's popularity among those he most strongly satirizes.

To describe Pelevin's writing as amoral would, however, represent a basic misreading, since as Kornev points out, following critics like Kostyrko and Genis, who note the nascent didacticism in Pelevin's early writing, his work is 'classically postmodernist' only in form, concealing a very firm ideological position which he propounds with increasing confidence and vehemence. This view of Pelevin's writing contradicts that of, for example, Chuprinin, who describes his work as 'pure art', defined as art which is neither burdened with an ideological message nor designed for mass entertainment, but is concerned only with telling stories, a view echoed by Dalton-Brown (see Chuprinin 1993: 182–3.) The debates about whether such art can ever exist will not be rehearsed here, but as Pelevin's Buddhist didacticism becomes increasingly overt with each new work, the term proves decreasingly appropriate in his case. Pelevin's exploitation of postmodernist techniques in effect mirrors Chapaev's advice to Pet'ka near the end of the novel, understood as an implied authorial artistic credo: 'Wherever you find yourself, live by the laws of the world in which you've ended up, and use these laws to free yourself from them' (Pelevin 1996: 324–5).

Chapaev heals Pet'ka by teaching him to recognize the inherent emptiness of all phenomena, to cease clinging to phenomena which are impermanent and cause suffering, including what Peter Harvey, in his analysis of the understanding of the self in early Buddhist texts, calls 'the conditioned factors of personality, which are *not*-self' (Harvey 1995: 43). In *Chapaev i Pustota*, Pelevin portrays the schizophrenic condition described by Laing not only as a positive state, but also as the 'true' way of seeing, the perfect expression of what Harvey terms the 'selfless mind'. Harvey notes how the quest for self-knowledge in the Upanishads is a quest to 'attain liberation from the age-old round of re-births', to come to knowledge of the Universal Self, defined as a 'transcendent, yet immanent reality that was a person's true nature.' (Harvey 1995: 1) Pet'ka's gradual recognition of the world as a series of competing fragments of text constitutes a rejection of the conventional equation of words with physical objects, the first, critical stage on a journey towards the final abandonment of that world in the 'eternal non-return' of Nirvana, the 'ultimate empty thing' (ibid.: 52), also depicted in Ivanchenko's novels.

Comparing Pelevin's notion of emptiness with that of Foucault, Kornev writes:

> The emptiness of Foucault and the emptiness of Pelevin are two different notions of being, each subject to its own separate internal law. Foucault's emptiness is Western emptiness, Pelevin's is Eastern. Western emptiness, unsatisfied and mocking, Eastern emptiness self-absorbed [*samouglublennaia*] and calm.
>
> (Kornev 1997: 253)

Foucault's notion of emptiness corresponds in effect to that represented by the blank pages and self-deleting 'frame-breaks' in Sorokin's writing, since, according to Kornev, Foucault's emptiness does not simply represent the absence of God, but 'itself replaces Him, wielding ontological supremacy over everything else' (ibid: 252). Where Foucault's emptiness represents a disturbing, ever-present origin, Pelevin's represents a happy ending, a longed for reunion with what Kahuda calls 'nameless timelessness'.

Kahuda only mentions Eastern philosophy explicitly once, in an admiring reference in *Houština* to a work colleague who practises Buddhist teachings and is described as an 'artist of life'. However, particularly in *Veselá bída* and *Houština*, he also pursues what Zuzana P. Krupičková calls the 'liberation of the mind' from its attachment to a finite physical conception of itself and the world (Krupičková 2000: 5). Kahuda toys with the reader's need for a tangible experience of existence, using dense descriptive language, which acts upon the reader's senses of smell and touch, producing an intensely physical experience of what are only words. His writing may be compared to a form of meditation, in which the mind attempts to rid itself of its attachment to an inventoried reality. Harvey writes: 'Contemplation of phenomena as impermanent, suffering and not-self is a way of undermining craving for and clinging to such phenomena. By seeing things "as they really are", attachment and its attendant suffering will be undermined' (Harvey 1995: 44–5).

In *Veselá bída*, a narrating consciousness moves through Prague one night, documenting what it observes. The work cannot be reduced to the account of a man's night-long walk through the city, though that appears to be its basis, because the narrating consciousness 'sees' and 'knows' far more than the human eye could. The consciousness both describes in fine detail and expands on its subjects, recording their feelings, motives, past and future actions. It is not witnessing, but creating, understood as the disgorging of products of consciousness. In *Houština*, this journey from dusk to dawn underpins the chronological account of a life, presented not as an accumulation or preservation of a Self, but as the redemption of the mind from this dark delusion. The language produced by this activity of human consciousness, working to fill the void of existence, constitutes the 'thicket' of the novel's title. At one point, the narrator disturbs the grave of the early twentieth-century Czech writer, Ladislav Klíma, a moment of self-conscious authorial irony, since the title of Klíma's philosophical tract, *Svět jako vědomí a nic* (The world as consciousness and nothingness, 1904), encapsulates a central premise of *Houština*. Klíma's work, the title of which parodies the title of Schopenhauer's *The World As Will and Representation*, seeks to take to its extreme Schopenhauer's suggestion that what is perceived as reality is the creation of the human mind. The heritage of subjective idealism is never far from Balla and Pelevin's work either; Balla also quotes Klíma, while both, like Klíma, make reference to Berkeley, Schopenhauer and Nietzsche.

Kahuda never refers directly to the work of writing in *Houština*, but many of the jobs which he describes serve as metaphors for his understanding of the writer: the night watchman as the observer, even the voyeur, of the products of his own consciousness, the gravedigger who traces decomposition and exhumes and buries the past, and the sewage engineer who gets rid of waste material. In the final chapter, the narration switches from the first- to the third-person, in Novotný's view signalling an 'escape from the prison of personal history' (Novotný 2000: 5), and therefore some progress in the process of emptying. In a manner reminiscent of Hodrová's description of Sofie Syslová's growing awareness of the nature of the self in *Kukly*, the new narrator comments of the former narrator: 'The man is experiencing a spreading feeling that there is more of him. He is made up of many. The result of past lives. A transitional location for current existences' (Kahuda 1999: 424). However, as in Pelevin, this initiation into the nature of existence constitutes only a stage in the process of liberation, which culminates in the final pages with the declared intention to abandon language: 'He must abandon these hackneyed configurations, he must divest himself of the tattered garments of words' (ibid.: 499). The re-attainment of 'nameless timelessness' is reflected, as in *Veselá bída*, by the image of the dawn at the end of the work, a happy release from the meaningless activity of consciousness depicted over the previous five hundred pages.

In contrast to the fiction of both Kahuda and Pelevin, Balla's fiction contains no prospect of escape, presenting writing as an endless process of emptying equated with being itself. As the very structure of *Leptokária* as a collection of discrete prose pieces suggests, to write is to take repeated dips into consciousness, understood as a chaos of language, which in 'Večerná úzkosť. Pieseň plavecká.' is described as an 'unhealthy, poisonous environment' where texts incubate and from which they are then expelled. The 'unhealthy, poisonous environment' of consciousness is reflected in the title of the first story in the collection, 'Infekcia'. In the story, the narrator inherits his parents' home, perhaps a metaphor for Freud's *Über-Ich*, but, feeling infested by its contents, strips out the furniture and carpets and burns them. Each time he moves in new contents, however, he feels the infestation again, until the narrator comes to realize that he is the infection. Balla thus presents the self as an empty shell which consciousness constantly fills and the writer constantly seeks to empty.

In the final piece in *Leptokária*, the narrator describes a road blocked by burnt furniture, an old fridge, an acrid stench and foul weather. In the context of the piece, these items belong to the aftermath of a fire, but they all come from earlier pieces in the collection, which the writer has already 'expelled' from himself. The narrator comments:

> From inside I'm even more filthy than on the surface. Nothing in the world can wash it away! I throw out my dung and another chestful, another bodyful of it is born…A pregnancy of dung and vomit and ethereal perversions, of the detritus of knowledge and degenerate ethics.
>
> (Balla 1996: 144)

Of the three writers discussed here, the emptiness portrayed in Balla's fiction resembles most closely that explored by Foucault, but it is presented not as an ever-present abyss, as in Sorokin, but as a promise of eternal creation. In 'Večerná úzkosť, pieseň plavecká', a narrator remarks: 'Below the surface let the talk be of great love for emptiness as the only possibility of love. Emptiness is a place for fruitful forces' (ibid.: 38–9).

The Russian, Czech and Slovak writers of the Changes essentially seek to liberate the writer from his traditional function in each literature as a teacher of life, making him instead a demonstrator of art. In the context of this division running through all three literatures, Pelevin stands on the opposite side from Balla and Kahuda. Kornev writes that Pelevin is 'in terms of ideas and content no postmodernist, but a bona fide Russian classical writer-ideologue like Tolstoy or Chernyshevsky' (Kornev 1997: 245), in Balla's terms a creator of a surface illusion of order. To return to the Pascal quotation with which this chapter began, whereas Pelevin asserts that the emptiness can be filled by a new understanding of what that emptiness means, the writing of Balla and Kahuda retains an awareness that all creation strives against that emptiness in vain. In both

Leptokária and *Houština*, the writer is characterized as an impotent wanderer in the products of consciousness which constitute existence and which he is incapable of changing. It is only upon the quality of his work in recycling and waste-disposal that he can be judged.

Conclusion

To speak or not to speak

The attempt in the fiction of the Changes to abandon the 'principle of "using" literature for an extra-literary purpose' and the scorning of 'all ideologies, missions and services to people or anyone' resulted in an intense self-consciousness about the act of putting pen to paper, encapsulated in the question which Kolenič's narrator poses to himself at the beginning of *Mlčať*: to speak or not to speak. The Czech fiction of this period exhibits a striking 'fear of stopping speaking', most obviously in Hodrová or Topol, but also, for example, in the garrulous narrators used by mainstream writers not discussed in detail here, like Šabach and Viewegh. For these writers, in keeping with the implicit reference to *Hamlet* in *Mlčať*, writing becomes a vital metaphor for the continuing presence, and often preciousness, of being.

The 'fear of stopping speaking' is evident also in the work of Pišťanek, Klimáček and Petrushevskaia, and may be said to have reasserted itself in Russian fiction in the 1990s, notably in the monologue narrations *Trepanatsiia cherepa* (Trepanning the skull, 1995) by Sergei Gandlevskii (b.1952), or *Svoboda* (Freedom, 1998) by Mikhail Butov (b.1964). Gandlevskii's short autobiographical novel, ultimately an affirmation of life in the face of life-threatening surgery, which won the Little Booker Prize in 1996, may be considered a response to Popov's *Dusha patriota*, in which the ironization of the 'underground' is replaced by its sentimentalization. By contrast, Butov's novel, which won the main Booker Prize in 1999, was received as a 'sober' reflection on the socio-political and literary liberation of the early 1990s, lacking the extravagant euphoria of Pelevin's earlier works, but not entirely pessimistic. In all these writers, the 'fear of stopping speaking' reflects a refusal to accept the defeat of literature expressed in works like *Moskva–Petushki* and *Příliš hlučná samota*. Both Hrabal, arguably the original source of this 'fear of stopping speaking' in contemporary Czech literature, and Venedikt Erofeev suggest that the coming society has no understanding of the 'sacrality' of literature as an expression of being, indeed of the soul, and therefore feels no need for it. The 'fear of stopping speaking' often underlies an attempt to preserve or restore this awareness of the 'sacrality' of literature, and therefore of the individual human existence.

The enduring faith of Czech writers in literature is reflected in their preference for very long novels (Topol, Matoušek), trilogies (Hodrová, Kratochvil) and a tetralogy (Macura), which by their very nature suggest that literature remains, in their view, consequential. By contrast, the frequent use of shorter forms by Russian and especially Slovak writers of the Changes, continuing a trend apparent in sanctioned 'urban' fiction since the Thaw, indicates the modesty of their aspirations in comparison with the 'big' official, dissident and nationalist writers, an assertion of the undesirability or impossibility of an epic, collective perspective that often becomes an expression of doubt that there is anything to say.

Writers like Petrushevskaia and Pišťanek are exceptions to the dominant 'fear of speaking' in the Russian and Slovak fiction of the Changes. In the Russian fiction discussed here, this 'fear of speaking' frequently derives from a sense of literature's complicity in tyranny, its potential to do harm. At the end of *Moskva–Petushki*, Venichka is pierced through the throat, the Russian writer silenced to prevent his dreams of a perfect world causing further barbarity. The novel's intertextuality reflects a nostalgia for a time before literature lost its innocence, seen also in contemporaneous writers like Bitov and Terts. Erofeev subsequently wrote only a few short pieces, and the slim single volume of his collected works consists mainly of unrealized fragments and notes. By contrast, in the work of Conceptualists like Sorokin, the effort to subvert the potency of words by emptying them of meaning reflects a view that the act of creation is never innocent. The handsome three-volume collected works of Sorokin, like Prigov's attempts to write thousands of poems, in effect demonstrate the monolithic emptiness of accumulated culture, parodying the revered collected works of great writers which grace the bookshelves of Russian intellectuals.

The suggestion that words affect the external world only for the worse co-exists in the fiction of the Changes with the perception that literature has no influence on the world outside itself, often directly influenced by the post-Structuralist dislocation of signifier and signified. While this perception underpins the assertion that literature has been 'misused' in the service of various ideologies, in the works of writers like Tolstaia and Popov it is accompanied by a disappointed, though ironized, sense of the futility of writing and of human existence. This perspective dominates the Slovak fiction of the Changes, in which this futility is presented as hateful or at best ridiculous in writers like Mitana, Kolenič, the Barbarians or the Genitalists before Balla, where the unceasing flow of language in the writer's head appears to mock the writer, thwarting the desire to cease speaking, and serving as a wretched substitute for meaningful, as it were 'god-like', being.

Barthes and Foucault present the loss of the notion of Author as a happy release, a cause for celebration, promising a new approach to writing and a new way of interpreting earlier writing. In his essay, 'What is an author?', Foucault argues that '[the author] is a certain function by which, in our culture, one limits, excludes, and chooses; in short, by which one impedes the free circulation, the free manipulation, the free composition, decomposition and recomposition of fiction' (Foucault 1998: 221). That 'freedom' underpins the approach of the writers who 'fear stopping speaking'. For those writers who 'fear speaking', however, the rejection of the belief that the writer could or should shape or instruct the world was experienced not as a liberation, but as a defeat, perhaps even a failed liberation from writing itself. In consequence, their models of the writer are, if not Venichka's corpse, then, for example, Tolstaia's wretched 'fakir' or Kolenič's morbid 'dilettante', who, like Popov's narrator-*flâneur* in *Dusha patriota*, wander aimlessly amid the relativity which remains.

Such metaphors perhaps ultimately reflect the implicit difficulty that certain writers of the Changes had in reconciling themselves to the changed status of literature and the writer which they themselves propounded. Despite their claims to the contrary, these writers mourned the loss of the special place accorded to literature in Russian or Slovak culture. In a paper presented at the Czech Embassy in London in January 2003, Petr A. Bílek makes a similar point about the Czech writers of the Changes period, noting that they too had been 'brought up under the paradigm that literature means something and expected an immediate, serious reaction to their books'. One might even argue that their didacticism about the role of literature, the writer and the limits of the human being suggested that, far from embodying the new literature, their work represented the last gasp of the old, a final chance for literature to 'speak', if only to call for silence. In the fiction of writers who 'fear stopping speaking', the playful expression of liberation is sometimes undermined by a fear of being silenced that makes their writing equally neurotic, as, for example, in Brabcová's *Daleko od stromu* or Hodrová's *Théta*, or in the endless, compulsive to-ing and fro-ing of Ajvaz's sculptor or Balla's swimmer.

In the early 1990s, Russian critics, who had embraced what they called 'other fiction' more loudly and exclusively than their Czech and Slovak counterparts in the first place, began to express weariness with its strategies. In an article tellingly entitled 'A za prazdnik – spasibo!' (But thanks for the fun!), published in 1992, Lipovetskii expressed disappointment that the inspiration of the 'other fiction' writers had apparently fizzled out so quickly:

> Liberation from illusions and dogmas, and from ideology of any sort, and, above all, the attempt to embody, or more precisely, to model a genuinely free relationship between the human being and the world through a playful relationship with culture; these are the elements which create the atmosphere in which the whole 'new wave' lived and breathed, and define its [...] historical meaning. But here too lies the source of weakness of this poetics.
> (Lipovetskii 1992: 4)[1]

Lipovetskii argued, for example, that in Tolstaia's most recent stories, 'Limpopo' (1990) and 'Siuzhet' (1991), her style had appeared strained, while Popov and others had become 'slaves to their own intonation' (ibid.). After the disastrous attempt to change direction in the overtly metafictional 'Siuzhet', Tolstaia produced no more new fiction until the publication of her first novel, *Kys'* (2001, dated as written 1986–2000), which contained a far bleaker depiction of human beings' relationship with literature than her earlier stories. Popov returned to critical favour with his parodic 'novel-commentary', *Podlinnaia istoriia 'Zelenykh Muzykantov'* (The true story of the 'Green Musicians', 1998).

In a later article, highly critical of Russian 'postmodernist' writers, Pavel Basinskii contended that their work reflected Soviet man's sense of inferiority to the West, brought on by 'corrective' policies such as Egor Gaidar's economic 'shock therapy'. Having provided literature with its own 'shock therapy', however, these writers, according to Basinskii, had nowhere else to go (Basinskii 1995: 222). Rather like Lipovetskii, Basinskii blamed this apparent inability to develop on the eradication of all limits, or the assertion of their arbitrariness, which underpinned these writers' work, arguing that the 'limit is an essential category, without which the world cannot live' (ibid.: 223). His comments are coincidentally mirrored in Vilikovský's review of *Mlčať*, in which Vilikovský, arguing that Kolenič had pointedly denied himself any possibility of development, quotes the Czech poet Vítězslav Nezval (1900–58):

> In the yard is heard a shriek
> It's the shriek of a little hysteric
> He's put his head straight through a wall
> And now doesn't know where to go at all.
> (Vilikovský 1992: 20)[2]

In reviews of novels like Topol's *Anděl* or Hodrová's *Ztracené děti*, Czech critics warned against the danger of becoming repetitive. Kratochvil declared his novel *Noční tango* (Night tango, 1999) to be the beginning of his search for a new style.

Given that nearly all the writers discussed in this study are still alive and publishing, to suggest that any are finished would be a mistake. However, whereas the tension in the fiction of the Changes initially stemmed from its subversive engagement with dominant conventions, as this study seeks to show, once these had been transgressed, its writers faced the problem of turning their techniques from weapons of conflict into tools of the trade, of being playful without becoming superficial. Writers emerged like Boris Akunin (Grigorii Chartishvili, b.1956), Miloš Urban and Michal Hvorecký, who exploit popular forms, responding in effect to the new 'censorship of the market' and, in Fiedler's terms, attempting to 'close the gap' between 'high' and 'low' literature. While Akunin's fiction turns the Conceptualist imitation of styles into a production-line of vaguely knowing but formulaic detective novels, Urban (who also writes detective fiction) and most obviously Hvorecký (who views the present or near-future through the prism of science fiction) aspire at the same time to comment on contemporary society. Together with writers like Pelevin and Juráňová, and also Topol and Kratochvil, whose *Lehni, bestie!* (Down, beast!, 2002) constituted the first Czech literary response to the attacks of 11 September 2001 in New York, they suggested a 're-engagement' of literature with the external world. The urgency of the need to re-define the writer, fundamental to the fiction of the Changes, appeared for the moment to have receded.

Notes

1 The fiction of the Changes

1 Leonid Brezhnev was general secretary of the Communist Party from 1966 until his death in 1982. He was followed by Iurii Andropov and Nikolai Chernenko, neither of whom lived long enough to make a major impact.

2 For a general account of the Soviet literary situation in this period, see, for example, Brown 1993: 1–18 and Shneidman 1995: 35–57.

3 For a more detailed discussion of the *Metropol'* episode, see Porter 1994b: 26–30.

4 The topos of the mental hospital appears in Russian novels from this period including Sharov's *Do i vo vremia* and Pelevin's *Chapaev i Pustota*, and also in Czech novels, beginning with Němec's *Hra na slepo* in 1982 and continuing after the Changes with Brabcová's *Daleko od stromu* and *Zlodějina* and Šabach's *Zvláštní případ Františka S.* (The strange case of František S., 1995). The motif of schizophrenia is discussed later in this study. particularly in the context of works by Ivanchenko, Kratochvil and Pelevin.

5 For a discussion of the prominence of the adolescent in Czech fiction of this period, see Pynsent 1984: 65–86.

6 Susanne Roth argues in her monograph on Hrabal that the text of the *Tvorba* interview, which she reproduces, was amended before publication (see Rothová 1993: 163–5). At the time, the interview provoked dismay, prompting students to burn Hrabal's books in public.

7 *Revolver Revue*, founded in 1985 as *Jednou nohou* but re-named after five issues, became legal after the Changes, and remains one of the most respected Czech literary periodicals.

8 In his study of the Czech literary underground in the postwar period, Martin Pilař describes Martin C. Putna's account of the four 'steps' which make a writer 'underground': '(1) hostility to the official world and its culture; (2) departure from it; (3) forming a group with like-minded people; (4) creating another, parallel world with another culture and other values' (Pilař 1999: 14.) Pilař's book draws attention to the continuity in Czech underground writing from the late 1940s to the 1980s, which could trace its roots back through the wartime underground to the prewar Poetist and Surrealist Avant-garde.

9 By 'artistic' and 'artificial', Kratochvil appears to mean literature which focuses on the processes of its own creation. František Gellner (1881–1914), uncle of Ernest Gellner, was an early twentieth-century anarchist poet.

10 At least in his study, entitled 'Jedna česká literatura? K některým tendencím "oficiální", samizdatové a exilové prózy', Bock puts 'official' in quotation marks. The only sanctioned writers about whom Jungmann wrote positively were Vladimír Körner, who continued to publish his historical fiction after the Thaw, and writers of

essentially one controversial sanctioned book like Pávek's *Simulanti* or Jana Červenková (b.1939), whose *Semestr života* (A term in life, 1982) describes the gradual destruction of the idealism of a young pro-Communist teacher who takes up her first post in the ideological 'virgin lands' of the south-western Czech border.

11 Jan Lukeš caused controversy in 1982 with the sanctioned publication of a collection of articles, *Prozaická skutečnost*, in which he articulated the concerns and strategies of writers like Dušek (see Lukeš 1982). For a similar survey in English, which earned a highly critical *samizdat* review from Jungmann for a perceived lack of discrimination between major ('grey') and minor ('official') writers, see Pynsent 1986: 1–36.

12 In fairness to Erofeev, the 1997 anthology of 'new' literature which he edited, *Russkie tsvety zla* (Russian flowers of evil), included Astaf'ev and a broad range of unsanctioned writers from the 1970s, including Mamleev, Sergei Dovlatov (1941–90) and Varlam Shalamov (1907–82) (see Erofeev (ed.): 1997).

13 During this period, Vilikovský was, however, a prominent translator and editor, and in 1976 joined the editorial board of the leading sanctioned periodical *Romboid*, ensuring its increasingly liberal direction in the 1980s.

14 In the 1990s, these last three, with the writer and painter Robert Bielik (b.1963) and, initially, Kolenič, formed the self-styled 'Barbarian Generation', but their collective contribution, though provocative, was ultimately slight.

15 For a range of reactions, see *Literárny týždenník* 1989: 5. Urban pointed out that Lehenová's work was not unprecedented in the context of recent Czech and Slovak poetry, recalling the earlier controversy in Czech literature caused by the collection *Říkají mi poezie* (They call me poetry, 1987) by Svatava Antošová (b.1957) (see Urban 1989: 4). The polarized reactions to Antošová, Lehenová and indeed Narbikova reflect the extent to which their portrayals of sexually aware women challenged the contemporaneous stereotype of the female.

16 For a discussion of Czech sanctioned poetry in the 1970s and 1980s, see Bílek 1991. For a discussion of its Russian counterpart, see Epshtein 1986: 40–72 and Postnikova 1995. Postnikova begins her study by describing how, in the early 1980s, young poets working in the traditions of poetry in the 1920s and 1930s broke into sanctioned publication, and notes the 'unconventionality and boldness of artistic imagination, open *épatage* with regard to embedded literary tastes, the complexity of their poetic vision of the world, and the incorporation into poetry of the clash of different cultural and historical layers' (Postnikova 1995: 5).

17 In the first issue of *Literárny týždenník*, Urban wrote a short piece pointing out how often his mental state had been questioned and asking for the views of psychiatrists. (See Urban, J., 'Čo na to psychiatri?', *Literárny týždenník*, I, 1988, 1, p. 4.)

18 Ján Solovič was the head of the Slovak Writers' Union during the Normalization. Readers saw *Literárny týždenník* as the symbolic revival in all but name of *Kultúrny život*, one of the most widely read pro-reform cultural weeklies of the 1960s, which ceased publication in the autumn of 1968, but briefly returned between 1990 and 1993 as *Literárny týždenník* came increasingly to reflect the agenda of the conservative/nationalist camp in post-1989 Slovak literature.

19 In the 1990s, *Dotyky*, though notionally a forum for the work of young writers and critics, in an implicit gesture of solidarity between like-minded writers of different generations, often included interviews, reviews and articles by or about writers like Dušek and Mitana.

20 The attempted coup by Communist hard-liners in August 1991, and Boris Yeltsin's subsequent conflicts with the Communist/Nationalist-dominated Russian Parliament in 1993 and 1995 indicate the seriousness of the confrontation, which was perceived to have been won with Yeltsin's re-election in 1996, but has re-surfaced in the arts under Vladimir Putin's leadership.

21 Works by Venedikt Erofeev, Tolstaia, Sorokin and Pelevin have also been published in book form in Czech since 1990, but the orientation of Czech readers in this period has

inevitably shifted westwards. Of the Czech and Slovak works discussed here, only Hrabal's *Příliš hlučná samota* has been published in Russian to date (April 2004).

22 Zajac's comments come in a foreword to an essay introducing the term 'postmodernism' by the German theorist Wolfgang Welsch, whose work greatly influenced Slovak and also Czech writers and critics in the subsequent period.

23 The extent of the liberalization in Slovakia by this time is evident in Žilka's reference to the unsanctioned *Nesnesitelná lehkost bytí* (The unbearable lightness of being, Toronto 1985) by Milan Kundera (b. 1929).

24 Lipovetskii's book also includes a chapter on Vladimir Nabokov (1899–1977) as an 'ancestor' of Russian postmodernism, which was omitted in the abridged English translation of the volume, published in 1999.

2 Deaths of authors

1 *Večne je zelený*...appeared in Vilikovský's first collection *Citová vychova v marci* (A sentimental education in March, 1965), and the novel was completed in 1972. An excerpt appeared in *Literárny týždenník* in November 1988. Excerpts from *Příliš hlučná samota* were sanctioned for publication in 1981 in a 'collage' called *Klub poezie*, together with excerpts from another unsanctioned work, *Něžný barbar* (The gentle barbarian, Cologne 1981 [as *Něžní barbaři*], Prague 1990). Earlier variants, one in verse, were published alongside the final prose version (which forms the basis of discussion here) in the ninth volume of Hrabal's collected works in 1994. For comparisons of the three versions, see Jankovič 1991: 171–89 and Rothová 1993: 117–22.

2 For a discussion of the novel in English in the context of postmodernist theories, see Beasley-Murray 1998: 266–78. By contrast, Darovec uses the term 'postmodernist' sparingly in his study, instead indicating the similarity between Vilikovský's method and those, in particular, of the nineteenth-century satirist Jonáš Záborský (1812–1876) in his comic novel *Faustiáda* (excerpt published in 1864, abridged version in 1912, in full 1953).

3 Gaiser-Shnitman draws attention to the semantics of *sueta*, which means both 'hustle-and-bustle' and 'vanity' in a Biblical sense (see Gaiser-Shnitman 1989: 46).

4 Venichka here quotes from 'Starukha Izergil'' (The old woman Izergil', 1895) by Maxim Gorky (1868–1936) – 'in life [...] there is always room for heroic deeds' (Gor'kii 1968: 87) – which became a Soviet slogan and is quoted sarcastically by other writers of the Changes, including Popov and Pelevin.

5 *Moskva-Petushki* is thus linked coincidentally with another Czech novel implicitly written in response to the Warsaw Pact intervention, Ladislav Fuks's *Oslovení z tmy* (A call from the dark), amazingly sanctioned for publication in 1972 and unjustly neglected since. The text of *Oslovení z tmy* takes place in the mind of a young Jewish boy, fatally injured in what may be a nuclear attack, and describes the Devil's battle with a Jewish priest for his soul. The Devil is a master of rational argument backed by brute force, but the aged, feeble priest quavering prayers represents the strength of the soul's yearning for salvation, and ultimately wins out.

6 This encounter between the Devil and the intellectual is made explicit in Mitana's *Hľadanie strateného autora: Rozhovory s Luciferom* (In search of a lost author: Conversations with Lucifer, 1991), discussed in Chapter 4.

7 Vilikovský perhaps alludes here to the Czech prewar journalist and literary critic and postwar Communist hero, Julius Fučík, who, imprisoned by the Germans in occupied Prague, sabotaged their pursuit of the Communist resistance and delayed his own execution by feeding his interrogators false information and apparently teaching them about Marxist-Leninist ideals.

8 Gaiser-Shnitman's monograph constituted the first thoroughgoing analysis of the novel's intertextuality, which was expanded by later critics, culminating in Eduard

Vlasov's commentary to the 2001 Vagrius edition of the novel (see Vlasov 2001: 121–574).

9 The approach to literature of both Erofeevs may be contrasted with that of Vladimír Macura, who exploits intertextual parody and allusion in his novel *Občan Monte Christo* (The citizen of Monte Cristo, 1993, dated as written 1983) and *Ten, který bude* (The one who is to come, as a single volume 1999), a quartet of novels focusing on the lives of leading figures from the nineteenth-century Czech National Revival, on which Macura the academic wrote prolifically. While these novels express the same nostalgia for a more innocent time, and a sense of being born too late, they share with Vilikovský's fiction a notion of an enduring, eccentric spirit that deserves preservation.

10 The word 'pábitelé', the title of Hrabal's second collection of short stories, published in 1964, has frequently been used to denote Hrabal's narrators and other narrators who use a similar style. For Hrabal's own account of the origin of the word, see Jankovič 1996: 26–7.

3 Giving a shape to one's fate

1 *Dusha patriota* bears comparison with the near-contemporaneous *Český snář* (A Czech dream-book, Toronto 1983, Prague 1990) by Ludvík Vaculík (b.1926), a patchwork of diary entries, essays, autobiographical and fictional writing set in the Czech dissident community of the late 1970s. Rather as Popov frequently alludes to the failure of attempts to secure the sanctioned publication of the *Metropol'* anthology, Vaculík's book reflects the mood of despair following the failure of the Charter 77 petition calling for greater human rights in Czechoslovakia.

2 For a discussion of this passage as an example of Soviet absurdity, see Lipovetskii 1999a: 192–3.

3 Chuprinin's assessment applies more to a writer like Vladimir Voinovich (b.1932), whose political satire in works like *Zhizn' i neobychainye prikliucheniia soldata Ivana Chonkina* (The life and unusual adventures of the soldier Ivan Chonkin, Paris 1975) or the essentially autobiographical *Ivan'kiada* (The Ivankiad, Ann Arbor 1976), favourably contrasts the basic common sense of the individual human being with the absurdity of the supposedly rational Soviet state. Like Voinovich, Popov set his early fiction in rural Siberia. However, while Voinovich consistently perceives virtue in 'native wit', in his short stories Popov emphasizes the incorrigible absurdity of human beings, reflected both in individual behaviour and in the social systems they devise for themselves.

4 *Medorek* marks a move away from the use of the adolescent as a moralizing device for social criticism in Czech fiction of the period. In the 1970s and 1980s, sanctioned writers like Václav Dušek, Bedřich Hlinka (b.1951) or Radek John (b.1954) favoured adolescent characters because, as Pynsent points out, they constituted a 'natural outsider', through whom the problems of contemporary society could be explored (see Pynsent 1984: 65). As Martin Machovec points out, the adolescent narrator of Jan Pelc's hugely controversial émigré novel *...a bude hůř* (...the worst is yet to come, Cologne 1985, Prague 1990), who rebels against his conformist father and falls into petty crime, hard drinking, drugs and sexual promiscuity, fulfils an extreme version of the same function (see Dokoupil and Zelinský (eds) 1994: 299). By the time of its first publication in post-Communist Czechoslovakia, alongside *Medorek*, in 1990, it already appeared outdated; Pavel Janáček contrasts what he considers the 'anti-Normalisation didacticism' of Pelc with the 'light pen' of Placák (Janáček 1991: 7).

5 Both *Medorek* and *...a bude hůř* reflect the attempt of younger writers in the 1980s to break with the views of the dissident establishment. Pelc's narrator describes the Charter 77 signatories as Communists in disguise, a reference to the Communist past and essentially left-wing views of the most prominent post-Thaw dissidents. In *Medorek*, Placák presents the 'underground' generation not as a practically minded and

courageous opposition, but as disparate gangs engaged in mysterious enterprises and cultivating alternative lifestyles. In this respect his novel continues a trend begun by Egon Bondy (b.1930) in his *Invalidní sourozenci* (Invalid siblings, Toronto 1981, Prague 1991), a dystopian allegory in which Bohemia is depicted as an island slowly being submerged. (In *Medorek*, Placák also half-heartedly suggests that the action of the novel is taking place in the distant future in an island city threatened by an apocalyptic flood.) Bondy satirizes the high-minded intellectualism of the dissidents, who are paid invalidity benefit by the state because they are ineffective workers, and live in a hippie commune at the highest point of the island. Bondy and Placák are also linked through the 1970s underground rock band, The Plastic People of the Universe, who set some of Bondy's poems to music and feature in *Invalidní sourozenci* and *...a bude hůř*, and for whom Placák wrote and played during the 1980s.

6 Pišťanek's numbering of his sequels owes more to cinema, especially low-grade commercial films, than to literature, as the title of this second sequel, reminiscent of the *Nightmare on Elm Street* series, indicates. (In 1995 and 1996, Pišťanek contributed a series of survey articles on cinematic genres to *Dotyky*.)

4 Subverting realism

1 Both Andrei Gimein and Ellen Chances note the influence of Bakhtin's notions of authorship, as described in his *Problems of Dostoevskii's Poetics*, published in 1963, on Bitov's *Pushkinskii dom*, the archetypal example of this 'author-seeking' type of Russian metafiction (see Gimein 1979: 369 and Chances 1993: 232–3).

2 For a discussion of Tolstaia's exploitation of the Tristram and Yseult myth in this story, see Goscilo 1997: 69–80.

3 'Fakir' coincidentally resembles Havel's unsanctioned play, *Vernisáž* (A private view, 1976), which also describes a visit to a beautifully decorated flat. In Havel's play, however, the implied authorial criticism is directed towards the *embourgeoisement* of the couple who are showing off the flat, who criticize their dissident-visitor (implicitly Havel himself) for his failure to have children, to decorate his home properly and to keep up with fashion. Their superficiality and their unthinking complicity with the Normalization regime contrast with the sacrifices made by the dissident, who cannot give up 'being true to himself', a possibility entirely absent from Tolstaia's stories. In its criticism of 'resurgent bourgeois values' and advocacy of 'true' and 'false' ways of living, Havel's play is entirely in keeping with sanctioned literature of the same period. Tolstaia's didacticism is no less strong, but is implicitly directed against the pretensions of both the official and dissident establishments.

4 The name Sonia, which also means 'sleepy-head', suggests that the character lives her life in a dream. Liudmila Ulitskaia (b.1943) uses the same name in her short novel *Sonechka* (1992), in which literature is also portrayed as a pure means of escape that loses its magic when ideas are imposed on it. In the novel, while Sonechka's awareness of the 'other world' of books enables her to accept cruel reality with equanimity, her artist-husband's judgemental, intellectual approach to art and life leaves him constantly disappointed.

5 Denisov's battle to remove Australia coincidentally recalls the title story of Petr Šabach's collection *Jak potopit Austrálii*, in which two schoolchildren play a practical joke on their geography teacher by removing Australia from the map of the world. For both writers, Australia appears to possess a sufficient air of unreality for their purpose. Whereas in 'Somnambula v tumane', Denisov's efforts to re-order the globe reflect his desire to resist what he experiences as the oppressive certainty of existence, the pupils' action in fact rescues their teacher, who had long lacked confidence in the rational explanations which he is expected to teach. By depicting the uncertainty of such a notionally authoritative figure, Šabach implies, like Tolstaia, that human knowledge may be only invented, though his teacher is not even sure about this.

6 The notion that human attempts to explain merely create a fog also appears in an episode in Pelevin's *Chapaev i Pustota*, in which a character wanders through fog produced by CNN's live broadcast of the 1993 bombing of the Russian Parliament, which obscures rather than clarifies the situation.
7 Mitana's concern about being supplanted is also reflected in his introduction to an extract from the novel, published in *Literárny týždenník* in January 1989, in which he describes the novel's protagonists as 'representatives of a generation which is surprised that yesterday they were rebels and today they have their own children growing up who are rebelling against them. One of the characters says: "I went to bed as an emerging prose writer and woke up as a writer of the middle generation"' (Mitana 1991: 166).

5 Writing as being

1 The quotation at the end of this passage comes from Eva Le Grand's 1998 study of Milan Kundera's novels, *Kundera aneb Paměť touhy*. Hodrová translated Bakhtin into Czech (*Román jako dialog*, 1980) and his thinking has had a fundamental impact on both her theory and her fiction.
2 This preoccupation remains evident, for example, in two of the most widely discussed, and very different, works of the late 1990s: *Pestré vrstvy* (Diverse seams, 1998) by Ivan Landsmann (b.1949) and *Sedmikostelí* (Sevenchurch, 1999) by Miloš Urban (b.1967). The experience of the 1970s and 1980s features prominently in *Hľadanie strateného autora*, but disappears in mid-1990s Slovak fiction, according to Pynsent because of continuing political uncertainties there, a suggestion which might equally be applied in the Russian context (see Pynsent 2000: 107).
3 In the eighth chapter of Kratochvil's third novel *Avion* (1995), the narrator, Hynek, accuses his uncle of this action, suggesting that it was motivated by jealousy because the uncle thought Hynek was a better writer than he, and anger that Hynek was not prepared to compromise his literary principles in support of the dissidents. The passage cannot, however, be read as anything other than a scarcely veiled attack by Kratochvil on his uncle, Antonín, who emigrated in 1952, the same year as Kratochvil's father. In emigration, Antonín Kratochvil (b.1924) wrote prolifically, particularly on Catholic writers whose existence was not acknowledged by the Communist regime. His work culminated in a three-volume documentary account of Communist oppression, *Žaluji* (J'accuse, 1973–7 abroad, 1990 in Czechoslovakia), which Kratochvil evidently parodies in the accusatory tone of the chapter.
4 Many of Kratochvil's short stories from the 1960s and 1970s, finally published in the collection *Orfeus z Kénigu* (The Orpheus of König, 1994), feature the word in their titles, as do his fourth and fifth novels, *Siamský příběh* (A Siamese story, 1996) and *Nesmrtelný příběh* (An immortal story, 1997).
5 Like Kratochvil, both Hodrová, with *Perunův den* and Topol, with *Anděl* (Angel, 1995), have published novels which endeavour to simplify their normal style in an attempt to reach a wider audience without abandoning their poetics.
6 Kratochvil alludes here without irony to Erich Fromm's *The Fear of Freedom*, a Marxist Freudian analysis of why people accepted Nazism, which greatly influenced Czech intellectuals in the 1960s.
7 The Abrahamites, a sect combining the beliefs of Protestant Christians and of Jews, appeared in Moravia in the early 1730s. In the 1780s, those who refused to be circumcised were deported to Transylvania.
8 The loss of a child as a metaphor for the loss of completeness and the destabilization of identity is central to Hodrová's fifth novel, *Ztracené děti* (Lost children, 1997), in which the style and techniques developed in the trilogy appeared exhausted.
9 Hodrová here not only reminds the reader, after Barthes, of the origins of the word 'text', but also evokes the medieval Czech dispute-cum-novel *Tkadleček* (Weaver,

*c.*1408, author unknown), based on *Der Ackermann aus Böhmen*, in which the Weaver, representing Emotion, and Misfortune, representing Reason, debate the extent to which a human being is able to dictate his fate, and the Weaver loses. As in Hodrová's writing, *Tkadleček*'s patchwork of intertextual references serves as a metaphor for the labyrinth of terrestrial existence and its playful assertion of the impotence of the human being in general and the writer in particular.

10 Hodrová's assertion of writing as resistance to stasis recurs in the prose piece *Rozžhavená kra* (A white-hot ice floe, 1993) by Jaromír Typlt (b.1971). Typlt argues that the poetic image, as indicated by his title, represents not 'fixedness' but 'action caused by the fact in the image itself, the image is opposed by DISINTEGRATION, the unceasing destroyer of manifestations and meanings' (Typlt 1996: 35). (This notion may be compared with Kratochvil's metaphor of the 'lamb in bear's clothing'.) In the piece, which he describes as a 'vratifest', returning the blow struck by the manifestos of the Avant-garde, and in his much discussed article, 'Devadesátá léta mezi zátiším a bojištěm', Typlt criticizes the modest aspirations of contemporary poets and poetry critics, whom he accuses of 'neo-classicism' (see Typlt 1993: 1). He calls instead for a return to the energy of the Avant-garde combined with an awareness of the inevitability of defeat.

11 A similar strategy is employed by Hodrová's husband, Karel Milota (1937–2002), who, in his *nouveau-roman*-influenced novel *Sud* (Barrel, 1993, dated as completed 1980) uses recurring motifs and characters to persuade the reader of a hidden pattern underlying the work. The reader's search for this pattern corresponds to the central character's vain attempts to avert the course of Fate (*osud*), whose constant presence is represented in the work by the sound of barrels rolling, also perhaps indicating the imminence of the Last Judgement (*Poslední soud*).

12 This remark coincidentally resembles that of the young writer in Balla's short story 'Večerná úzkosť. Pieseň plavecká', who longs to be part of a nation of people who cannot make themselves understood to each other. (This story is discussed in detail in Chapter 7.)

13 Psice's name fits with the recurring Native American motif in the novel. In 1997, Topol published a book of translations of Native American legends entitled *Trnová dívka* (The thorn girl). In *Sestra*, however, Topol draws more, not only on children's literature about the Wild West, like Karl May's *Vinnetou*, but also on Czech children's literature about gangs of boys playing cowboys-and-Indians-type games, like *Bylo nás pět* (There were five of us, 1946) by Karel Poláček (1892–1944) or the newspaper cartoons *Rychlé šípy* (The swift arrows) by Jaroslav Foglar (1907–99). At one point, Potok becomes confused with Pátek, meaning not only 'Friday', in reference to Daniel Defoe's *Robinson Crusoe*, but also the 'fifth one', as in Poláček's novel. By implicitly equating the activities of Potok's gang, conducting a mixture of cut-throat capitalism and multi-cultural community building in post-1989 Prague, with the games of children, Topol provides an ironic characterization of his own various 'projects' under and after Communism.

14 Topol retains this model of the cyclical recurrence of evil in his second novel, *Anděl*, in which the absence of the stone angel at the crossroads in Prague which bears its name signifies a world which has lost its spirituality and gone over to evil. At the end of the novel, the central character, Jatek, burns to death a group of gangsters and religious fanatics brought together by a wondrous drug he once created, thus apparently eradicating through a burnt offering the evil he brought into the world. However, the threat of evil indicated in the first chapter of the novel in fact chronologically follows these events. The blood which appears in the corner of Jatek's eye and fills the sky recalls the red darkness which Potok sees in *Sestra*, symbolizing the cycle of evil and purification underpinning existence in this world.

15 Asked about the renewed debate surrounding the Czech expulsion of Sudeten Germans after the Second World War, Topol expresses his satisfaction that the media have now

made clear the extent of Czech brutality in that period: 'We have a victim complex: the Russians are bad, the Germans are bad, whereas we, with our *vesnička středisková*, we're really quite nice, we have clean hands and our Hrabalian beer' (Chuchma 2002: 8). Topol is attacking here not so much Hrabal himself as the Normalization interpretation of his works in still enormously popular family films like Jiří Menzel's *Postřižiny* (Clippings, 1980), and films in a similar style, not based on Hrabal's work, like Menzel's *Vesnička má středisková* (My sweet little village, 1985). These films essentially reduced Hrabal's style to a comfortable assertion of the harmless eccentricity of the good-hearted, bucolic Czechs. *Sestra* itself represents a rejection of this collectivizing, potentially chauvinistic type of art. Topol directly satirizes Czech nationalism in his later novel *Noční práce* (Night work, 2001).

16 Jan 'Eskimo' Welzl was a Czech Arctic explorer who became the chief of an Inuit tribe, and whose adventures may be parodied by Pišťanek in *Rivers of Babylon 3*. Two books of Welzl's memoirs were published by the journalists Bedřich Golombek (1901–61) and Eduard Valenta (1901–78) in 1932.

6 Empty words

1 For a brief survey of various critical interpretations of 'sots-art', see Lipovetskii 2000: 167–70. This volume contains articles analysing 'sots-art' and its major practitioners by the most prominent interpreters of the phenomenon.

2 Kolenič is therefore singled out for particular mockery in the volume. In one interview, he is described, along with Pišťanek and Jozef Urban, as the 'dried-up middle stream' of contemporary Slovak literature (Turan *et al.* 1998: 95).

3 The closest counterpart in contemporary Czech literature is the poet Jaroslav Pížl (b.1961), who often performs his verse accompanied by his own musical compositions, and who explores both Conceptualism and postmodernist theory in visual art in his essay *K otázkám nového expresionismu v české malbě 80. let* (1995).

4 Sorokin's assertion of the importance of his encounter with the Conceptualists for the development of his writing has led many critics to identify Sorokin entirely with Moscow Conceptualism. Mikhail Ryklin, however, argues that Sorokin differs from the Conceptualists in his 'romantic desire to shock, to be unacceptable, to embody in his writing the reverse of literature', which, in Ryklin's view, renders his relationship to the Russian literary heritage of equal importance (see Ryklin 1998: 738).

5 The immense critical interest in Sorokin in the West has frequently surprised Russian critics. Vladimir Novikov comments: 'if [Sorokin] lacks [readers] in Russia, then abroad will help. Sorokin has been published there many times both in Russian and in translation, and he has there if not an army, then at least an élite guard of admirers among professional Slavists' (Novikov 1997: 272).

6 *Subbotnik* refers to the Soviet tradition of voluntary work undertaken on a Saturday by, and usually for the benefit of, the local community. The definitive version of this collection, containing twenty-nine stories, appears in the 1998 collected works. Seventeen of these stories appeared in the untitled collection from 1992, but in the interview appended to this earlier edition Sorokin refers to a different, presumably *samizdat* collection called 'Pervyi subbotnik', the title of which may indicate that it contains some of Sorokin's earliest work (see Rasskazova 1992: 119).

7 This device in its Socialist Realist incarnation is also parodied by Pišťanek in *Rivers of Babylon* and 'Mladý Dônč', and by Pelevin, particularly in *Omon Ra* and *Chapaev i Pustota*.

8 Strictly speaking, the first text in the 1998 version of the collection is the foreword, a parody of the ideological stamp of approval accompanying recommended works by unknown writers. Sorokin uses the less overtly political, moralistic tone of such forewords in the later Soviet period without obvious hyperbole, and thus the

uninitiated reader may not appreciate the parody until he encounters the 'frame-break', which in the case of this first text is represented by the rest of the collection.

9 The plot and themes of *Tridtsataia liubov' Mariny* closely resemble Páral's *Profesionální žena*; however, the contrast between them sharply highlights the distinction between what Lipovetskii calls the 'conceptualist' and the 'neo-Baroque'. Like *Tridtsataia liubov' Mariny*, *Profesionální žena* is at once a social satire and a literary burlesque in which the heroine, more Angélique than Emanuelle, repeatedly escapes the clutches of various corrupt, *embourgeoisés* gangsters successfully plying their trade in Socialist Czechoslovakia, before finally becoming a model Socialist worker. At the same time as she frees herself from these undesirable characters, she also frees herself from her 'creator', a mysterious stranger, Manek Mansfeld. For much of the novel, Mansfeld dictates her actions through letters and telegrams, but he turns out to be only a certain Josef Novák, living with his parents in a Prague suburb, like Tolstaia's 'fakir' combining his private fantasies with his favourite works of fiction. While Sorokin's work ultimately expresses the inescapable harmfulness of the text, in *Profesionální žena*, Páral, on the contrary, seeks to rid literature of pretensions to power over the individual, showing the writer's apparent aristocratic potency to be the mask of a humble, though basically harmless figure. In effect, the sentiment of Páral's novel corresponds to that of Ronald Sukenick in his contemporaneous short story 'The Death of the Novel' (1969): 'What we need is not great works but playful ones… A story is a game someone has played so you can play it too' (quoted in Waugh 1984: 34). While Páral, like Manek/Josef, seeks to rejuvenate the novel by freeing it of its heavy didacticism, Sorokin, though frequently playful, ultimately seeks to crush the novel under its own weight.

10 Sorokin's implicitly consensual use of the concept 'homo sovieticus' popularized by the dissident writer Aleksandr Zinov'iev (b.1922) gives credence to Bakhyt Kenzheev's comparison of *Norma* with Zinov'iev's classic of 1970s dissidence, *Ziiaiushchie vysoty* (The yawning heights, 1976) (see Kenzheev 1995: 203).

11 This episode, which 'breaks the frame' of reverence through which Russian culture conventionally remembers the Soviet war effort, coincidentally resembles a scene in Quentin Tarantino's 1994 film, *Pulp Fiction*, which similarly 'breaks the frame' of liberal righteousness through which the Vietnam War has come to be perceived by American cinematic culture in particular. In the scene, a general solemnly gives a little boy a gold watch, passed down through generations. In order to protect the watch while a prisoner of war, the boy's father had hidden it in his rectum, and when he died, the general ensured that it reached his son by keeping it in the same place. Tarantino's films, which attracted enormous critical interest as well as commercial success in Russia, reached the wider public there shortly after Sorokin's fiction, and the similarity in method has been noted by critics such as Petr Vail' and Gillespie (see, in particular, Vail' 1995: 4).

12 Topol breaks a comparable Czech cultural taboo in *Sestra* by suggesting that ordinary Czechs willingly collaborated in Auschwitz. The equation of German fascism with Stalinism occurred earliest in Slovak fiction, in Bednár's collection of stories *Hodiny a minúty* (Hours and minutes, 1956), and can be found in Czech literature in Ivan Klíma's novels of the early 1960s.

13 Litvák also uses the concept of 'mother' in *Samoreč* as a means to shock the implied reader and as a metaphor for language or literature, notably in the piece entitled 'Ľútosť ', in which the narrator physically and perhaps sexually assaults his mother, kicking her in the face to destroy his own resemblance to her. This act not only serves to complete his alienation from other human beings, but also reflects his 'defacement' of the notion of literature in the work.

14 Bátorová interprets Kolenič's novel as a moralizing attack on the contemporary human being. The ironic manner in which she criticizes the work reflects the apparent

difficulty experienced by critics in this period, particularly in Russia and Slovakia, who wished to object on moral grounds but did not want to be associated with the moralizing of the former 'official' and 'dissident' critical establishments.

15 The Underground Man remarks: 'Let's say, let's say I'm a chatterer, a harmless, annoying chatterer, like we all are. But what else is to be done if the real and only function of any intelligent man is chatter – that is, a deliberate pouring out of emptiness into void' (Dostoevsky 1956: 147).

16 Kolenič's preoccupation with shocking the reader may be compared with the approach of Igor' Iarkevich (b.1962), who briefly scandalized the mainstream Russian intelligentsia with his pastiche of Tolstoy's trilogy *Childhood* (1852), *Adolescence* (1854) and *Youth* (1857): *Kak ia obosralsia* (How I shat myself, 1991), *Kak menia iznasili* (How they raped me, 1991) and *Kak ia zanimalsia onanizmom* (How I masturbated, 1994). Somewhat in the spirit of Sorokin, Iarkevich suggests that he has been raped by Russian culture, which seeks to turn him into an ideologue, and advocates masturbation as a metaphor for the activity of the writer who abandons his traditional social role.

7 Learning to live with emptiness

1 Hodrová, indeed, alludes herself, through the character of Jan Paskal in *Podobojí*, to Pascal's assertion of the insurmountable intermediacy of human existence 'suspended in the mass which nature has given him between the two abysses of the infinite and of nothingness' (Pascal 1991: 249). Paskal's desperate attempts to invent a lasting identity for himself typify the vain activity of filling emptiness described by Pascal, a definition of writing from which neither Pascal's nor Hodrová's own writing is excluded.

2 In *Exhumace* (Exhumation, 1998), a collection of short fiction written mainly in the 1980s, Kahuda does not, however, link this behaviour explicitly with the regime, looking forward to the more general rejection of physical existence, particularly in *Houština*, in which many episodes from the stories in *Exhumace* are re-used.

3 Much sanctioned and unsanctioned fiction in the 1970s and 1980s was preoccupied with diagnosing the type of human being produced by Socialist society. Kahuda's Slezák to some extent recalls the central character, Zderad, in the novel *Mrchopěvci* (Toronto 1984, Prague 1990) by the émigré writer Jan Křesadlo (1926–1995). The neologism *mrchopěvec* refers sarcastically to Zderad's work, singing at funerals, since *mrcha* may mean 'carrion' or 'worn-out nag', but also evokes *mrchožravec*, meaning 'scavenger', and therefore necrophagy. At the same time, *mrcha* is also a common insult equivalent to 'bastard' or 'bitch'. Zderad consents to lick the anus of a Communist official whenever required to evade imprisonment for writing an anti-Stalin poem at school. His name, meaning 'happy here', indicates his complete submission not only to the regime, but also to terrestrial existence, from which, in a parody inversion of Socialist Realism, he is eventually rescued by his heroic wife. The sarcastic, satirical approach of Kahuda and Křesadlo closely resembles that of unsanctioned Russian writers like Iuz Aleshkovskii (b.1929) or Iurii Mamleev.

4 The desire to return to the 'basic sound of the universe' recalls Ajvaz's 'Koncert', in which the organist moves from a multitude of notes to a single note which apparently 'contains all other sounds' and therefore corresponds in effect to the Vedic 'om'. In contemporary Czech fiction, Ajvaz's writing exhibits the most serious leanings towards Oriental philosophy.

5 The instructors' names recall that of Pavel Korchagin, the hero of the Socialist Realist classic, *Kak zakalialas' stal'* (How the steel was tempered, 1934) by Nikolai Ostrovskii (1904–36). However, taken together they also evoke the slapstick characters Bobchinskii and Dobchinskii in Gogol's *The Government Inspector* (1836),

whose mistaken assertion that Khlestakov is the Government Inspector sets the farce in motion.

6 The image of the old woman as a symbol of the ugliness and transience of physical existence recurs in Pelevin's writing. In 'Khrustal'nyi mir' (The crystal world), the last story in *Sinii fonar'*, the link between this existence and Marxism-Leninism is made through the depiction of Lenin disguised as an old woman.

7 Kratochvil's attempt to realize his notion of 'self-subverting' short stories in the collection *Má lásko, Postmoderno* finds comparable expression in Slovak literature in the similarly Borges-influenced collection of short 'tales of the unexpected', *S odstupom času* (In hindsight, 1995) by Pavol Rankov (b.1964). Like Sorokin in his short fiction, Rankov relies on twists that expose the reader to the chaos beneath the apparent surface order, an objective he shares with Balla and indeed with the fiction of the Changes in general. His appeal to certain Slovak critics lay, however, in his interest in story-telling (also shared with Balla) and his lack of reliance on taboo-breaking, which distinguished him from his Barbarian or Genitalist contemporaries. On the basis of this first collection, Dana Kršáková described Rankov as a writer who 'is able to draw the reader into a world of absurdity, contrast and total relativization without shocking verbally' (Kršáková 1996: 69). This renewed interest in story-telling is also reflected in Horváth's subsequent prose, beginning with *Niekoľko náhlych konfigurácií* (Some sudden configurations, 1997).

8 In the early 1990s, Chapaev was also the subject of a short story by the Riga-born Russian writer Andrei Levkin (b.1954), entitled 'Chapaev: Mesto rozhdeniia – Riga (Novoe o G.I. Gurdzhieve)' (Chapaev: Place of birth – Riga (New findings about G.I. Gurdzhiev), 1993). In the manner of Borges, the story takes the form of a parody of a piece of obscure historical research. Chapaev here is portrayed as the product of a mysterious Georgian's experiments during the First World War to produce a homunculus without sexual, high intellectual or high emotional 'centres', who could therefore be relied upon to function effectively in military situations, without unnecessary dissipation of energy. Rather like Kratochvil in *Avion*, which also describes the manufacture of a homunculus by an evil genius, Levkin satirizes Stalin's 'engineering' of human souls, but also, through his description of the homunculus's character, the preferred Socialist literary type. At the same time, however, Levkin's story provides further evidence, along with Pelevin, of how the Conceptualist assertion of the manufactured nature of the Soviet system may be rendered creative.

Conclusion

1 The title of Lipovetskii's article coincidentally foreshadows the sentiments of a petition in the Czech Republic calling for the mass resignation of the political establishment which had overseen the first ten years of post-Communist transition, entitled 'Děkujeme – odejděte!' (Thank you, now go!).

2 Czech critics reacted similarly to Typlt, who appeared to have burnt himself out with his *Rozžhavená kra*.

Bibliography

1 The fiction of the Changes in English translation (original titles in square brackets where different)

Erofeev, Ven. (2001) *Moscow Stations* [*Moskva–Petushki*] trans. Stephen Mulrine, London: Faber & Faber.

Erofeev, Vik. (1992) *Russian Beauty*, trans. Andrew Reynolds, London: Hamish Hamilton.

Hrabal, B. (1991) *Too Loud a Solitude*, trans. Michael Henry Heim, London: Deutsch.

Makanin, V. (1996) *The Escape Hatch* [*Laz*] and *The Long Road Ahead*, trans. Mary Ann Szporluk, Ann Arbor: Ardis.

Pelevin, V. (1994) *Omon Ra*, trans. Andrew Bromfield, London: Harbord.

Pelevin, V. (1999) *The Life of Insects*, trans. Andrew Bromfield, London: Faber & Faber.

Pelevin, V. (1999) *The Clay Machine Gun* [*Chapaev i Pustota*], trans. Andrew Bromfield, London: Faber & Faber.

Pelevin, V. (2001) *The Blue Lantern*, trans. Andrew Bromfield, London: Faber & Faber.

Pelevin, V. (2001) *Babylon* [*Generation P*], trans. Andrew Bromfield, London: Faber & Faber.

Petrushevskaya, L. (1994) *The Time: Night*, trans. Sally Laird, London: Virago.

Popov, E. (1994) *The Soul of a Patriot*, trans. Robert Porter, Evanston: Northwestern.

Sorokin, V. (1988) *The Queue*, trans. Sally Laird, London: Readers International.

Tolstaya, T. (1989) *On the Golden Porch*, trans. Antonina W. Bouis, London: Virago.

Tolstaya, T. (1992) *Sleepwalker in a Fog*, trans. Jamey Gambrell, London: Virago.

Tolstaya, T. (2003) *The Slynx* [*Kys'*], trans. Jamey Gambrell, Boston: Houghton Mifflin.

Topol, J. (2000) *City Sister Silver* [*Sestra*], trans. Alex Zucker, North Haven: Catbird.

Ulitskaya, L. (1998) *Sonechka and other stories*, trans. Arch Tait, Birmingham: Glas.

Vilikovský, P. (2003) *Evergreen Is…*, trans. Charles Sabatos, Evanston: Northwestern.

2 Fiction and non-fiction by writers of the Changes

Ajvaz, M. (1992) *Druhé město*, Prague: Mladá fronta.

Ajvaz, M. (1997a) *Tyrkysový orel*, Prague: Hynek.

Ajvaz, M. (1997b) *Tajemství knihy*, Brno: Petrov.

Ajvaz, M. (2000) *Návrat starého várana*, Prague: Hynek.

Balla, V. (1996) *Leptokária*, Banská Bystrica: Drewo a Srd.

Balla, V. (1997) *Outsideria*, Banská Bystrica: Drewo a Srd.

Berková, A. (1988) *Knížka s červeným obalem*, 2nd edn, Prague: Práce.

Bitov, A. (1989) *Pushkinskii dom*, Moscow: Sovremennik.
Bondy, E. (1991) *Invalidní sourozenci*, Bratislava: Archa.
Brabcová, Z. (1991) *Daleko od stromu*, Prague: Československý spisovatel.
Brabcová, Z. (1995) *Zlodějina*, Prague: Český spisovatel.
Butov, M. (2000) *Svoboda*, St Petersburg: Inapress.
Erofeev, Ven. (1995) *Ostav'te moiu dushu v pokoe*, Moscow: AO 'Kh.G.S.'.
Erofeev, Vik. (1996) *Strashnyi sud*, Moscow: Soiuz fotokhudozhnikov Rossii.
Erofeev, Vik. (ed.) (1997) *Russkie tsvety zla*, Moscow: Podkova.
Erofeev, Vik. (1998) *Russkaia krasavitsa*, Moscow: Podkova.
Gandlevskii, S. and Prigov, D. (1993) 'Mezhdu imenem i imidzhem', *Literaturnaia gazeta* 19: 5.
Gandlevskii, S. (1995) *Trepanatsiia cherepa*, St Petersburg: Pushkinskii fond.
Hodrová, D. (1989) *Hledání románu*, Prague:Československý spisovatel.
Hodrová, D. (1992) *Město vidím...*, Prague: Euroslavica.
Hodrová, D. (1993a) *Perunův den*, Prague: Hynek.
Hodrová, D. (1993b) *Román zasvěcení*, Jinočany: H&H.
Hodrová, D. (1994) *Místa s tajemstvím*, Prague: Koniasch Latin Press.
Hodrová, D. (1997) *Ztracené děti*, Prague: Hynek.
Hodrová, D. (1999) *Trýznivé město*, Prague: Hynek.
Hodrová, D. (2001) *...na okraji chaosu...*, Prague: Torst.
Horváth, T. (1992) *Akozmia*, Bratislava: Kalligram.
Horváth, T. (1997) *Niekoľko náhlych konfigurácií*, Levice: L.C.A.
Horváth, T. (2000) *Dušan Mitana*, Bratislava: Kalligram.
Hrabal, B. (1994a) *Kafkárna*, Prague: Pražská imaginace.
Hrabal, B. (1994b) *Hlučná samota*, Prague: Pražská imaginace.
Hrabal, B. (2000) *Obsluhoval jsem anglického krále*, 6th edn, Prague: Mladá fronta.
Hrúz, P. (1990) *Chliev a hry*, Bratislava: Smena.
Hvorecký, M. (1998) *Silný pocit čistoty*, Levice: L.C.A.
Hvorecký, M. (2001) *Lovci a zberači*, Bratislava: Techno.sk.
Iarkevich, I. (1996) *Kak ia i kak menia*, Moscow: Proza Press.
Ivanchenko, A. (1987) *Iabloko na snegu*, Moscow: Sovetskii pisatel'.
Ivanchenko, A. (2000) *Golos bezmolviia*, Ekaterinburg: U-Faktoriia.
Johanides, J. (1995) *Trestajúci zločin*, Bratislava: Slovenský spisovateľ.
Juráňová, J. (2001) *Utrpenie starého kocúra*, Bratislava: Aspekt.
Kahuda, V. (1997) *Veselá bída*, Brno: Petrov.
Kahuda, V. (1998) *Exhumace*, Brno: Petrov.
Kahuda, V. (1999) *Houština*, Brno: Petrov.
Kahuda, V. (2000) *Technologie dubnového večera / Příběh o baziliškovi*, Brno: Host.
Klimáček, V. (1991) *Ďalekohladenie*, Bratislava: Slovenský spisovateľ.
Klimáček, V. (1997) *Panic v podzemí*, Levice: L.C.A.
Kolenič, I. (1992) *Mlčať*, Bratislava: Slovenský spisovateľ.
Kolenič, I. (1993) *Porušenie raja*, Bratislava: Slovenský spisovateľ.
Kolenič, I. (1996) *Ako z cigariet dym*, Bratislava: Slovenský spisovateľ.
Kratochvil, J. (1990) *Medvědí román*, Brno: Atlantis.
Kratochvil, J. (1992) *Uprostřed nocí zpěv*, Brno: Atlantis.
Kratochvil, J. (1993) *Avion*, Brno: Atlantis.
Kratochvil, J. (1994a) *Orfeus z Kénigu*, Brno: Atlantis.
Kratochvil, J. (1994b) *Má lásko, Postmoderno*, Brno: Atlantis.

Kratochvil, J. (1995) *Příběhy příběhů*, Brno: Atlantis.
Kratochvil, J. (1996) *Siamský příběh*, Brno: Atlantis.
Kratochvil, J. (1999a) *Noční tango*, Brno: Petrov.
Kratochvil, J. (1999b) *Urmedvěd*, Brno: Petrov.
Kratochvil, J. (2002) *Lehni, bestie!*, Brno: Petrov.
Kremlička, V. (1999) *Zemský povídky*, Prague: Hynek.
Landsmann, I. (1999) *Pestré vrstvy*, Prague: Torst.
Lehenová, T. (1989) *Pre vybranú spoločnosť*, Bratislava: Slovenský spisovateľ.
Litvák, J. (1992) *Samoreč*, Bratislava: Fragment.
Macura, V. (1991) 'Román Prahy', *Tvar*, II, 32: 5.
Macura, V. (1993) *Občan Monte Christo*, Prague: GMA 91.
Macura, V. (1999) *Ten, který bude*, Prague: Hynek.
Makanin, V. (1999) *Dolog nash put'*, Moscow: Vagrius.
Milota, K. (1993) *Sud*, Prague: Československý spisovatel.
Mitana, D. (1991) *Hľadanie strateného autora*, Bratislava: Smena.
Mitana, D. (1993) *Slovenský poker*, Bratislava: Hevi.
Pelevin, V. (1991) *Sinii fonar'*, Moscow: Tekst.
Pelevin, V. (1996) *Chapaev i Pustota*, Moscow: Vagrius.
Pelevin, V. (1997) *Zhizn' nasekomykh*, Moscow: Vagrius.
Pelevin, V. (1998) *Zheltaia strela*, Moscow: Vagrius.
Pelevin, V. (1999) *Generation P*, Moscow: Vagrius.
Petrushevskaia, L. (1996) *Sobranie sochinenii* (in 5 volumes), Kharkov, Moscow: Folio/TKO ACT.
Pisťanek, P. (1991) *Rivers of Babylon*, Bratislava: Archa.
Pisťanek, P. (1994) *Rivers of Babylon 2 alebo Drevená dedina*, Bratislava: Champagne Avantgarde.
Pisťanek, P. (1995) *Skazky o Vladovi*, Bratislava: Fénix.
Pisťanek, P. (1998) *Mladý Dônč*, 2nd edn, Levice: L.C.A.
Pisťanek, P. (1999) *Rivers of Babylon 3 alebo Fredyho koniec*, Bratislava: Fénix.
Placák, P. (1997) *Medorek*, 2nd edn, Prague: Hynek.
Popov, E. (1990) *Prekrasnosti zhizni*, Moscow: Moskovskii rabochii.
Popov, E. (1994) *Dusha patriota ili Razlichnye poslaniia k Ferfichkinu*, Moscow: Tekst.
Popov, E. (1998) *Podlinnaia istoriia 'Zelenykh Muzykantov'*, Moscow: Vagrius.
Rankov, P. (1995) *S odstupom času*, Levice: L.C.A.
Šabach, P. (1999) *Jak potopit Austrálii*, 5th edn, Prague: Paseka.
Sharov, V. (1995) *Do i vo vremia*, Moscow: L'Age d'Homme/Nash dom.
Sorokin, V. (1998a) *Sobranie sochinenii v dvukh tomakh*, Moscow: Ad Marginem.
Sorokin, V. (1998b) *Goluboe salo*, Moscow: Ad Marginem.
Tále, S. (2001) *Kniha o cintoríne*, Levice: L.C.A.
Tolstaia, T. (1997) *Liubish' – ne liubish'*, Moscow: Oniks-OLMA-Press.
Tolstaia, T. (2001) *Kys'*, Moscow: Podkova/Inostranka.
Topol, J. (1994) *Sestra*, Brno: Atlantis.
Topol, J. (1995) *Anděl*, Prague: Hynek.
Topol, J. (2001) *Noční práce*, Prague: Torst/Hynek.
Turan, A., Bielik, R., Zbruž, K. and Litvák, J. (1998) *Barbar(u)ská ruleta*, Bratislava: Vydavateľstvo Spolku slovenských spisovateľov.
Typlt, J. (1993) 'Devadesátá léta mezi zátiším a bojištěm', *Tvar*, IV, 16: 1,4.
Typlt, J. (1996) *Rozžhavená kra*, Olomouc: Votobia.

Ulitskaia, L. (1998) *Medea i ee deti*, Moscow: Vagrius.
Urban, J. (1988) 'Čo na to psychiatri?', *Literárny týždenník*, I, 1: 4.
Urban, J. (1989) 'O psoch a karaváne', *Literárny týždenník*, II, 12: 4.
Urban, M. (1999) *Sedmikostelí*, Prague: Argo.
Vilikovský, P. (1989a) *Večne je zelený*..., Bratislava: Slovenský spisovateľ.
Vilikovský, P. (1989b) *Eskalácia citu*, Bratislava: Tatran.
Vilikovský, P. (1992) 'Na nádvorí je počuť krik', *Dotyky*, IV, 8: 20.
Vilikovský, P. (1993) 'Správy z cesty (do plytčín noci)', *Dotyky*, V, 8: 18–19.
von Kamin, T. (1995) *I., alebo Žltý penis*, Levice: L.C.A..
Zbruž, K. (1993) *Spitý imidž*, Levice: L.C.A.

3 Other works used

Al'tshuller, M. (1982) '*Moskva–Petushki* Venedikta Erofeeva i traditsii klassicheskoi poemy', *Novyi zhurnal*, 146: 75–85.
Aleksandrov, Nikolai D. (1997) 'Novaia eklektika', *Literaturnoe obozrenie*, 3: 27–34.
Alenka, A. (1994) 'Já jsem někdo jiný, čili Agent Jícha potká v Potoku syna člověka', *Literární noviny*, V, 29: 6.
Azhgikhina, N. (1990) 'Razrushiteli v poiskakh very', *Znamia*, 9: 223–7.
Bakhtin, M. (1984a) *Problems of Dostoevsky's Poetics*, translated and edited by Caryl Emerson, Manchester: Manchester University Press.
Bakhtin, M. (1984b) *Rabelais and His World*, translated by Hélène Iswolsky, Bloomington: Indiana University Press.
Bakhtin, M. (1990) *Art and Answerability*, trans. Vadim Liapunov, edited by Michael Holquist and Vadim Liapunov, Austin: University of Texas Press.
Balina, M., Condee, N., Dobrenko E. (eds) (2000) *Endquote: Sots-Art Literature and Soviet Grand Style,* Evanston: North Western University Press.
Barthes, R. (1976) *The Pleasure of the Text*, trans. Richard Miller, London: Jonathan Cape.
Barthes, R. (1977) *Image–Music–Text*, trans. Stephen Heath, London: Fontana.
Basinskii, P. (1995) 'Pafos granitsy', *Novyi mir*, 1: 221–3.
Bátorová, M. (1993) 'Nekrižujte Krista, netetujte Máriu', *Romboid*, XXVIII, 3: 57–9.
Beasley-Murray, T. (1998) 'Postmodernism of Resistance in Central Europe: Pavel Vilikovský's *Večne je zelený*...', *Slavonic & East European Review*, 76, 2: 266–78.
Beasley-Murray, T. (1999) 'Jacques Lacan, Ivan Kolenič – imaginárne a symbolické v próze *Mlčať*', *Romboid*, XXXIV, 7: 37–41.
Beasley-Murray, T. (2000) 'Contemporary Slovak Literature, the Devilish Pact with Theory, and the Genitalists' in Williams, K. (ed.), *Slovakia after Communism and Mečiarism*, London: School of Slavonic and East European Studies–UCL: 79–88.
Bergson, H. (1911) *Laughter: An Essay on the Meaning of the Comic*, trans. Cloudsley Brereton and Fred Rothwell, London: Macmillan.
Berry, E.E. and Miller-Pogacar, A. (eds) (1995) *Re-entering the Sign: Articulating New Russian Culture*, Ann Arbor: University of Michigan Press.
Bílek, P.A. (1991) *'Generace' osamělých běžců*, Prague: Československý spisovatel.
Bock, I. (1992) 'Jedna česká literatura? K některým tendencím "oficiální", samizdatové a exilové prózy', *Česká literatura*, 40: 67–84.
Bogdanova, O.V. (2002) Moskva–Petushki *Venedikta Erofeeva kak pratekst russkogo postmodernizma*, St Petersburg: Filologicheskii fakul'tet Sankt-Peterburgskogo gosudarstvennogo universiteta.

Borges, J.L. (1970) *Labyrinths*, Harmondsworth: Penguin.

Boym, S. (1993) 'The Poetics of Banality' in Goscilo, Helena (ed.), *Fruits of Her Plume: Essays on Contemporary Russian Women's Culture*, Armonk, N.Y., London: M.E. Sharpe: 59–83.

Breisky, A. (1996) *Střepy zrcadla*, edited by Luboš Merhaut, Prague: Thyrsus.

Brooks, P. (1984) *Reading for the Plot: Design and Intention in Narrative*, Oxford: Clarendon.

Brousek, A. (1991) 'Román jako otevřený systém', *Literární noviny*, II, 35: 4.

Brown, D. (1993) *The Last Years of Soviet Russian Literature*, Cambridge: Cambridge University Press.

Burkhart, D. (ed.) (1999) *Poetik der Metadiskursivität: Zum postmodernen Prosa-, Film- und Dramenwerk von Vladimir Sorokin*, Munich: Sagner.

Calabrese, O. (1992) *Neo-Baroque: A Sign of the Times*, Princeton: Princeton University Press.

Calinescu, M. (1987) *Five Faces of Modernity*, Durham, NC: Duke University Press.

Camus, A. (1988) *The Myth of Sisyphus*, trans. Justin O'Brien, Harmondsworth: Penguin.

Chances, E. (1993) *Andrei Bitov: The Ecology of Inspiration*, Cambridge: Cambridge University Press.

Chrobáková, S. (1992) 'Konfrontácia Č/Ch', *Romboid*, XXVII, 5: 75.

Chuchma, J. (2002) 'Jáchym Topol: Snad se v nás neprobudí démoni', *Mladá Fronta Dnes*, 3 May, Section B: 8.

Chuprinin, S. (1989a) 'Drugaia proza', *Literaturnaia gazeta*, 6: 4–5.

Chuprinin, S. (1989b) 'Prochitannomu verit'', *Volga*, 2: 77–89.

Chuprinin, S. (1993) 'Sbyvsheesia nebyvshee', *Znamia*, 9: 181–8.

Chvatík, K. (1992) 'Medvědí román anebo Nezničitelnost epiky', *Tvar*, IV, 6: 6–7.

Clark, K. (1981) *The Soviet Novel: History as Ritual*, Chicago, London: University of Chicago Press.

Čúzy, L. (1992) 'Konfrontácia Č/Ch', *Romboid*, XXVII, 5: 74.

Čúzy, L. (1997) 'Metafora o živote generácií', *Romboid*, XXXII, 8: 87–8.

Dalton-Brown, S. (1997) 'Ludic Nonchalance or Ludicrous Despair? Viktor Pelevin and Russian Postmodernist Prose', *Slavonic & East European Review*, 75, 2: 216–33.

Darovec, P. (1996) *Násmešné rozmlúvanie*, Levice: L.C.A.

Dedkov, I. (1991) 'Mezhdu proshlym i budushchim', *Znamia*, 1: 231–40.

Deleuze, G. and Guattari, F. (1984) *Anti-Oedipus: Capitalism and Schizophrenia*, trans. Robert Hurley, Mark Seem and Helen R. Lane, London: Athlone.

Deutschmann, P. (1999) 'Der Begriff der Norm bei Sorokin' in Burkhart, D. (ed.), *Poetik der Metadiskursivität: Zum postmodernen Prosa-, Film- und Dramenwerk von Vladimir Sorokin*, Munich: Sagner: 37–52.

Docherty, T. (1983) *Reading (Absent) Character: Towards a Theory of Characterization in Fiction*, Oxford: Clarendon.

Dokoupil, B. and Zelinský, M. (eds) (1994) *Slovník České prózy 1945–1994*, Ostrava, xx: 1994.

Dostoevsky, F. (1956–8) *Sobranie sochinenii* (in 10 volumes), Moscow: Khudozhestvennaia literatura.

Eliade, M. (1954) *The Myth of the Eternal Return*, trans. Willard R. Trask, New York: Pantheon.

Epshtein, M. (1986) 'Pokolenie, nashedshee sebia', *Voprosy literatury*, 5: 40–72.

Epshtein, M. (1991) 'Posle budushchego. O novom soznanii v literature', *Znamia*, 1, 217–30.

Epshtein, M. (1995a) 'Posle karnevala, ili Vechnyi Venichka' in Erofeev, Ven., *Ostav'te moiu dushu v pokoe*, Moscow: AO 'Kh.G.S.': 3–30.

Epshtein [Epstein], M. (1995b) *After the Future: The Paradoxes of Postmodernism and Contemporary Russian Culture*, trans. Anesa Miller-Pogacar, Amherst: University of Massachusetts Press.

Eshelman, R. (1997) *Early Soviet Postmodernism*, Frankfurt-on-Main, Berlin, Bern, New York, Paris, Vienna: Peter Lang.

Exner, M. (1991) 'Šíře a hloubka metafory', *Tvar*, II, 35: 14.

Fiedler, L. (1971) 'Cross the Border – Close the Gap' in *The Collected Essays of Leslie Fiedler*, vol. II, New York: Stein and Day: 461–85.

Foucault, M. (1998) *Aesthetics, Method, and Epistemology*, edited by James Faubion, trans. Robert Hurley, Harmondsworth: Penguin.

Fromm, E. (1942) *The Fear of Freedom*, London: Kegan Paul, Trench, Trubner.

Gaiser-Shnitman, S. (1989) *Venedikt Erofeev 'Moskva–Petushki' ili 'The rest is silence'*, Berne, Frankfurt-on-Main, New York, Paris: Peter Lang.

Gammelgaard, K. (1997) *Spoken Czech in Literature*, Oslo: Scandinavian University Press.

Genis, A. (1999) 'Borders and Metamorphoses: Viktor Pelevin in the Context of Post-Soviet Literature' in Vladiv-Glover, Svetlana M. (ed.), *Russian Postmodernism: New Perspectives on Post-Soviet Culture*, New York, Oxford: Berghahn: 212–24.

Gillespie, D. (1997) 'Sex, Violence and the Video-Nasty: The Ferocious Prose of Vladimir Sorokin', *Essays in Poetics*, 22: 158–75.

Gimein, A. (1979) 'Nulevoi chas', *Kontinent*, 20: 369–73.

Givens, J.R. (1993) 'Reflections, Crooked Mirrors, Magic Theaters: Tat'iana Tolstaia's "Peters"' in Goscilo, H. (ed.), *Fruits of Her Plume: Essays on Contemporary Russian Women's Culture*, Armonk, N.Y., London: M.E. Sharpe: 251–70.

Goethe, J.W. (1998) *Faust: Part One*, trans. David Luke, Oxford, New York: Oxford University Press.

Gor'kii, M. (1968), *Polnoe sobranie sochinenii* (in 25 volumes), Moscow: Nauka.

Goscilo, H. (1988) 'Tat'iana Tolstaia's "Dome of Many-Coloured Glass": The World Refracted Through Multiple Perspectives', *Slavic Review*, 47, 2: 280–90.

Goscilo, H. (1993a) 'Perspective in Tatyana Tolstaya's Wonderland of Art', *World Literature Today*, 67, 1: 80–90.

Goscilo, H. (ed.) (1993b) *Fruits of Her Plume: Essays on Contemporary Russian Women's Culture*, Armonk, N.Y., London: M.E. Sharpe.

Goscilo, H. (1997) *The Explosive World of Tatyana N. Tolstaya's Fiction*, Armonk, N.Y., London: M.E.Sharpe.

Grant, R.M. (1959) *Gnosticism and Early Christianity*, New York, London: Columbia University Press.

Grekova, I. (1988) 'Rastochitel'nost' talanta', *Novyi mir*, 1: 252–6.

Groys, B. (1992) *The Total Art of Stalinism*, trans. Charles Rougle, Princeton: Princeton University Press.

Halvoník, A. (1989) 'Figový list výrečnosti', *Literárny týždenník*, II, 26: 4.

Haman, A. (2001a) *Prozaické surfování*, Olomouc: Votobia.

Haman, A. (2001b), 'Vyznání s puncem generačního programu', *Tvar* XII, 9: 1,4.

Harvey, P. (1990) *An Introduction to Buddhism*, Cambridge: Cambridge University Press.

Harvey, P. (1995) *The Selfless Mind*, Richmond, Surrey: Curzon Press.
Hausenblas, O. (1994) 'Placákův *Medorek* jako čin lingvistický', *Naše řeč*, 77, 1: 6–13.
Havel, V. (1990) *O lidskou identitu*, Prague: Rozmluvy.
Havel, V. (1999) *Hry* (*Spisy*, Vol.2), Prague: Torst.
Henderson, K. (2002) *Slovakia: The Escape from Invisibility*, London, New York: Routledge.
Heřman, Z. (1992) 'Ambiciózní próza', *Tvar*, III, 4: 14.
Hosking, G. (1980) *Beyond Socialist Realism*, London: Elek.
Hume, D. (1978) *A Treatise of Human Nature*, Oxford: Clarendon.
Hutcheon, L. (1988) *A Poetics of Postmodernism*, New York, London: Routledge.
Hutcheon, L. (1989) *The Politics of Postmodernism*, London: Routledge.
Iser, W. (1974) *The Implied Reader*, Baltimore, London: Johns Hopkins University Press.
Ivanova, N. (1989) 'Namerennye neschastlivtsy?', *Druzhba narodov*, 7: 239–53.
Ivanova, N. (1991) 'Neopalimyi golubok', *Znamia*, 8: 211–23.
Ivanova, N. (1993) 'Peizazh posle bitvy', *Znamia*, 9: 189–98.
Ivanova, N. (1998) 'On the Mound of Returned Tickets: The Newest Russian Prose', trans. Julian Graffy, *Artes*, 5: 77–85.
Jameson, F. (1991) *Postmodernism or The Cultural Logic of Late Capitalism*, London, New York: Verso.
Janáček, P. (1991) 'Kulatá ouzkost. Tři prozaické debuty ve zkoušce ohně', *Lidové noviny*, 10 July: 7.
Janáček, P. (1994) 'Božská komedie po výbuchu času', *Lidové noviny*, 31 December, supplement *Národní 9*: IV.
Jankovič, M. (1996) *Kapitoly z poetiky Bohumila Hrabala*, Prague: Torst.
Jankovič, M. (1991) *Nesamozřejmost smyslu*, Prague: Československý spisovatel.
Janoušek, P. (1994) 'Dejte mi pevný bod aneb Za společenský román krásnější', *Tvar*, V, 12: 3.
Janoušek, P. (1996) 'Proměny literární atmosféry v době postlistopadové', *Tvar*, VII, 18: 10–11.
Janoušek, P. (2001) *Time-out*, Brno: Host.
Jedličková, A. (1992) 'Mnou vchází se do trýznivého textu', *Tvar*, III, 51–2: 19.
Jenčíková, E. and Zajac, P. (1989) 'Situácia súčasnej slovenskej literatúry', *Slovenské pohľady*, 105, 2: 45–71.
Jungmann, M. (1988) *Cesty a rozcestí*, Purley: Rozmluvy.
Jungmann, M. (1990) 'Česká proza v normalizační tísni', *Česká literatura*, 39, 2: 145–58.
Jungmann, M. (1993a) 'Kudy kam z chaosu', *Literární noviny*, IV, 4: 7.
Jungmann, M. (1993b) 'Hazardér české prózy', *Literární noviny*, IV, 17: 6.
Jungmann, M. (1997) *V obklíčení příběhů*, Brno: Atlantis.
Kantůrková, E. (1988) 'Karel Medor, hrdina naší doby', *Kritický sborník*, 8, 2: 41–51.
Kautman, F. (1993) 'Skica Daniely Hodrové', *Literární noviny*, IV, 9: 6.
Kenzheev, B. (1995) 'Antisovetchik Vladimir Sorokin', *Znamia*, 4: 202–4.
Klíma, L. (undated) *Svět jako vědomí a nic*, Bratislava: Súvislosti.
Kočka, F. (1987) '*Medorek*. Značně opožděný ohlas stejnojmenného prozaického díla', *Revolver Revue*, 6: first page (unpaginated).
Kornev, S. (1997) 'Stolknovenie pustot: mozhet li postmodernizm byt' russkim i klassicheskim?', *Novoe literaturnoe obozrenie*, 28: 244–59.
Kostyrko, S. (1992) 'Chistoe pole literatury', *Novyi mir*, 12: 250–60.
Křesadlo, J. (1999) *Mrchopěvci/Gravelarks*, Prague: Maťa.

Kříž, J. (1993) 'Druhé město', *Tvar*, IV, 37–8: 7.

Kršáková, D. (1996) 'Zábava intelektuálneho razenia', *Romboid*, XXXI, 3: 69–70.

Krupičková, Z.P. (2000) 'Román o biologickém fenoménu', *Tvar*, XI, 3: 5.

Kuritsyn, V. (1993) 'My poedem s toboiu na "A" i na "Iu"', *Novoe literaturnoe obozrenie*, 1: 296–304.

Kuritsyn, V. (1997) 'Gruppa prodlennogo dnia' in Pelevin, V., *Zhizn' nasekomykh*, Moscow: Vagrius: 7–20.

Kuritsyn, V. (1999) 'Telo teksta' in Burkhart, D. (ed.), *Poetik der Metadiskursivität: Zum postmodernen Prosa-, Film- und Dramenwerk von Vladimir Sorokin*, Munich: Sagner: 61–4.

Kuritsyn, V. (2000) 'Skuchno pisat' odinakovo' in Ivanchenko, A., *Golos bezmolviia*, Ekaterinburg: U-Faktoriia: 615–22.

Kustanovich, K. (1997) 'Venichka Erofeev's Grief and Solitude: Existentialist Motifs in the *Poema*' in Ryan-Hayes, K. (ed.), *Venedikt Erofeev's Moskva–Petushki: Critical Perspectives*, New York: Peter Lang: 123–51.

Laing, R.D. (1969) *The Divided Self*, Harmondsworth: Penguin.

Laird, S. (1999) *Voices of Russian Literature*, Oxford: Oxford University Press.

Latynina, A. (1987) 'Zhestkaia proza', *Literaturnaia gazeta*, 24: 4.

Latynina, A. and Dewhirst, M. (2001) 'Post-Soviet Russian Literature' in Cornwell, N. (ed.), *The Routledge Companion to Russian Literature*, London, New York: Routledge: 234–50.

Lehár, J., Stich, A., Janáčková, J. and Holý, J. (1998) *Česká literatura od počátků k dnešku*, Prague: Lidové noviny.

Likhachev, D. (ed.) (1984) *Smekh v drevnei Rusi*, Leningrad: Nauka.

Lipovetskii, M. (1989), 'Svobody chernaia rabota', *Voprosy literatury*, 9: 3–45.

Lipovetskii, M. (1991) 'Zakon krutizny', *Voprosy literatury*, 11–12: 3–32.

Lipovetskii, M. (1992) 'A za prazdnik – spasibo!', *Literaturnaia gazeta*, 46: 4.

Lipovetskii, M. (1997) *Russkii postmodernizm*, Ekaterinburg: Ural'skii gosudarstvennyi pedagogicheskii institut.

Lipovetskii [Lipovetsky], M. (1999a) *Russian Postmodernist Fiction: Dialogue with Chaos*, Armonk, N.Y., London: M.E.Sharpe.

Lipovetskii, M. (1999b), 'Russkii postmodernizm v 1990-e gody', paper presented at BASEES Twentieth Century Group seminar, Oxford, September 1999.

Lipovetskii [Lipovetsky], M. (2000) 'Vladimir Sorokin's "Theatre of Cruelty"' in Balina, M., Condee, N. and Dobrenko, E. (eds) *Endquote: Sots-Art Literature and Soviet Grand Style,* Evanston: North Western University Press: 167–70.

Literární týždenník (1989) II, 4: 5.

Lotman, I. (1988) 'Myslenie kritiky', *Literárny týždenník*, I, 9: 9.

Lukavská, K. (2002), *Navrať se do domu srdce svého... aneb Jiří Kratochvil – 'Postmoderní' literatura*, supplement to *Tvar*, XIII, 3.

Lukeš, J. (1982) *Prozaická skutečnost*, Prague: Mladá fronta.

Lyotard, J.-F. (1984) *The Postmodern Condition: A Report on Knowledge*, trans. Geoff Bennington and Brian Massumi, Manchester: Manchester University Press.

Machala, L. (2001) *Literární bludiště: Bilance polistopadové prózy*, Prague: Brána.

Macura, V. (1991) 'Román Prahy', *Tvar*, II, 32: 5.

Malura, J. (1993) 'Město nepřiznané', *Tvar*, IV, 33–4: 20–1.

Matejovič, P. (1996) 'Povinné čítanie', *Romboid*, XXI, 7: 68.

McCannon, J. (1997) 'Positive Heroes at the Pole: Celebrity Status, Socialist Realist Ideals and the Soviet Myth of the Arctic, 1932–1939', *Russian Review*, 56, 3: 346–65.
McCausland, G. (2000) 'Viktor Pelevin and the End of Sots-Art' in Balina, M., Condee, N., Dobrenko, E. (eds) (2000) *Endquote: Sots-Art Literature and Soviet Grand Style*, Evanston: North Western University Press: 225–37.
McHale, B. (1987) *Postmodernist Fiction*, New York, London: Methuen.
Mertl, V. (1993) 'Obnovení řádu v české literatuře', *Literární noviny*, IV, 1: 6–7.
Mikula, F. (1989) 'Krajnosťou k miernosti, obscénnosťou za lepšiu budúcnosť', *Slovenské pohľady*, 105, 8: 41–7.
Minár, P. (1992) 'Smrť subjektu po slovensky', *Dotyky*, IV, 8: 20.
Moravčík, Š. (1992) 'Pochutnal som si na svojej nicote', *Dotyky*, IV, 10: 36.
Nefagina, G. (1998) *Russkaia proza vtoroi poloviny 80-kh-nachala 90-kh godov XX veka*, Minsk: Ekonompress.
Němec, L. (1982) *Hra na slepo*, Brno: Blok.
Nemzer, A. (1998), *Literaturnoe segodnia: O russkoi proze. 90-e*, Moscow: Novoe literaturnoe obozrenie.
Nicholas, M.A. (1996) 'Dmitrij Prigov and the Russian Avant-Garde, Then and Now', *Russian Literature*, XXXIX: 13–34.
Novikov, V. (1997) *Zaskok: Esse, parodii, razmyshleniia*, Moscow: Knizhnyi sad.
Novotný, V. (1995a) 'Nová česká literature (1990–1995)', *Tvar*, VI, 15: 24.
Novotný, V. (1995b), 'Nová česká literature (1990–1995)', *Tvar*, VI, 16: 24.
Novotný, V. (2000) 'Zdali nám bude dáno světlo v houštinách', *Tvar*, XI, 3: 5.
Novotný, V. (2002) *Mezi moderností a postmoderností*, Prague: Cherm.
O'Connor, B. (ed.) (2000) *The Adorno Reader*, Oxford, Malden, Massachusetts: Blackwell.
Opelík, J. (ed.) (2000) *Lexikon české literatury*, 3 [I], Prague: Academia.
Otčenáš, I. (1992), 'Nech žije holá veta', *Dotyky*, IV, 2: 39–40.
Ovid (1955) *The Metamorphoses*, trans. Mary M. Innes, Harmondsworth: Penguin.
Páral, V. (1998) *Profesionální žena*, 5th edn, Prague: Baronet.
Pascal, B. (1991) *Pensées*, Paris: Bordas.
Pelc, J. (1996) *...a bude hůř*, 3rd edn, Prague: Maťa.
Peterson, N.L. (1997) *Subversive Imaginations: Fantastic Prose and the End of Soviet Literature 1970s–1990s*, Boulder, Colorado, Oxford: Westview Press.
Petrík, V. (1991) 'K charakteru Vilikovského prózy', *Romboid*, XXVI, x: 16.
Pilař, M. (1999) *Underground: Kapitoly o českém literárním undergroundu*, Brno: Host.
Píša, V. (1991) 'Medvědi nevědí...', *Tvorba*, II, 26: 15.
Piskunova, S. and Piskunov, V. (1988) 'Uroki sozerkal'ia', *Oktiabr'*, 8: 188–98.
Pohánková, K. (1996) 'Směřování mladé generace v próze osmdesátých let', *Česká literatura*, 44, 2: 181–7.
Porter, R. (1994a) 'Translator's Introduction' in Popov, E. (1994) *The Soul of a Patriot*, trans. Robert Porter, London: Harvill: v–x.
Porter, R. (1994b) *Russia's Alternative Prose*, Oxford, Providence: Berg.
Postnikova, T.V. (1995) *'Esli ty nosish' nachalo vremen v ushakh' (Avangardnaia poeziia 80-kh-90-kh gg.)*, Moscow: Rossiiskaia gosudarstvennaia biblioteka.
Potapov, V. (1989) 'Na vykhode iz "andergraunda"', *Novyi mir*, 10: 251–7.
Pynsent, R.B. (1984) 'Adolescence, Ideology and Society: The Young Hero in Contemporary Czech Fiction' in Wallace, I. (ed.), *The Adolescent Hero*, Dundee: GDR Monitor: 65–86.

Pynsent, R.B. (1986) 'Social Criticism in Czech Literature of 1970s and 1980s Czechoslovakia', *Bohemia*, 27, 1: 1–36.

Pynsent, R.B. (1990) 'Ballek a Vilikovský', *Romboid*, XXV, 12: 120–8.

Pynsent, R.B. (1997) 'Killing, Laughing and Observing: Three Trends in Contemporary Slovak Literature' in Navrátil, I. and Pynsent, R.B. (eds), *Appropriations and Impositions: National, Regional and Sexual Identity in Literature*, Bratislava: Národné literárne centrum: 195–220.

Pynsent, R.B. (1999) 'What about the Slovaks?' in Kollar, Miro, (ed.), *Scepticism and Hope: Sixteen Contemporary Slovak Essays*, Bratislava: Kalligram: 9–25.

Pynsent, R.B. (2000) 'Video Nasties: The Last Decade of the Slovak Twentieth Century through the Eyes of Peter Pišťanek' in Williams, K. (ed.), *Slovakia after Communism and Mečiarism*, London: School of Slavonic and East European Studies–UCL: 89–109.

Pytlík, R. (1998) *...a neuvěřitelné se stalo skutkem: O Bohumilu Hrabalovi*, Prague: Emporius.

Rasskazova, T. (1992) 'Tekst kak narkotik' in Sorokin, V., *Vladimir Sorokin*, Moscow: Russlit: 119–26.

Rédey, Z. (1994) 'Mladý Dônč – starý syndrom', *Romboid*, XIX, 4: 56–60.

Resutík, M. (1990) 'Ex libris', *Romboid*, XXV, 3: 124.

Richterová, S. (1991) *Slova a ticho*, Prague: Československý spisovatel.

Rodnianskaia, I. (1993) 'Gipsovyi veter', *Novyi mir*, 12: 215–31.

Rodnianskaia, I. (1996) '...i k nei bezumnaia liubov'...', *Novyi mir*, 9: 214–15.

Roll, S. (1996) 'Stripping Socialist Realism of its Seamless Dress: Vladimir Sorokin's Deconstruction of Soviet Utopia and the Art of Representation', *Russian Literature*, XXXIX: 65–77.

Romboid (1988) XXIII, 5: 114–22.

Rose, M.A. (1993) *Parody: Ancient, Modern and Postmodern*, Cambridge: Cambridge University Press.

Rothová, S. (1993) *Hlučná samota a hořké štěstí Bohumila Hrabala*, trans. Michael Špirit, Prague: Pražská imaginace.

Ryklin, M. (1998) 'Medium i avtor' in Sorokin, V., *Sobranie sochinenii v dvukh tomakh*, vol.2, Moscow: Ad Marginem: xx.

Ryšavý, M. (1993) 'Zasvěcení do textu', *Tvar*, IV, 37–38: 18–19.

Sakwa,R. (1990) *Gorbachev and His Reforms 1985–1990*, New York, London, Toronto: Philip Allan.

Sartorti, R. (1995) 'On the Making of Heroes, Heroines and Saints' in Stites, R. (ed.), *Culture and Entertainment in Wartime Russia*, Bloomington: Indiana University Press.

Shapoval, S. (1998) '"V kul'ture dlia menia net tabu..."' in Sorokin, Vladimir, *Sobranie sochinenii v dvukh tomakh*, vol.1, Moscow: Ad Marginem, 1998: 7–20.

Shklovskii, E. (1988) 'Idushchie vosled', *Znamia*, 4: 217–26.

Shneidman, N.N. (1995) *Russian Literature 1988–1994: The End of an Era*, Toronto, Buffalo, London: University of Toronto Press.

Shtokman, I. (1989) 'Vkus podlinnosti', *Literaturnaia gazeta*, 16: 4.

Skoropanova, I. (1999) *Russkaia postmodernistskaia literatura*, Moscow: Flinta/Nauka.

Slávik, I. (1989) 'Náčrt súčasnej situácie mladej českej prózy druhej polovice 80. rokov', *Dotyky*, I, 8: 21–2.

Sloboda, R. (1992) 'Niekoľko poznámok k Riekam Babylonu', *Dotyky*, IV, 2: 39–40.

Šofar, J. (2000) 'The Fool on the Hill', *Tvar*, XI, 3: 1.

Solovič, J. (1988) 'Nezostať v závetrí', *Literárny týždenník*, I, 1: 1.

Součková, M. (1994) 'Slovenský bestseller', *Romboid*, XIX, 2: 63–5.
Spivak, P. (1988) 'Vo sne i naiavu', *Oktiabr'*, 2: 201–3.
Sternbergová, K. (1993) 'Čas v Thétě Daniely Hodrové', *Tvar*, IV, 27–28: 9.
Šútovec, M. (1989) 'Umenie nosiť bremená' in Vilikovský, P., *Eskalácia citu*, Bratislava: Tatran.
Tao Te Ching (1954), trans. J.J.L. Duyvendak, London: John Murray.
Terts, A. (1982) *The Trial Begins*, trans. Max Hayward, and *On Socialist Realism*, trans. George Dennis, Berkeley, Los Angeles: University of California Press.
Tiutchev, F. (1984) *Sochineniia v dvukh tomakh*, Moscow: Khudozhestvennaia literatura.
Uch«li, D. (1992) 'Svet podľa Pišťanka', *Dotyky*, IV, 3: 43.
Urnov, D. (1989) 'Plokhaia proza', *Literaturnaia gazeta*, 6: 4–5.
Vaca, K. [–kv-] (1988) 'Boží prostota?', *Kritický sborník*, 8, 3: 55–6.
Vaculík, L. (1992) *Český snář*, Brno: Atlantis.
Vail', P. (1995) 'Konservator Sorokin v kontse veka', *Literaturnaia gazeta*, 5: 4.
Vail', P. and Genis, A. (1988) 'Popytka k begstvu', *Sintaksis*, 24: 116–31.
Vail', P. and Genis, A. (1989) 'Novaia proza: ta zhe ili "drugaia"?', *Novyi mir*, 10: 247–50.
Vasilevskii, A. (1988) 'Nochi kholodny', *Druzhba narodov*, 7: 256–8.
Vladiv-Glover, S.M. (ed.) (1999) *Russian Postmodernism: New Perspectives on Post-Soviet Culture*, New York, Oxford: Berghahn.
Vlasov, E. (2001) 'Bessmertnaia poema Venedikta Erofeeva "Moskva–Petushki". Sputnik pisatelia' in Erofeev, Ven., *Moskva–Petushki*, Moscow: Vagrius: 121–574.
Vohryzek, J. (1995) 'Výlet k nádražní hale', *Literární noviny*, VI, 43: 5.
Voinovich, V. (1993) *Maloe sobranie sochinenii* (in 5 volumes), Moscow: Fabula.
Vojtěch, D. (1994) 'Příběh naší zkušenosti', *Literární noviny*, V, 27: 6.
Vrbová, A. (2001) *Koncepty prostoru v románových trilogiích Daniely Hodrové a Jiřího Kratochvila*, supplement to *Tvar*, XII, 2–3.
Waugh, P. (1984) *Metafiction: The Theory and Practice of Self-Conscious Fiction*, London, New York: Routledge.
Wilde, O. (1986) *De Profundis and Other Writings*, Harmondsworth: Penguin.
Williams, K. (ed.) (2000) *Slovakia after Communism and Mečiarism*, London: School of Slavonic and East European Studies–UCL.
Wordsworth, W. (1994) *Selected Poems*, Harmondsworth: Penguin.
Zajac, P. (1989a) 'Incognito, ergo sum', *Literárny týždenník*, II, 26: 4–5.
Zajac, P. (1989b) 'Postmodernizmus', *Romboid*, XXIV, 6: 102–3.
Žilka, T. (1989) 'Postmodernizmus v próze', *Romboid*, XXIV, 9: 18–24.
Žilka, T. (1990) 'Recepčné relácie súčasnej prózy', *Romboid*, XXV, 1: 83–91.
Zolotonosov, M. (1987) 'Mechty i fantomy', *Literaturnoe obozrenie*, 4: 58–61.
Zorin, A. (1989) 'Prigorodnyi poezd dal'nego sledovaniia', *Novyi mir*, 5: 256–8.
Zvonnikova, L. (1996) '"Moskva–Petushki" i pr. Popytka interpretatsii', *Znamia*, 8: 214–20.

Index